the finest of Sunday mornings. The sun basked the mean streets of South Central Los Angeles in its warm glow; enough to be felt on exposed skin, but not hot enough to release the odor of the offal in the dumpsters and trash As Marva walked to church, many of the aged dwellings she passed were in an advanced state of disrepair. Here ere, like skipped teeth, were garbage strewn empty lots where the city had demolished boarded-up apartments.

tire landscape resembled a ne. And there was never an nce or ceasefire. Sociologists it as a continuing struggle ward mobility by the under Pundits dubbed it an urban ground instituted by drugs rime. But Marva knew it for it was: the ultimate war for between Good and Evil.

was an unsettling absence ds and trees. All animal life he exception of humans and n had vanished from South al long ago. Would mankind ally become an endangered ? With every home boarded demolished, the low income it was shrinking. Population y was on the increase. With er the inner city became a re cooker about to explode.

The inner city, South Central Los Angeles, 1984

"The entire landscape resembled a war zone."

essness was pervasive. Few believed that conditions would ever improve. The infrequent politician or religious who attempted to make improvements was almost always overwhelmed by the enormity of the task.

ocked our puritantical forbears and lost our work ethic. We traded our high standard of living for cheap thrills as drugs and sex. When we lost touch with God, our social structure crumbled, and the institutions which our thers had so lovingly labored to build began to fall apart. Our culture needs to rediscover morals and ethics, re- o the faith that made us strong. People must be made to realize that their wicked ways hurt everyone, including Change or perish; everybody needs to be reborn in Jesus Christ. Jesus is the Great Recycler. He makes it right.

e lapsing into sleep, Condo Don thought about what he had said. Something terrible had gone wrong in his life. had recycled him. Jesus was here. There was still hope for mankind.

LARGE PRINT

ISBN 978-1-58345-004-8 90000

9 781583 450048

The Gospel According to Condo Don

by Fred Dungan

DUNGAN BOOKS

The Gospel According to Condo Don

- An eyewitness account of the Second Coming of Our Savior, Jesus Christ

As told to Fred Dungan

The Gospel According to Condo Don

—An Eyewitness Account of the Second Coming of Our Lord and Savior, Jesus Christ

A DUNGAN BOOKS PUBLICATION

by Fred Dungan

3749 Myers Street
Riverside, CA 92503-4280
(951) 688-1396
fdungan@fdungan.com
Large Print Second Edition, July 2011

This is a work of Christian fiction. As such, the author has taken considerable license, albeit striving to stay within the limits of Scripture, in this depiction of the Second Coming. Matthew 24:36 says "But of that day and hour no one knows, not even the angels of heaven, nor the Son, but the Father alone." Thus, this novel is merely one of an infinite number of possible scenarios. Nevertheless, our faith shall not waiver because Revelation 22:7 assures us that "...I am coming quickly."

ISBN: 978-1-58345-004-8

Published under an agreement with Lulu.com.

TO MY SON -
CHE PETER DUNGAN
DUTY, HONOR, COUNTRY

TABLE OF CONTENTS

PREFACE		5
CHAPTER 1	South Central Los Angeles	13
CHAPTER 2		18
CHAPTER 3		27
CHAPTER 4	Washington, D.C.	31
CHAPTER 5		35
CHAPTER 6		47
CHAPTER 7		64
CHAPTER 8	Orange County, California	68
CHAPTER 9		75
CHAPTER 10	Skidrow, Downtown Los Angeles	95
CHAPTER 11		101
CHAPTER 12		114
CHAPTER 13		137
CHAPTER 14	MacArthur Park, Los Angeles	141
CHAPTER 15	The Salton Sea	163
CHAPTER 16		176
CHAPTER 17	Aerial Gunnery Range	190
CHAPTER 18	Chicago and Washington, D.C.	214
CHAPTER 19	Ontario International Airport	220
CHAPTER 20	Pelican Bay State Prison	235
CHAPTER 21		247
CHAPTER 22		251
CHAPTER 23	Medvedev Institute, Leningrad	260
CHAPTER 24	The Mojave Desert	270
CHAPTER 25	Boiling Mud Pots	285
CHAPTER 26		292
CHAPTER 27	Oasis, North Salton Sea	296
CHAPTER 28	Following the Eternal Flame	302
CHAPTER 29	Interstate 40, East of Barstow	319
CHAPTER 30		323
CHAPTER 31	Entering the Cube	341
ACKNOWLEDGEMENTS		345
MAP OF CALIFORNIA STATE PRISONS		350
MAP OF CALIFORNIA HOLY LANDS		351
ABOUT THE AUTHOR		352

PREFACE

Although it is almost 3 AM, the solitary gnarled and weathered prisoner who sits hunched over a grimy stainless steel pull down table in a spartan windowless dank cell has no way of knowing the time because the naked bulb in the center of the featureless ceiling burns 24 hours a day. Sensing the inanimate hardened coldness of the metal beneath his leathery palms, he grasps tighter the chewed-up stub of a pencil that he has meticulously sharpened by twisting the graphite point at an acute angle against the rough concrete floor while tediously rubbing away the wood and, in large misshapen block letters like an overly careful kindergartner might make, begins to write ever-so-slowly, as if it pains him deeply to do so:

August 8, 2008
Security Housing Unit
Pelican Bay State Prison
Crescent City, California 95531

I was pushed into this world on the dawn of Armageddon, 0530 hours, July 16, 1945, at an Army Air Force hospital near Alamogordo, New Mexico. As the doctor held me in the air by the ankles, the shock wave from the Trinity atomic blast struck the building with a roar, shattering a window in the delivery room. Startled, the obstetrician lost his grip and I fell nearly three feet head first and bounced on the linoleum floor.

They christened me Donald Thaddeus Stearns III. It was a big name and my parents expected me to grow into it. Each generation had produced at least one famous and successful Stearns. There was Rear Admiral H. Lucius Stearns of the Spanish-American War, Lieutenant General Byron Stearns of World War I, and my father, Colonel Peter Stearns, chief of security at Alamogordo Army Air Base, who is primarily remembered for alerting America to Soviet espionage of Manhattan Project secrets. My family spoiled me rotten. We were quite well off and I always had the latest games, the best toys and the most fashionable clothes as I was growing up.

I was an average child, but average just wasn't good enough for my mother and father. When I received "C's," they clamored for "A's." When I made the Junior Varsity football team, they pressured me to make Varsity.

Since I wasn't capable of doing anything right, I began to do things wrong. I joined a gang and was arrested for shoplifting. A week later, the coach caught me using cocaine in the locker room. To get even, I broke into the gymnasium and redecorated the walls with graffiti. But no matter what I did, my parents were able to buy my way out of it.

Despite my overtly destructive behavior, I managed to graduate from high school. I had planned to travel for a year or so before I went to college, but my father wouldn't hear of it. He made some kind of a deal with a Congressman and I was appointed to the Air Force

Academy at Colorado Springs. My father hoped that strict military discipline would make a man out of me.

My first year at Colorado Springs was pure misery. I hated the Academy and everyone in it. My knuckles were scabbed from innumerable fights. It didn't matter to me how big or powerful my opponents were—I just wanted to punch someone. Although fighting earned me demerits, it also earned me a place on the Varsity Boxing Team. For the first time in my life I had found something I was good at.

My grades were horrible, but the coach got me a tutor. I was surprised when I heard that I had survived the first year's cut. By the time I left for home and summer vacation, I was beginning to feel that I might someday fill my father's shoes.

I was a lot more confident and self-assured my second year. Some of my bad old habits such as drinking and shoplifting returned. But I figured that I was a whole lot smarter now and could get away with it.

At 0330 one Tuesday morning, they woke the entire academy for a surprise drug test. I pissed into a bottle like everybody else and didn't give it another thought. Four days later I was hauled before a Cadet Board of Conduct and charged with amphetamine and barbiturate abuse. I was shocked because I had been clean for almost two weeks before the test. This time my father's money couldn't save me. They kicked my young ass out of the Air Force Academy.

From Colorado Springs the road led downhill. There wasn't enough alcohol in the entire world to drown my shame or curb my self-pity. I didn't want to return home in disgrace, so I hung out in the streets. I slept in doorways and in parks; I didn't bathe or shave for weeks; and I managed to snort, shoot and squander every penny my family sent me.

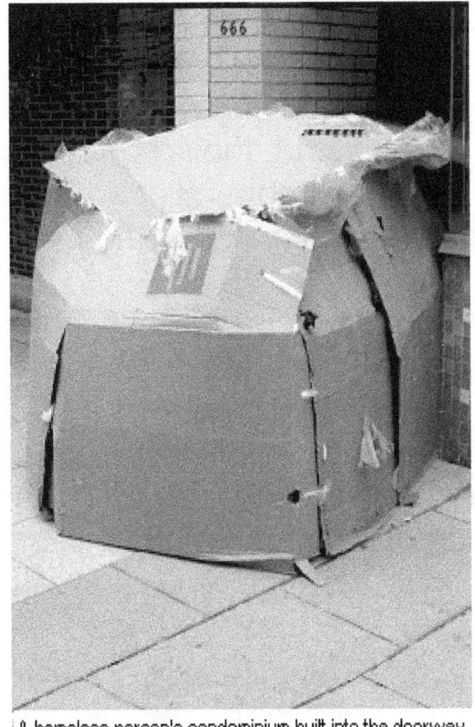

A homeless person's condominium built into the doorway of a boarded up business on Skidrow, Washington, D.C.

I drifted from place to place in the underworld of the bums and the homeless. Yet even there, I could never lose myself completely. No matter how low a person goes, his companions still demand that he do his share. A number of bums are good at panhandling, some in scavenging and others in dealing with the authorities. Due to the knowledge of engineering that I had acquired at the Academy, my specialty became shelter. I had a talent for carving rooms from riverbanks, constructing tents of plastic sheeting and camouflaging the huts I built alongside freeways. But my most outstanding achievements were the inner city dwellings I built on sidewalks and vacant lots using large, discarded appliance boxes and scavenged building materials. They were condominiums for the homeless and earned me the nickname "Condo Don." It was short enough that I could live up to it.

Jesus was not the first person who tried to save me from myself. There were scores of others. High, mighty, and pious, they came slumming for a short time and then returned to their comfortable lives with rich tales about how ungrateful people like me were. I could spot the patronizing, condescending bastards from a mile away. Preaching to the downtrodden inflated their egos and they always secretly smiled when someone slipped from the grasp of their helping hand and fell back into the mire.

Thirty years of heavy drinking and drug abuse had taken its toll on my body. Deep crow's feet etched my face beneath bloodshot eyes. What few teeth I had left were stained and encrusted. Puss oozed from open sores resulting from a vicious venereal disease that over the years had withstood massive doses of antibiotics. Arthritis inflamed my joints and left me stiff on cold mornings. Jaundice lent my puffy skin a yellow tinge.

When animals sense that a member of the herd is dying, they abandon it so as not to endanger the rest. So it was with me. As I slept on a park bench in a municipal park adjacent to the Crystal Cathedral one night, my friends crept away and left me to my fate. But I was a fighter and refused to die. Like an aged toothless lion, I began to concentrate on easy prey, intimidating old ladies, little children, and the disabled into giving me a handout.

Jesus looked like an easy mark. I figured him to be no more than twelve or thirteen years of age and a mommy's boy due to his squeaky clean appearance in a pressed suit and a tie. I didn't particularly care for black people or their culture, but race is never a factor when a predator spots its victim.

I will save the story of my salvation for a later and more appropriate part of this testimony. Suffice it to say that I was near enough to death that I figured I had nothing to lose by giving God a try. I must confess that at the time I was openly hostile towards religion and would not have given a dime for my immortal soul.

God only knows the transformation that Jesus wrought in me. Like Lazarus, I was miraculously brought back from the dead. I will always wonder why Jesus chose me to save. No other human being could have been so unwilling, so set in his vile ways, and so determined to destroy himself. No one was less worthy of His attention.

Following the destruction of the Crystal Cathedral by an earthquake, Jesus bid me to roam the world with the message of His coming. I did so with a buoyant heart and sureness of purpose that made my task easy. I no longer feared the police or what they could do to me.

Shielded by the armor of truth, I felt immune to the barbs of my fellow men. Many were the times that I walked into the toughest bar in a blighted neighborhood and began to seek converts for Jesus. Making my way into abandoned boarded up buildings, I confronted heroin addicts as they were fixing and showed them the tracks on my own arms. There were many people who either didn't listen to me or thought I was crazy. But no one ever doubted my sincerity.

I must atone for the heads I busted, arms I broke, and any other damage I may have caused while evangelizing. Turning the other cheek never became a specialty of mine and those who angered or assaulted me inevitably got worse than they gave. I confess that there is something about my nature that attracts violence. Despite prayers for patience and serenity, my temper still occasionally gets the best of me.

Much of what I will relate I got first hand. I was privileged to spend years accompanying Jesus in his ministries. Every word He spoke is burned into my memory and comes back to me as clear as if He were speaking to me at this very moment. When I close my eyes, I can visualize him shaking my hand the day I departed and I can feel the power surging through my body.

The story of Jesus which follows is rendered with attention to accuracy and detail. Whenever possible, I have corroborated it with others who witnessed His miracles.

The only peace I have known in this life was the days I spent with Jesus. May His words also bring you comfort. No man is so low or degraded as to escape His notice; no man so exalted or powerful as to be beyond His judgment. Salvation is impossible unless you open your heart to Him.

I am told that I will die in this prison. If it be His will, so be it. It would be a great honor to give my life for Jesus. The people who run this place do not yet believe in His healing powers. They think that the miracle of my physical regeneration should be credited to some kind of scientific mumbo-jumbo. There are those among them who wish to speed my death in order to dissect my corpse and discover the means by which Jesus cured my afflictions. I forgive them and pray that they may yet see the truth.

The blinding light by which I entered the material world pales in comparison to the Almighty Eternal Light that awaits me at the exit.

May the grace of Our Living Savior be with you the rest of your days and may He dwell in your heart forever. Amen.

Condo Don

PART ONE

MOTHER MARVA

"... Blessed art thou among women ..." Luke 1:42

Chapter 1

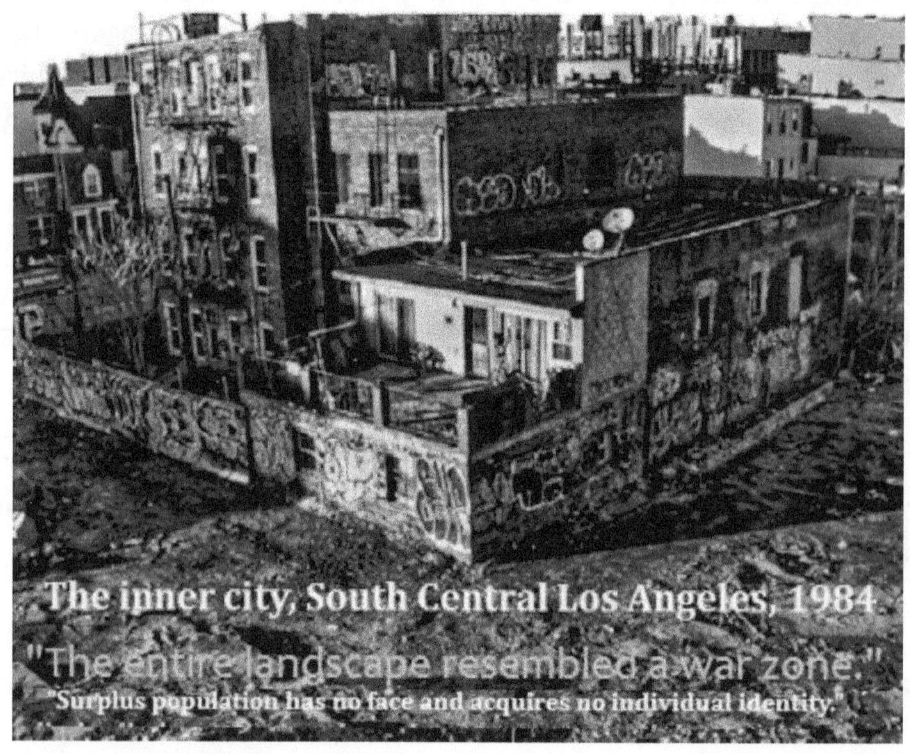

The inner city, South Central Los Angeles, 1984
"The entire landscape resembled a war zone."
"Surplus population has no face and acquires no individual identity."

South Central Los Angeles—1984

The wall was pink. Marva knew this with certainty

because whenever she lifted either of the two religious objects from the wall, its silhouette remained in the original color. Fly specks, dust, smoke, and grease had conspired over the years to turn the remainder of the wall into an ugly, dark, uneven rose. The two icons had shielded a portion of it from the grime and pollution of the urban atmosphere. Marva truly believed they had likewise shielded her for sixteen years against the rampant drugs, crime, and violence of the inner city hell in which she lived.

On the upper left hung a large, bare wooden cross. It was originally rough and unfinished, but years of constant handling had smoothed it until it fairly glistened. Marva's father had given it to her for her second birthday shortly before dying from something which her mother termed "consumption." As she pressed it to her breast, she searched her memory for a picture of her father. But the only image that came to mind was from a faded black and white photograph her mother had once shown her. He was tall, black, and muscular. Marva thought that he was the second most handsome and kindly man who had ever walked the earth.

A lithographed likeness of the first and best man was centered on the wall in a gilded frame. Marva wasn't sure where it had come from. No matter where she stood in the small bedroom, her glance was returned by Jesus. Even now, as she lay on the brass bed directly beneath the portrait, His eyes lovingly met hers. It made her feel all warm and secure to know that Jesus was always watching her, even when she slept. Her relationship with Jesus was of a personal, one-on-one nature. He talked to her from within her mind and never let her stray from the path of righteousness. Jesus loved all children. And Marva knew in her heart of hearts that Jesus especially adored her.

The small room was divided in half by a green blanket draped over a clothesline that ran between opposing walls. The other half of the bedroom had belonged to her older brother, Marcellus, before he had perished in a drive-by shooting several years back. The blanket was an imperfect partition. Any tall person could see over it and any small child could easily peer beneath it. When her mother entertained "gentlemen friends" at night in the combination living room-kitchen-den area of their one bedroom apartment, Marva sat quietly on her bed to avoid notice. The blanket gave no protection from the odor of alcohol or the stench of drugs. She would often hold the cross tightly to her breast in the darkness and pray that everything happening in the other room would soon go away.

The brass bed was the only thing left to remind her of her brother. When they had shared the bedroom, it had been his and she had slept on a mattress on the floor. The bed wasn't really brass. In the eighth grade she had done a science project on ferrous metals and had found that a refrigerator magnet stuck to the bed. Besides, real brass didn't rust.

Marva believed her mother had been glad when

Marcellus died. He was big and tough and belonged to a gang. Sometimes he called his mother a whore and threatened to kill her when he came home and found her under the influence of drugs. Once he had pistol whipped a gentleman friend and had slapped her repeatedly until she fell to the floor. He even stole money from her purse and flushed her drugs down the toilet. Terrorizing his mother would have been a non-stop ritual, except that Marcellus had preferred to spend as little time as possible at home. He usually ignored Marva except to advise her to escape from their mother as soon as possible.

The day after the shooting, several gangsters from the Rolling '60's Crips gang had dropped by the apartment. They had pressed a wad of money into Marva's mother's hand and told her it was to cover the funeral expenses plus a little extra for "party money." She had wept, repeating over and over again how lucky Marcellus had been to have such good friends.

The blanket and the clothesline had remained in place following Marcellus' death. Marva's mother told her that the apartment was too cramped and she needed the extra space for storage. All of Marcellus' personal belongings had been thrown into the trash. In their place were now a broken television set, odds and ends of furniture, and an enormous steamer trunk filled with every losing lottery ticket her mother had ever purchased.

With Marcellus gone Marva's mother no longer had any controls on her life. She made no attempt to hide her drug habit and her gentlemen friends became bolder and visited with increased frequency. Quite often the partying continued throughout the night.

It wasn't easy to get to sleep amid the racket. After she said her prayers, Marva would curl up in a fetal position upon the bed and commence a ritual that had begun many years before. She would say "good night" to all of the inanimate objects in the bedroom until she fell asleep:

"Good night Jesus. Good night, Holy Cross. Good night, floor. Good night ceiling. Good night light bulb. Good night dresser. Good night, blue dress. Good night, black dress. Good night shoes. Good night, scarf. Good night, mattress. Good night, pink wall. Good night, brass bed. Good night pillow. Good night blanket. Good night, Bible. Good night, white socks."

As the inventory progressed, it became slower. Soon, Marva began her nightly journey through a wonderful world of enchanted dreams that erased the day's pain. She walked with Jesus, talked with her father, and flew with angels. Always, when she woke in the morning, she was smiling and looking forward to another day.

Chapter 2

It was the finest of Sunday mornings. The sun basked the city in its warm glow—warm enough to be felt on exposed skin, but not hot enough to release the odor of the offal scattered about the streets. Nothing broke the blue skyline above the rooftops except for an occasional billboard touting the manly virtues of imbibing a particular brand of alcoholic beverage.

"¡Ron Cortez—Que Bueno Es!" exclaimed a bikini-clad, perspiring model as she offered a muscle bound hunk an iced glass of a rum concoction in the Caribbean paradise pictured on the billboard atop an apartment building. Latino immigrants had been moving into the traditionally black neighborhood for the past decade. Although they were still a small part of the community, their influence was becoming noticeable. The white models in the billboard advertisements were airbrushed brown almost as often as they were airbrushed black. However, the blonde hair and the Nordic features of the billboard dwellers lent both them and the products they were hawking an alien tinge. The billboard dwellers were painted bigger than life—hedonistic, two-dimensional gods in the fantasy Mount Olympus that existed above the mean city streets. A substantial number of the mortal men below believed that by purchasing the billboard dwellers' products, they, too, could become part of a better world. But the streets, even on this, the finest of

Sunday mornings, bore testimony to the degradation of drugs and alcohol, as sunken-eyed derelicts sat on the neighborhood stoops with their brown paper bags between their feet.

Marva nearly stumbled into one such derelict as she exited her apartment building. The pile of dirty clothing before her stirred and looked up, showing that it still retained some vestige of the humanity God had bestowed upon it.

"Yo, mama," the derelict said, "that white lacy number is absolutely divine. You has won your heart's desire with such finery," and he held the paper bag out towards Marva as if to invite her to share his elixir. She quickly stepped past him and was rid of everything about him but his voice as she reached the street. "You is brutal, mama. Is you in such a hurry that you can't stop a minute to socialize with your main man?"

Marva wished she had waited for one of the older church ladies to pass by before she ventured out on the street. The vermin seemed to melt into the asphalt whenever they spotted one of the venerable matrons walking towards them. Sharp tongued and armed with weighty purses, they were capable of tearing a man to shreds who did not show them proper respect. Viewing their world with black and white severity, they trod on the unrighteous and unjust as they strode towards church on Sunday morning. But Marva was no longer a little girl and she knew it was time to learn to protect herself from the harsh environment. Transfixing her features into chiseled stone and glaring straight ahead as fiercely as she could manage, she set off at a fast pace down the sidewalk towards the storefront church.

Many of the buildings she passed were abandoned. Not being able to generate the revenue for their absentee owners that it took to maintain them, they had, consequently, decayed beyond the point where they could attract tenants. They had become shooting galleries for addicts and breeding grounds for rats. Here and there, like skipped teeth, were garbage strewn empty lots where the city had demolished boarded-up buildings. The entire landscape resembled a war zone. And there was never an armistice or cease-fire. These streets had already claimed a dozen additional victims since Marcellus met his tragic fate. Sociologists viewed it as a continuing struggle for upward mobility by the disadvantaged. Sociologists and politicians dubbed it an urban battleground instituted by drugs and crime. But Marva knew it for what it was—the ultimate war between Good and Evil.

As she walked, Marva passed neither trees nor birds. All living things except man and vermin had vanished from the inner city long ago. Human beings were now the endangered species. With every building boarded-up or demolished, their habitat shrank. New immigrants were continually searching for cheap housing. Many of the older residents on fixed incomes sublet space in their cramped apartments to help pay their rent. The population density was soaring. In summer the entire inner city became a non-air conditioned pressure cooker waiting to explode. Periodic riots such as the Rodney King riot in 1992 vented steam and accomplished little else. A sense of hopelessness pervaded the community. Few believed that conditions would ever get better. The occasional politician or religious leader who attempted to make improvements was almost always overwhelmed by the enormity of the task.

Formerly Stroud's Discount Furniture, the Missionary Baptist Church was indistinguishable from the buildings it adjoined. Built of unreinforced brick and mortar, it had the same crumbling appearance as the majority of older downtown buildings. What made it a community landmark, however, was not its looks. The indefatigable spirit of the church, personified by the Reverend Solomon Harms, acted as a magnet that attracted the faithful from the surrounding community on Sunday mornings. Competition was fierce for the hard-backed folding seats and it was not unusual to have a large number of people standing in the rear of the church as the Reverend Harms beseeched Almighty God to show them His mercy by restoring peace to the community.

People came early, congregating under an awning outside the entrance. Gossip flowed freely as church matrons deplored the decadent state of the neighborhood. Marva ran the gauntlet of ladies, speaking politely to those who spoke to her, and took her usual seat in the sixth row. Before long, Carlos Ortiz, a clerk whom she knew from the market where her mother spent their food stamps, sat down next to her.

Carlos was light skinned with dark wavy hair. His family had fled for their lives from Central America, crossing the border illegally from Mexico some six years before. They lived in constant fear of being discovered and deported. Carlos worked hard at the market and gave much of his earnings to an immigration lawyer who claimed that legal residency was only a few payments away. Carlos had been attracted to Marva because she was totally unlike the other women he had met in America. She was quiet and introspective and carried with her an aura that demanded respect. He was careful not to touch her and limited his conversation to religious matters.

Marva was well aware of Carlos' attraction to her. When he had first sat next to her four weeks before, she had almost stood up and moved to another chair. There was something about him, however, that told her he was sincere. He did not attempt to force his attentions on her and he talked of religion rather than himself. Marva had begun to look forward to the precious minutes of conversation they shared before the sermon began.

Of course, Marva suspected that she and Carlos had become a source of gossip for the church matrons. But she knew that it was only talk. The previous Sunday, following services, one of them had actually pressed her arm and whispered, "He's such a nice boy."

The Reverend Harms had no doubts as to the forces which composed the universe. Everything was either positive or negative—Good or Evil. There were two classes of people—the sinners and the redeemed. The latter would enjoy everlasting pleasure in Heaven and the former would roast in Hell for eternity. Either an individual gave himself to God or he was consumed by Evil. One could read it in the Bible and one could see it in the streets. Alcohol, drugs, easy money, and a hundred other temptations of the flesh were waiting to destroy and devour anyone who failed to put his faith in God. It was Reverend Harms' job—his sacred God given mission—to share this certain knowledge with anyone who would listen.

Nobody described in greater detail or with more relish the punishments of Hell. Fire and brimstone flowed from Reverend Harms' sermons like lava from a volcano. Demons ripped apart lost souls while the tormented screamed in anguish. As his voice rose, one could almost smell the sulfur and feel the heat from the flames. This was the fate that awaited the majority of mankind. Only by reaching out to God, through His Son, Jesus Christ, could anyone achieve redemption. Jesus would come again and gather up the pimps, whores, drug addicts, alcoholics, money-gouging slumlords, bigots, corrupt politicians, rapists, and sodomizers and cast the lot of them into the fiery furnace.

Today's sermon was entitled "Original Sin." Adam had sinned and all men had inherited his sin. By succumbing to temptation in the Garden of Eden, Adam had sealed Man's fate. God now viewed mankind as tarnished and unclean and would only accept those individuals into Heaven whom His Son, Jesus Christ, had found sincerely repentant. The great of this world would tremble before the Gates of Heaven and those judged unfit would be denied admittance. Heaven was likened to an exclusive country club where Christian acts, rather than money, purchased membership. Those who gave willingly of themselves for their brethren, those who were persecuted in life for preaching the Word of God, and those who were born again in the Spirit of Jesus, would be forgiven all sin and admitted into the presence of the Lord. Only they would taste the cool, sweet waters of redemption and know everlasting Peace. And those who failed the extensive screening process had nobody but themselves to blame. The Word of God surrounds Man; he need but open his ears and heart to reach Glory.

Following the sermon, several ushers passed a collection plate among the congregation. Marva always dreaded this moment. She spent most of the money she made from babysitting on school supplies. Her offering usually consisted of one or two quarters which she would cup in her hand in the hope that nobody would notice the paucity of her contribution. Everyone was watching her, she felt, and she longed to become invisible whenever the collection plate approached. Her discomfort was compounded when she noticed that Carlos had placed folding money in the plate. Had she looked closer, she might have spotted two slugs and a bus token at the bottom.

What the congregation failed to contribute to God in money, it more than made up for in song. The small choir was the envy of many larger churches in more affluent sections of the city. Over the years, it had gained a reputation that reached far beyond the brick and mortar walls of the storefront church. Marva, too, had a fine lilting soprano voice and planned to join the choir someday. As the congregation sang The Old Wooden Cross and Rock of Ages, the strains carried for blocks. Pedestrians on the sidewalk outside the church would stop to listen. All the misery and frustration that came from life in the inner city was vented in those hymns. Not since the psalms of the Israelites in bondage had there been such a harmonious appeal to God. The hymns of the Missionary Baptist Church were a cry from God's long suffering children to fulfill the promises that He had made to mankind. They were truly urban Christian soldiers and the tensions of the battlefield in which they lived burst forth in their songs.

When the services ended and everyone stood to leave, Marva remained seated and turned towards Carlos.

“Do you ever study the Bible?” she asked.

“It's very hard to study with all my brothers and sisters running around—I try sometimes.”

“I often study the Bible on the roof where I live,” Marva

stated. "It's quiet there and I feel like I am closer to heaven when I am outside. I close my eyes and I can feel His presence."

"You are blessed," commented Carlos, "I wish I had such a special place."

"I would like to share it with you, if you could find the time to come to my home," Marva offered.

With a slight blush Carlos said, "I would be honored."

Chapter 3

Temblors was what the evening news called them. Small earthquakes that did little or no damage were shaking Southern California with increased frequency. In the previous week there had been eight temblors with a magnitude greater than 3.0 on the Richter scale.

The television reporters claimed that the temblors were beneficial, serving to relieve stress along the numerous fault lines that criss-crossed Southern California and decreasing the likelihood of a destructive quake.

If anyone had surveyed them, most of Los Angeles' residents would have disagreed with the conclusions of the experts. The majority perceived the series of small earthquakes as a warning. Panic was beginning to grip them. People who had the resources were moving from the earthquake zone to safer locations in the Southwest. But the inhabitants of the inner city could only roll with the temblors and wonder how much more punishment their unreinforced brick and mortar buildings could absorb before they crumbled and buried their occupants beneath mounds of rubble.

The Reverend Harms was quick to seize upon the earthquakes as divine punishment for the sins of man. He visualized the ground opening and the wicked being swallowed by the earth.

But Marva did not find the temblors to be threatening. As she was climbing the last of the steps to the roof, a jolt had thrust her into the sturdy arms of Carlos and he had carried her out onto the flat roof. The shaking had stopped but her body still trembled. Carlos thought that she was afraid and sought to reassure her that it was over and she was safe. He was not aware that her tremors were caused by his own proximity and that she was struggling to regain control of her emotions. At that moment he could have taken advantage of her and she would not have resisted. But Carlos was not that type of man. Concern for her safety, rather than animal lust, motivated his actions.

When Marva's heart finally slowed, she started to go back down the stairs to get the Bible she had forgotten to bring with her. Carlos stopped her. He did not want her to traverse the stairs alone in case of another earthquake. "Besides," he said looking across the rooftops, "we need nothing more than our senses to share the wonders of God's creation." And as he spoke, two white doves flew down and landed on the parapet. Marva was indeed overcome by the wonders of God's creation in a way she had never experienced before. Silently, she thanked God for bringing her Carlos.

Carlos and Marva remained on the roof for hours. The sunset was spectacular. Each particle of pollution in the urban sky bent the angled light from the waning sun like a miniature prism to produce colors that were unequaled even in the tropics.

The doves flew away and Carlos knew it was time to say goodbye. He started to bend down to kiss Marva's willing lips, but instead mumbled a few parting words and then bolted down the stairs.

* * *

Marva's mother was waiting for her when she entered their apartment. "Everybody says you been making a fool of yourself with some wetback on the roof," her mother accused.

"He's not a wetback."

"They're all wetbacks. Why can't you find yourself a man of your own color. If your brother were still alive, he'd have skinned that wetback for sure."

"That's why he died—anger and hatred killed him."

"You best have some respect for your poor, departed brother. Remember, your father died from a bullet, too. And he was every bit as high and mighty of a self-righteous religious fool as you."

"You said Daddy died of 'consumption'."

"That's right," Marva's mother snickered, "he tried to consume a bullet, but it consumed him first. During the riots, he went around preachin' peace and stickin' his nose where it didn't belong. And, when he got shot, God deserted him. He bled to death in my arms." She began to sob and pointed a scrawny, gnarled finger at her daughter. "At least he was a black man," she cried, "how dare you disgrace his memory with some filthy greaser?"

Marva stopped arguing. It never did any good and only served to provoke her mother. She reached out to hug, but her mother abruptly pulled away.

Grabbing her sequined purse and throwing a thin jacket around her shoulders, Marva's mother turned towards the door. As she exited, she took one last parting shot at Marva:

"I'm goin' out. And when I come back, I'm bringin' me a real man—a black man—not some foreign trash. He'll have a black face, and black hands, and a black pecker. He won't be the color of a turd that you flush down the toilet!"

The door slammed in Marva's face, almost catching her outstretched fingers. Running to the bedroom, Marva quickly slipped under the green blanket, flung herself onto the bed, and cried for hours until finally, exhausted and soaked by warm, salty tears, sleep mercifully claimed her.

Chapter 4

Washington, D.C.

Although Janet Carson had been appointed Attorney General by the President of the United States, she considered him neither her mentor nor a man for whom she had any particular respect. She judged him to be a morally deficient womanizer who had cheated on his wife numerous times. Her appointment was a sop to the National Organization of Women who had supported the President's candidacy as the lesser of two evils. Now, following his successful election, they were pressing him for their fair share of the political spoils.

Janet Carson had cut her teeth in the rough and tumble world of feminist politics. Unlike the President, who seemed to shift with the political wind, she intended to use her office as a tool to enforce civil rights for women and to expand the influence of the feminist movement on government.

At the close of the previous session, Congress had narrowly passed a bill permitting doctors to perform abortions upon demand. Although the bill contained no provisions for funding abortions, it had angered religious organizations and resulted in the mass picketing of abortion clinics throughout the United States. There had been several incidents of violence and, as one of her first acts in office, Janet Carson had directed federal marshals to provide security for any abortionist who felt threatened. She had also personally telephoned the President and requested him to call out the National Guard to prevent protesters from forming impassable cordons around abortion clinics. Her impassioned plea had met with a "We'll wait and see how the situation develops" from the President. He had no intention of becoming embroiled in a battle with organized religion and suggested that she reconsider her decision to employ federal marshals as bodyguards.

Janet Carson firmly believed that all women had the right to abort unwanted fetuses. When an unplanned pregnancy had threatened her ability to attend law school, Janet had not hesitated to get an abortion. She considered her body, like that of all women, to be her exclusive property to do with as she wished. As she watched the presidency vacillate on issues concerning women's rights, she felt a need to redouble her efforts to force the public to accept feminist values, regardless of the political cost to herself and the Administration. She felt that if she could not enforce the abortion rights of women, the pro-abortion issue would lose momentum as fast as the Equal Rights Amendment had in a previous decade. Abortion had become her personal crusade.

* * *

Nobody had ever mistaken Carl Utz for a crusader. With close cropped gray hair, short arms and legs, and a stocky body, Carl resembled a bulldog. And like the bulldog, Carl plodded methodically after his opponents until he sunk his teeth into them. Short on bark and big on bite, he was a gruff veteran of 32 years on the Philadelphia Homicide Squad.

Forced to retire, Carl Utz had chosen to become the head of a newly formed federal law enforcement agency rather than rust in a rocking chair. As chief of the Genetic Enforcement Service (GES), it was his responsibility to arrest anyone who had committed a biological crime in violation of federal statutes, especially those involving unauthorized alteration of DNA, and turn them over to the Justice Department for prosecution. Although he had at first imagined this to mean tracking down assorted Frankenstein monsters, he soon discovered that for the most part his duties consisted of preventing potentially dangerous genetic alterations of fruit and vegetables. His first case had involved a biologist who had attempted to market an apricot that was the size of an apple. It was firmer and sweeter than any conventional apricot and had only one drawback—it contained enough strychnine to make it potentially lethal to anyone who ate large quantities of the fruit. When confronted with the evidence, the unwitting offender had readily signed an Agreement to Desist. Because the altered apricot had yet to be marketed, nobody had been injured and Carl hadn't even bothered to prosecute the biologist for a misdemeanor.

It was difficult to accept that after a stunning 32 year career as a homicide detective in which he had single-handedly brought to justice the notorious Parkway Strangler, Carl now found himself working as a glorified agricultural inspector. Chief in name only, his entire workforce consisted of a buxom secretary and a geneticist who spent most of her working hours perusing obscure biological journals for evidence of criminal activity. His $165,000 per annum budget was the smallest agency budget in Washington, D.C. and had resulted in GES having to be headquartered in a rented one-room office in the far from upscale Adams-Morgan District. His request for a 9 mm standard police issue handgun had been turned down by the Government Accounting Office as an unnecessary expenditure.

Carl's boss was Attorney General Janet Carson. They had never met and he would not have recognized her if he had passed her in a hallway. Considering the vast scope of her responsibilities, it was doubtful that she was aware that GES was part of her domain. Isolated and obscure, Carl Utz felt like the straight man in some bureaucratic joke. How he missed Philadelphia!

Chapter 5

The Reverend Solomon Harms was a mortal man, made of flesh and blood. He experienced the same urges and temptations as other men. Many was the time when he had succumbed to sin, but he was always sorry afterwards and prayed to God for forgiveness. And God had forgiven him—not seven times, but more than seven times seven.

And so it was on this dismal night that Solomon Harms had felt the Forces of Evil transform him into Mr. Hyde and had gone out into the streets to seek relief from his torment. Sitting in a corner of a sleazy, darkened bar, he found his Jezebel.

After a few drinks, she suggested he accompany her to her apartment. Soon, they were in the backseat of a taxi, indulging their passions.

Somehow, however, in the light of her apartment, the magical feeling had vanished. He could now see the wrinkles beneath the makeup and the purple stains of varicose veins. Downing drink after drink in the futile hope that the distilled potion would transform the scrawny hag in his arms into a vision of loveliness, Solomon Harms at last achieved numbness. In a blissful state of Nirvana with the walls circling around him, he began to slip from the sofa onto the floor.

But as he went down, his blurred vision focused on the luscious, curvaceous outline of a feminine figure that seemingly beckoned to him from behind a thin green backlit blanket in an adjoining room. Here was the vision of loveliness he craved, the Madonna of his dreams. On hands and knees he wobbled towards the goddess, and then reached up to possess her.

Marva awoke screaming. She stood up on her bed and stomped on the clutching hands. Grabbing the wooden cross from the wall, she swung it like a pickax against the head of the inebriated cleric. Blood gushed from a scalp wound and his body slumped to the floor. Marva's mother, shocked sober from her stupor, ran into the bedroom and cradled the bloody head in her arms.

"You keep your filthy hands off my man," she screamed at Marva.

"He attacked me," she blurted between sobs.

"A man don't go after a woman unless she beckons him. Next time, you stick to your Mexican trash or I'll throw you out on your black ass."

After stopping the bleeding with a towel, Marva's mother splashed cold water on the Reverend's face until he regained consciousness. The Right Reverend Harms kept blubbering something about forgiveness as she struggled to get him down the stairs and put him in the back of a taxi.

Marva's mother bounded back up the stairs, taking two steps at a time. Bursting into the apartment, she hit the blanket divider full force, pulling the clothesline from the wall. Pouncing on Marva's sobbing, prone body, she proceeded to pommel Marva, pulling Marva's hair and gouging Marva with her long fingernails.

Marva offered no resistance. She continued to sob and attempted to bury her head in her pillow. Finally, Marva's mother quit beating her and stood up, yelling, "You worthless bitch, how could you?" But the stream of tears continued unabated.

Marva's mother reached down, grabbed her daughter by the hair and turned her over on the bed, screaming, "Listen to me when I talk to you!"

Marva curled into a fetal position and whispered, "No."

"No what, you ungrateful little slut—no you're not sorry or no you're not listening?"

"Mama, he's a bad man."

"You listen to me. Hes a good man, an educated man, a true man of God. He's a real gentleman. He treated me like a lady. How dare you seduce my man?"

"Mama, he's not a man of God."

"Oh, no?," Marva's mother sneered, pulling a $100 bill from her bra. "And I suppose this wasn't heaven sent. Look at it child. Do you know how much money this is?"

"Four hundred quarters," Marva sobbed, recalling her ordeal with the collection plate. She flipped over and again buried her face in the pillow.

Marva lay, sobbing, amidst the blood-soaked sheets for what seemed to be an eternity before she drifted into sleep. In her dreams she saw herself rising above a tumultuous battlefield towards the peaceful meadow where she normally met either Jesus or her father. This time, a stranger in a flowing robe awaited her. He seemed kindly and with his smile the pain drifted away.

"Fear not," he said. "I am the Lord's messenger, Gabriel, and I bring you good news. God has found you to be the most worthy of women. You shall suffer no longer. Rejoice! God has chosen you to bear His Son. You will be the mother of the Savior, who as He promised two thousand years ago, will return to reveal to man the meaning of creation."

A warm glow overcame Marva as her soul reentered her body. She awoke completely refreshed with a new purpose in life. God had favored her. She had fallen asleep as a girl and awoken as a woman. Something wonderful was now growing inside her. She was truly blessed!

* * *

Marva sat with her hands folded in her lap, staring at the textured patterns on the opposite wall. It was freshly painted. Everything in the lobby was new. The carpet, the chairs, and the other furnishings were luxurious and bespoke an opulence seldom seen in a commercial office.

Marva had come to Planned Parenthood, Incorporated, to make certain that her baby would be born healthy. A lady for whom she sometimes babysat had told her that Planned Parenthood offered free prenatal services for low income women.

After registering at the receptionist's window and filling out several forms and a long questionnaire, a nurse had taken samples of her blood and urine. She was then directed to take a seat in the lobby until the tests were processed and she could then discuss the results with a counselor.

All the other girls in the lobby were younger than Marva. She thought that one of them could not have been more than eleven years old. Several had their mothers with them, but most had come alone. One was accompanied by her boyfriend.

While Marva's attention was fully engrossed in deciphering the textured pattern of the opposite wall, she was startled to hear her name called. Turning to her left, she saw an open door in which stood a tall, blonde, tanned, and immaculately dressed young white woman who was the epitome of the billboard people she had seen in liquor advertisements. Marva stood and walked into the office where the billboard lady asked her to take a seat.

"Hi, I'm Tina Miller and I will be your counselor," the billboard lady said. "Anything you say to me will be completely confidential. We will be discussing the results of your tests and I will help you to reach solutions to any problems that they might present. Any decisions made will be entirely your own. I am here to assist you and answer any questions that you may have. Did anyone accompany you here today?"

"No, Ma'am."

"Please, call me Ms. Miller. You will have to trust me if I am going to be of any assistance to you. I hope that we will become friends. Feel free to ask me anything."

"Am I pregnant?"

"Your test results were positive. I need to clarify some of the information you provided on your questionnaire. It says here that the father of your child is God. Of course, God is the spiritual father of all children. What we need to know is the name of the physical father."

"My child was fathered by God," Marva stated confidently.

Ms. Miller started to say something and then closed her mouth. She looked closely at Marva and announced, "I'm going to show you a film that will help you understand your situation and answer my questions."

Ms. Miller pulled a screen down from the wall and dimmed the lights. After fumbling with a projector for several minutes, it made a whirring sound and Ms. Miller focused the image of two animated characters, one male and one female, on the screen. The film was explicit and the overtly anatomically correct cartoon figures engaged in sex while the narrator defined such complex terms as penis and vagina. Several charts detailing how the sperm swam up the fallopian tubes to fertilize the egg were also explained by the narrator. As the narrator began to warm to his subject and relate how the fetus developed in the womb, Ms. Miller switched off the projector and turned the lights back on.

"Now, Marva," Ms. Miller said gently, "I need to know the names of the men with whom you have had sex in the past several weeks."

"I've taken Biology in school and I'm not stupid," Marva stated. "If I had made love with a man, I would have told you about it. The baby that I carry within me is the Child of God."

Ms. Miller fumbled for a while with the pens on her desk. Marva was staring at her and Ms. Miller found it impossible to meet Marva's eyes. The silence lengthened until Ms. Miller finally stuttered, "Do you have a boyfriend?"

"I have the most wonderful boyfriend in the entire world," Marva replied with enthusiasm.

"And what is his name?" Ms. Miller ventured.

"Carlos Ortiz."

Ms. Miller erased "God" from the answer on Marva's questionnaire and substituted "Carlos Ortiz" as the child's father. As she put her pen down, the floor began to roll beneath her. "Earthquake!" she screamed and ran out of the office. Marva sat calmly in her chair until the shaking subsided. After several minutes, Ms. Miller returned red-faced and somewhat disheveled. "I'm so sorry," she apologized, "these earthquakes are frightening. I have had premonitions of the earth opening and swallowing me."

"Perhaps it shall," Marva replied coldly. And then, noticing how Ms. Miller was trembling, Marva took her hand and reassured, "We are all afraid at times. But we can find strength and courage in God."

Composing herself, Ms. Miller pulled away from Marva's grasp. "We need to be discussing your problems, not mine," she said. "I'm sorry I lost control. It won't happen again."

Ms. Miller paced the room. She felt her strength returning and picked up the questionnaire. "Have you given any thought as to whether or not you want to keep the child?" she resumed.

"I will be a good mother," Marva stated flatly.

"And how do you propose to support the child?"

"God will provide."

"That's hardly an answer and it certainly doesn't provide a solution."

"I place my faith in God," Marva repeated.

"Will God pay your doctor's bills, will God put food on your table, and will God pay child support?" Ms. Miller quipped.

"I have faith."

"Let me give you the benefit of my experience," offered Ms. Miller in a confidential tone. "Single mothers like yourself drop out of school and go on welfare. They curse their lives and often abuse their babies. But it doesn't have to be that way. Planned Parenthood can help you solve your problem. We can arrange for you to have an abortion. You can stay in school and live a normal life. Nobody needs to know."

"I would know," Marva replied. "I would have the blood of God's child on my hands."

"It won't cost you anything and it will rescue your life, countered Ms. Miller. Please take some time to think about it."

"No!" Marva insisted and the earth jolted violently. Ms. Miller once again ran from the room, but Marva remained seated. She watched intensely as several cracks appeared in the walls and began to lengthen. After several minutes, the shaking stopped. Marva stood, walked out the front door of the deserted building and caught the bus home. She had no intentions of ever returning to the clinic.

"God will provide," she kept repeating to herself on the bus ride home. "God will provide."

It was quite dark by the time Marva reached her apartment building. She shuddered in apprehension of what her mother would say about her being out so late. It was an unsolvable dilemma—she thought she could neither lie to her mother nor tell her the truth without adverse consequences.

As Marva climbed the unlit wooden stairs, she noticed a crowd at the top of the landing. Neighbors were milling around the hallway. Everyone seemed in a festive mood. Marva pushed her way to the open doorway of the apartment.

Catching sight of her daughter, her mother ran to Marva and flung her arms around her. Yelling, "I won, I won!" she spun round and round with her daughter until Marva's feet came off the ground. Never had Marva seen her mother this happy. After a few seconds of shocked jubilation, Marva managed to ask her mother what she had won.

"I won it all, child!" Marva's mother exclaimed. "All six numbers on the lottery—the big jackpot. I'm a multi-millionaire. No more ghetto garbage, no more nigger nonsense, no more having to kiss the white man's ass. I'm emancipated, darling, and nobody on earth is ever going to make me eat shit again."

Once more Marva's mother began to jump and dance around the small living room. "Lucky sixes," she cried. "Who would have thought that six sixes would be the winning numbers? I thought I had played every number combination there wass, but I never played my lucky sixes until now."

Gradually, Marva pieced together the entire story. Several days before, Marva's mother had been watching the evening news and noticed the number 666666 on a locomotive that had jumped the tracks, resulting in a disastrous chemical spill. The following day, she had gone to the market and bet the numbers on a lottery ticket. Less than an hour before Marva returned home, Marva's mother had learned that she had won $22.3 million, payable in annual installments over a twenty year period. At first she had refused to believe it. In ten years of constant play, she had never won more than a $100 prize. How often she had dreamed of winning the lottery. And now, suddenly, she had found the solution to all of life's problems. Marva's mother was heady with the sudden rush of freedom that winning had bestowed upon her. She again grabbed Marva, hugged her, and pranced around the floor screaming, "I won, I won!"

Chapter 6

The day after Marva's mother received her first check from the Lottery Commission, she threw the most extravagant party the neighborhood had ever seen—a fully catered, no-expense-spared bash to celebrate her good fortune. She was determined to leave the inner city and never return. Thoughts of Hawaii, Bora Bora, Jamaica, the Bahamas, the Virgin Islands, and a thousand other tropical paradises were jumbled in her mind. Maybe she would pick one, maybe she would visit them all. It didn't matter. The important thing was that she was leaving poverty behind. This was to be Marva's mother's bon voyage party—her personal way of communicating to her friends and the world that she was destined for better things.

Marva wasn't quite sure where she fit into her mother's plans. Whenever her mother mentioned the future, it was always prefaced by "I" rather than "we." Long ago she had learned life seldom offers guarantees. She would face the problem when she came to it.

Throughout the day, delivery men carried cases of liquor, stereo equipment, and food up the stairs. The apartment was overflowing before any of the guests arrived. Marva's mother kept busy ordering the men to "put it here" and to "be careful." She was obviously enjoying her new role and didn't notice when Marva slipped quietly into her bedroom.

There was no invitation list. Word about the party spread quickly by word of mouth. It was just beginning to get dark when the festivities started. Upon the arrival of some Crips whom Marva recognized as Marcellus' friends, she closed the bedroom door and slid a chest of drawers against it. A short time later somebody pounded on the door and tried his weight against it. She braced a chair against the chest of drawers and lay down on the brass bed.

Several hours later Marva was startled awake by gunfire. Someone was firing a handgun at the ceiling and loud voices were cheering him. There were sounds of glass bottles breaking and raucous, unrestrained laughter. Putrid odors wafted from the crack beneath the door. The combined stench of alcohol, drugs, and cigarette smoke caused Marva to gag. She got on her hands and knees and stuffed rags into the crack.

It was daylight when Marva next awoke. The noise of partying was gone and the silence was overwhelming. She quickly pushed the chair and the chest of drawers back where they belonged and opened the door.

Her eyes beheld an unnatural disaster. A cyclone could not have caused half the damage that Marva witnessed in the living room. Splintered glass from broken liquor bottles littered the floor. Great chunks of plaster had been knocked from the walls, revealing the wooden lath beneath. Two used sanitary napkins clung to a ceiling that was punctuated by numerous bullet holes. Gang graffiti interspersed with the numbers 666666 were spray painted everywhere. The front door had been pulled from its hinges and now hung haphazardly across the doorway. Someone had defecated on a cushion that rested atop an overturned sofa. The room smelled worse than a garbage dumpster on a hot day.

Where was her mother? Had she left with everyone else? Marva's eyes scanned the room and fell upon a lump beneath the soiled sheets on her mother's bed. Carefully picking her way through the broken glass and trash until she reached the bedside, she pulled back the sheets and froze in shock. Her mother lay curled on the bed clutching a hypodermic syringe in one hand. Blood seeped from her nostrils and pale green mucous marked the corners of her mouth. The numbers 666666 were scrawled on her forehead in red lipstick. A cockroach scurried to safety beneath the pillow.

Marva quickly dropped the sheet and ran screaming from the apartment. As she bounded down the stairs, she stumbled on the last flight and rolled down half a dozen steps. Crawling to the edge of the stairs, she put her head over the side and succumbed to the cold nausea convulsing her body.

Someone draped a coat over her shoulders. Looking up through blurred vision, she saw the comforting face of

Carlos. As she continued to shake uncontrollably, he took her in his arms and drew her towards him. They sat huddled together on the stairs until the police arrived. And Marva was still in Carlos' strong arms when the coroner appeared an hour later.

Marva was unable to answer many of their questions. Her mind was spinning. It all seemed so senseless. First, Marcellus, and now, her mother. After the officials finished and her mother's lifeless body had been wheeled away on a gurney, Carlos assisted Marva up the stairs to the apartment.

Everything in the front room had been destroyed, broken, or otherwise rendered useless. Carlos helped lug load after load of trash down the stairs. By the time they finished, the dumpsters were overflowing. Little was left in the living room; not even a chair to sit on.

While Marva swept and mopped the bare floors, Carlos studied the front door. The screws attaching the hinges to the frame had been jerked out, stripping the wood. Other than damage to the paint, Carlos could see nothing else wrong with the door. He collected wooden splinters from where they had fallen on the door sill. Borrowing some white asphaltic glue from Marva's school supplies, he carefully coated each splinter with white glue and inserted it into a hole in the doorframe. When he ran out of splinters, he used toothpicks to fill the remainder of the holes, painstakingly breaking them off flush with the frame.

Upon finishing, he set the door upright, lifting it while she placed shims underneath until the holes in the thick metal hinges aligned with the filled in holes in the wooden frame.

Marva searched and found a rusty screwdriver in a bin beneath the kitchen sink. After allowing sufficient time for the glue to dry, Carlos replaced the screws.

As he stood on a stack of books, screwing the topmost and final screw in place, a light tremor shook the building. Finishing quickly, Carlos and Marva stood in the doorway while the undulation continued. They watched in amazement as doors from neighboring apartments flung open and people raced down the hallway for the stairs. One man was in his undershorts. His wife still had on a mudpack and her hair was in curlers. Utter confusion reigned as they panicked and fled down the stairs. Marva and Carlos looked at each other and began to laugh. Carlos puffed out his cheeks and bugged his eyes until he resembled the lady with the mudpack, which made Marva laugh even harder.

Soon, Carlos had to leave for his job at the market. Marva looked around for something to use as a seat and pushed the steamer trunk from her bedroom into the front room. Out of curiosity, she lifted the lid and stood transfixed by what she saw. There, on top of the losing lottery tickets, were bundles of crisp $100 bills.

When Carlos next returned several days later, he was

ecstatic. At long last the immigration lawyer had obtained green cards for the entire Ortiz family. They were now legal residents and no longer had to live in fear of "La Migra" (the Border Patrol). Marva could not get the normally taciturn Carlos to shut up.

Carlos had every reason to be happy. An older brother and his father had found jobs as construction workers. He would no longer have to give every cent he made to his extended family. Thinking of the future made his head spin. There was no limit to what a man might accomplish in America.

While Carlos effervesced, giving vent to years of pent emotions, Marva brooded. Although she tried to share Carlos' happiness, she felt guilty about not having told him that she was pregnant. Try as she might, she could think of no easy way.

Perceiving her hesitancy, Carlos asked, "Is something wrong?"

"I'm pregnant," blurted Marva.

"So?" queried Carlos looking deep into her eyes.

"So, He is God's Child—you are not the father."

Carlos stood and began to pace the room. After an interminable silence he offered, "These things happen. Worrying about them doesn't do us any good."

"Yes, but it happened to me," said Marva. "I can imagine how you must feel. I should have told you sooner."

"It makes no difference," he declared with a shrug of his shoulders.

Carlos had averted his eyes from her gaze. The tone of his voice struck her as unconvincing. "It does make a difference," Marva said decisively. "If you never want to see me again, I will understand."

She began to cry. Carlos sat down next to her and took her head in his arms. He kissed the tears that ran from her eyes. "I want to be with you for the rest of my life," he whispered in her ear.

Marva stopped crying and kissed Carlos with all the passion that had accumulated within her. Before he could recover, she snatched his green card from his hand, waving it underneath his nose and daring him to try and get it back. Round the apartment they went, careening helter-skelter into walls and each other, until they both collapsed from exhaustion.

"Give it back!" demanded Carlos.

"What will you give me for it," laughed Marva.

"I will pledge my life to you. We going to get married and raise a wonderful family in this land of opportunity."

* * *

Staring through the storefront window of the Missionary Baptist Church the following evening, Marva spotted her prey at the pulpit, rehearsing his Sunday sermon. She flung open the door and descended upon Reverend Harms like an avenging angel.

"What do you want of me?" the Reverend stammered.

"There is nothing of you worth taking!" screamed Marva. "You took advantage of my mother and tried to rape me. You're a drunken fiend posing as a man of God."

"I'm only human; all men make mistakes" fumbled Reverend Harms in a barely audible voice that begged for pity. "God forgives."

"You're a despicable filthy animal!" Marva exploded. "You're not fit to utter the name of God. How many other girls have you molested?"

"Please, it's not what you think."

"Of course it isn't. In my worst nightmares I have never imagined a creature as slimy and repulsive as you. The fires of hell are not hot enough for you."

"Please . . .," begged the Reverend.

"God won't have mercy on your wretched soul, so why should I?" Marva said derisively.

"My congregation believes in me. I show them the path of righteousness. It matters not what I myself am."

"It matters to every woman who ever put her trust in you and had it betrayed. How many innocent girls have you polluted? How many have you scarred with your animal lust?"

All the time that Marva talked, she continued to stride towards the pulpit. As she met the Reverend Harm's gaze, her eyes shot fire and he partially shaded his vision with his right hand as if staring into brilliant sunlight. She now stood beside him and, smelling his breath, reached inside the pulpit for the bottle of rum that rested on a shelf. Breaking it against the pulpit, she pressed the jagged neck of the bottle against the Reverend Harms' genitals.

"I'll do anything," he blubbered.

"You will marry me and Carlos Ortiz for free in the finest wedding this city has ever seen," Marva ordered. "And after that I will decide what to do with your rotten carcass."

Marva dropped the bottle, turned on her heel, and strode back down the aisle with a gait and purpose that would have made a church matron proud.

* * *

Marva's mother did not leave a will. Her estate had to be processed through Probate Court. With the exception of the money she had discovered in the steamer trunk, this meant that Marva would not receive any of her mother's lottery winnings for quite some time. Although both Marva and Carlos longed to escape the inner city, they agreed that it would be best to remain where they were until the estate was settled.

Repairing the damage to the apartment was no easy task. Carlos mixed a large bag of Spackle with water and troweled it carefully over the holes in the plaster. After giving it several days to dry, they washed the walls with a solution of trisodium phosphate that removed layers of dirt, grease, and grime. Next, they painted the front room white and the bedroom aqua. When they finished, they could hardly tell it was the same place.

Marva furnished the apartment with used furniture purchased from a thrift store. It was sturdy and practical and would serve them well until they moved.

However, when it came to buying things for her expectant baby, Marva splurged. An oversized crib was made of genuine oak that exactly matched a high chair and a small chest of drawers. The small thermal blankets were woven of the finest cotton. And, she couldn't resist buying a perambulator with hard rubber tires that looked as if it belonged to Mary Poppins. The aqua bedroom was quickly converted into a nursery. All that remained of the past was the rough wooden cross and the portrait of Jesus.

Life with Carlos was a joy. Whenever he had time off from his job, he took her somewhere. They went to amusement parks and movies. She saw museums and art exhibits. At a street fair he bought her a large, ornate sombrero and won the unborn Baby a stuffed lamb at a ring toss booth. It seemed there was no end of new places to see and exciting things to do.

One Sunday Carlos took her on a long bus ride to the suburbs. They attended services at the Crystal Cathedral, a magnificent church built entirely of glass. Sonorous tones poured forth from a stainless steel carillon and Marva remarked that it was truly the sound of heaven. They were both so impressed by the church and the surrounding neighborhood that they agreed it would be an excellent community in which to raise a family. Before they left for home, Carlos picked a white rosebud and placed it in Marva's hair. She was indeed the most beautiful woman he had ever seen.

Pregnancy was not the dread disease that Marva had been led to believe it was. All her life she had heard women describe the ills of pregnancy. But she herself experienced none of these. There was no morning sickness or nausea. Marva was anything but moody; she couldn't remember any time in her life when she had been happier. Both her appetite and her sense of humor had sharpened. It was if the child growing inside her had rescued her from an otherwise inescapable dungeon of depression. Never before had she felt so free and alive. Sometimes for no reason at all she burst out singing while mopping the floor or preparing dinner.

But lingering doubts occasionally dimmed her spirits. She worried about Carlos. Had he understood what she meant when she had told him that this was God's Child? How could she convey to him that her pregnancy was not some accident, but an indelible covenant between herself and God? Did Carlos understand that this would be no ordinary child? How could she best prepare him for the enormous responsibility they would both share? And once Carlos finally realized the truth about the Child, would he be jealous of Him? The more Marva worried about these things, the more questions she raised. But she fretted needlessly, for Carlos was a simple man who lived his life to the full extent permitted by God. Worrying was not part of his nature and he would have been very surprised to learn of Marva's misgivings. Long ago in Central America he had learned to accept life as God willed it. To Carlos the unborn Child was already a part of his life and was no more alien than his own brothers and sisters.

Marva spent long hours staring at the portrait of Jesus. Was this how her Child would appear? She looked at the creamy white skin in the picture and tried to imagine it developing within her mulatto body. Her own hair was jet black and kinky. Could she possibly produce a Son with long, flowing golden-brown hair? She recalled a priest named Mendel from her high school Biology lessons. Mendel was the first to discover dominant and recessive genes and had determined that all offspring received their genetic structure from their parents. If this was true and God was as white as Michelangelo had painted Him in the Sistine Chapel, then maybe all her genes were recessive and the Baby would be as pale as Jesus in the portrait. Actually, she didn't really care what color His skin was; she would be content if He radiated the same kindness and warmth as the lithographed Savior.

Marva could feel Him thumping around inside her. She was 8½ months along and was beginning to carry low. When Carlos rested his head on her belly, he too could hear the Child moving.

It was Carlos' day off and Marva wanted to go to the zoo. Carlos was against the idea. He thought it would be too much walking for Marva. But she felt great and insisted on going.

Marva enjoyed the zoo. The only animals she had ever seen other than dogs and cats were in movies or on television. But the creatures in the petting zoo were darling. Rubbing her face against the soft fleece of a lamb, she begged Carlos to let her take it home. They did not leave until closing time and by then Marva's walk had slowed to a shuffle. Carlos led her gently to the bus stop, where she was glad to sit down.

It was a long bus ride. They had to transfer twice and each time Carlos had to push to help Marva up the stairwell. He joked that she would have to give birth soon or she would get too big to ride the bus.

They were only a few miles from home on the #4 bus, when Marva suddenly gripped Carlos' forearm and said, "He's coming."

Carlos was no stranger to childbirth. His mother had given birth at home to all his brothers and sisters and, as a boy in Central America, he had assisted farm animals in giving birth. Instinctively, he stripped off his coat and shirt and propped them under Marva's head for a pillow. He loosened her skirt and noted that the contractions were already coming very close together.

"¡Parada!," he yelled, "my wife is having a baby."

The bus driver looked in the mirror, saw Marva, and pulled to a stop at the curb. Grabbing the microphone on the dashboard, he radioed the dispatcher to send an ambulance. Then, turning to Carlos, he asked, "Can I help?"

"Give me your towel," requested Carlos, pointing at a dingy towel hanging from a visor. Reaching up, the driver grabbed the towel he kept there to wipe sweat from his palms.

Suddenly there were sirens and flashing lights all around as a Fire Rescue vehicle and a hook & ladder arrived. Just as the paramedics reached the stairwell, Marva gave one final push and the Baby was born. Thus, Our Savior was born on the Number 4 Rapid Transit District bus between 3rd and Pico, wrapped in a busman's towel, and heralded by flashing emergency lights and sirens.

Feeling elated but weak, Marva drifted in a haze of semi-consciousness. A warm, peaceful glow permeated her being. She was vaguely aware that a fireman was snipping the umbilical cord. Attempting to reach for her baby, she found that her arms would not respond and she sank deeper into the vinyl warmness of the bus seat.

A fireman dressed in a heavy slicker and hip boots was telling passengers to return to their seats. Soon, the hook & ladder left, leaving the paramedics to attend to the details.

One of the paramedics directed Carlos to an adjoining seat and began to question him. Carlos gave the paramedic the information he needed for his report while constantly craning his neck to look at Marva and the Baby.

"Don't worry," the paramedic attending Marva said, "both the mother and Baby are doing fine. It's a strong and healthy boy."

The first paramedic asked, “Do you have a name for Him?”

“Jeruzabellah,” Marva mumbled.

“Jesse, who?” asked the paramedic.

“She means Jesus,” laughed Carlos.

The second paramedic cleaned the newborn Jesus and wrapped Him in fresh linen. The infant Jesus had protested for a short time when the paramedic first handled Him, but now He was quiet and smiling.

“Are you the father?” the first paramedic queried. “No offense, but he sure doesn’t look like you.”

Carlos had seen that the Baby’s skin was darker than ebony, a deep black that almost shined. Now, glancing at the white skin of the paramedic, he quipped, “He doesn’t resemble you either.”

“We deliver two or three babies a month,” said the paramedic. “I normally carry cigars to celebrate the occasion, but I seem to be fresh out.” Reaching deep in a pocket, he pulled out a small paper and foil tube. “Here, have a breath mint,” he offered.

“Thanks,” said Carlos accepting. Then, turning to look at the Baby Jesus he ventured, “He’s so big and strong. Maybe He will grow up to be a fireman and save lives.”

Swiveling on the seat, the first paramedic took Jesus from his partner. He stood and raised Him over his head until the Baby's backside touched the curved metal ceiling of the bus. Studying the Infant's face, he commented, "With a name like Jesus he will have to save more than a few lives—more like the entire world!"

Chapter 7

It wasn't long before Carl Utz got his genetically engineered Frankenstein monsters. Fourteen hideous inhuman babies were born to Chicago area mothers within a three week period. National tabloids ran their pictures on the front page. People wanted swift justice.

Solving the case proved easy. A common thread linked the 14 mothers: all had undergone in vitro test tube fertilization and embryo transfers at the University of Chicago Medical Center.

Within an hour after landing at O'Hare International Airport in Chicago, Utz interrogated Emmanuel Feinstein, one of the Biology graduate students responsible for incubating the embryos until they were ready to be transplanted into their mothers' wombs. Feinstein, a timid, scruffy little man with a scraggly beard, unruly hair, and anodized gold wire rim spectacles, broke down almost immediately and confessed to having introduced pigeon culture into the embryos. Cells from pigeons were induced to fuse with human embryo cells, forming dual nuclei heterokaryons which, when they divided, produced hybrid pigeon-human cells and altered the genetic composition of the developing fetuses. Overcome with remorse, he claimed that he had not intended to create monsters. He had simply tried to combine the embryo transfers with a primate research project that had recently had its funding eliminated. Instead of effectuating primates with an infallible sense of direction, he had inadvertently unleashed a public distrust of scientists and genetics that threatened to doom him and his profession.

With a flare for the dramatic and an awareness of the value of public relations, Utz arranged for the feckless man's arrest to take place at the Federal Building in a room filled with bright lights and reporters. After advising him of his Miranda rights and placing him under arrest, Utz ordered Feinstein to stand. Too dazed to comprehend or comply, he could only remain seated. Grabbing Feinstein by his shirt, Utz lifted him bodily from the chair. The next day the New York Times ran the photo on the front page beneath the headline "G-Man Collars Monster." Seemingly overnight Carl Utz and the GES became famous.

Several weeks later the White House received a threat that terrorists had stolen a presidential blood sample from Walter Reed Hospital and were using it to clone perfect copies of the nation's leader. Although a Secret Service investigation found the threat to have been a hoax, the President was sufficiently disturbed to personally ask Utz what his agency would require to prevent something like this from actually taking place. Off the top of his head, Utz asked for 150 additional agents, a $40 million a year budget, a national DNA Identification & Research Center, and unprecedented police powers. To his amazement, Utz got more than he requested.

In less than a month Utz had gone from being an obscure bureaucrat to the nation's top G-man. Success agreed with Carl. He had even bigger plans in mind.

PART TWO

JESUS, THE GREAT RECYCLER

". . . You must be born again!" John 3:7

Chapter 8

Orange County, California

The Crystal Cathedral in Southern California, a modern Tower of Babel.

Marva knew all about heaven. Heaven had a 14 amp vacuum cleaner, a food processor, a trash compactor, a microwave oven, an automatic dishwasher, a garbage disposal, a hot air popcorn popper, waffle iron, frost-free refrigerator, electric skillet, four-slice toaster, large capacity freezer, stainless steel heavy duty front loading washing machine, four cycle clothes dryer, six burner self-cleaning gas range and oven, Water-pik, hair dryer, electric can opener, personal computer, and an electric wok. In heaven there was a cordless telephone with automatic redial, a digital answering machine, a big screen stereo television, lifelike digital 3D DVD, compact disc player, AM-FM console stereo radio, electronic security system, and a satellite dish antennae with more than 500 channels.

Heaven came complete with five bedrooms, two and a half bathrooms, large walk-in closets, enclosed patio, cinder block fence, 3 car garage, remote control garage door opener, automatic sprinkler system, custom kitchen cabinets, central air conditioning, forced air heating, intercom, family room, dining room, plush stain-resistant carpeting, brick fireplace, greenhouse kitchen window, skylight, hardwood floors, gilded bathroom fixtures, and a 100% fireproof concrete tile roof with a lifetime guarantee.

Heaven was in the suburbs, far away from drugs and crime. Heaven had good public schools within walking distance, twice a week trash pickup, nearby shopping centers, and a fire department that responded in less than 30 seconds when someone dialed 911.

Heaven was adorably landscaped with fruit trees and ground cover. Heaven was pastel pink stucco with chocolate brown trim and large brick planters. Heaven was the home that Marva had always longed for. And when the real estate agent showed Mr. and Mrs. Ortiz heaven, they instantly fell in love with it and considered it a bargain at only $198,000.

Marva and Carlos came to venerate technology. It made their lives easier. Although neither understood the mechanics of the appliances they owned, both regarded them with a fascination bordering on reverence. Never before had they been so comfortable. Dinner was cooked by the turn of a timer and entertainment was summoned with the flick of a remote control. Life in Central Los Angeles had been survival of the fittest. Life in the suburbs was pleasantly mellow. The contrast was so shockingly vivid that the past seemed almost a surreal dream. Neither Marva nor Carlos desired to ever wake again to the nightmare that was their former lives in the inner city.

God had created heaven and man had eventually managed to clone it. To Mr. and Mrs. Ortiz, like many others, the distinction was becoming blurred.

Carlos got a job as a cabinetmaker for custom homes. He was good at his work and much in demand. As the family prospered, it grew. Esteban was born one year after Jesus. Then came Carlos Jr., Christopher, David, and Paul.

Jesus was a strong and healthy child. As Marva watched Him play with other children, she attempted to convince herself that He was not different from them. But He was. He carried an aura that caused people to notice Him. A neighbor lady remarked that when she held the Infant Jesus, she felt a warm, tingling feeling, almost as if she had encountered an electrical field.

When Jesus was five, Marva registered Him for public school.

He was given the usual inoculations, a physical, and a blood test. There was a minor discrepancy in the results. Although Jesus seemed to be in perfect health, the doctor wanted to send the blood sample to the DNA Identification and Research Center for further analysis. There was nothing to worry about, he simply wanted to be safe.

Jesus did well in school. He made friends easily and was a natural leader. One of His teachers remarked that He had a knack for settling disagreements between other students. Although He did not make straight "A's", His grades were above average.

One day in the third grade during recess, Jesus was playing basketball when a member of His team inadvertently threw the ball on the roof of the cafeteria. Another player shinnied up a pole supporting an overhang in order to retrieve it. But when he went to get down, he found that he could not reach the pole. Some of the other third graders shouted at him to jump. For almost a minute he hesitated at the edge, unsure of what to do. More and more children yelled, "Jump!" Looking over the side, he lost his balance, slipped on the rain gutter, and fell to the asphalt head first. Many students later claimed that his head split open like a ripe melon on impact, spattering blood and gray matter everywhere. However, when the teacher reached the accident, Jesus was holding the victim's head in His arms and all that appeared to be wrong with him were some minor lacerations. The teacher said it was a miracle that anyone could fall head first from such a height without sustaining serious injury. Jesus just smiled.

After school and on weekends, Jesus helped Marva take care of His younger brothers. On Saturdays and holidays there were family outings. On Sundays they attended services at the Crystal Cathedral.

The Crystal Cathedral was twentieth century man's Tower of Babel. Pinnacles of glass rose to challenge the heavens. Like a giant multi-faceted prism, it refracted heaven's rays, dazzling the beholder. Its transparent radiance marred the boundaries between earth and sky. One could not gaze upon it without being impressed by overwhelming achievement. Architecturally, it was one of the wonders of the modern world.

The wonders of the Crystal Cathedral, however, were not limited to architecture. Besides a seating capacity of several thousand worshippers, it boasted an outdoor drive-in complex complete with rows of speakers and a 50 foot silver screen. For those who preferred the comfort and independence of their own automobiles, the drive-in Crystal Cathedral afforded the ultimate in convenience. Mothers changed their infants' soiled diapers without missing a single word of the sermon. And fathers could occasionally turn on the car radio to see how their favorite football team was doing.

The Crystal Cathedral was no mere local landmark to be seen once and then forgotten. Via a weekly syndicated television program, the Crystal Cathedral transmitted its evangelistic message throughout the United States and to 38 foreign countries. But it was perhaps best known for infomercials featuring starving Third World children with matchstick legs, distended bellies, and open sores who would soon die were it not for the monetary gifts of love being sent to a post office box in Orange County, California.

If God's benevolence could be measured in dollars, than the Crystal Cathedral was truly the Holy of Holies. Each week it received millions in offerings and donations. The Internal Revenue Service had attempted to revoke its tax-free, non-profit status on several occasions, only to be outmaneuvered by hefty contributions from the Cathedral to the reigning political party. When the President of the United States took the oath of office for his second term, he used a Bible given to him by the church's founder. Business was good for the Crystal Cathedral and having the right political connections made it even better.

The founder, pastor and Chief Executive Officer of the Crystal Cathedral was the Reverend Robert A. Schiller whose unique amalgamation of religion with technology, polemics and business savvy had begat personal success, fame and fortune. Sundays saw his benign image projected bigger than life on the drive-in's screen. Thanks to the electronic wizardry of television, he was also the guest of honor in tens of thousands of living rooms from Los Angeles to Yokohama. He had written 33 books—one of which had sold over a million and a half copies in the Orient alone. All the recognition, wealth, and respect that he had desperately craved as an only child growing up in a small Midwestern town had become his. But the Reverend Schiller was a fraud who benefited unduly from the donations he sought in God's name. And, although he had succeeded in deceiving others, he could not hide his heart from his maker. He was as transparent as the Cathedral that was about to come crashing down around him.

Chapter 9

On Sunday mornings Marva awoke early to cook a big breakfast. She placed two large platters in the center of the table heaped with waffles, bacon, and eggs. The younger children squirmed in their chairs in anticipation as the aroma wafted through the air, but nobody touched either platter until Carlos said grace. His prayers reflected the gratitude he felt for all that God had done for him and his family. Although there was more than enough food, Carlos served his youngest sons before passing the platters around the table.

After breakfast everyone dressed in their best clothes and got ready for church. It was a short drive to the Crystal Cathedral. Carlos dropped the children off at Sunday School while he and Marva attended regular services. The boys were divided into classes according to age groups; the younger ones colored biblical scenes with crayons while the older boys learned stories from the Bible and discussed religious principles with their teacher. Jesus was forever questioning everything. Jesus was especially interested in how various morals, ethics, and religious concepts applied to everyday modern life.

Jesus did not ask easy questions. Once, the teacher became so frustrated that he asked Jesus if He would rather teach the class. The entire class snickered. But Jesus apologized and said that He meant no disrespect—

He only wanted to make certain He clearly understood everything in the lesson.

Sunday School ended an hour before the regular services did. When the weather was decent, Jesus and His brothers would play in the park across the street from the church until it was time to rejoin Marva and Carlos. Taking off their coats, they carefully laid them on a picnic table to keep them from getting dirty before climbing the palo verdes, black oaks, and pepper trees that dotted the small park. Jesus took it on Himself to make certain that no one slipped and fell. He restricted the younger boys to an old spreading carob with low-lying branches until they developed the skills to join their older brothers.

Most times there were older people in the park, some walking dogs and others picnicking. And almost always there were homeless people pushing shopping carts containing their meager possessions. An elderly bag lady often smiled at the children, but never said a word. Occasionally, a bum attempting to nap on a park bench would curse if they made too much noise.

* * *

Jesus was running along the sidewalk towards a towering hollow pepper tree that Esteban and Carlos, Jr. were already ascending. As He passed a park bench a voice rasped, "Hey kid, you got a quarter?"

Upon reaching the pepper tree's gnarled base, Jesus

abruptly stopped and turned to face the disheveled ancient derelict who was slowly rising from the park bench. The bum was wearing a grungy sweatshirt emblazoned with a happy face and a pair of threadbare jeans. Both he and his clothes were in dire need of washing. "In the name of God, son, can you spare some change?" the derelict begged.

Staring at him for perhaps fifteen seconds, Jesus took in the long graying hair beneath the Chicago Cubs baseball cap, the three day growth of beard, and the partially laced tennis shoes. Then His gaze penetrated the man's surface features and peered at his soul. Maintaining eye contact, Jesus advanced toward him, asking, "What is it about your life that you would like God to change?"

The bum looked startled. Rarely had he encountered such self-confidence in one so young. Taking a step backwards, he mumbled, "That's not what I meant."

"No," Jesus said, getting in the bum's face, "what you want is money for liquor so you can commit slow suicide."

Recovering, the bum leaned forward and said, "You think you're a right smart little know-it-all, speaking to your elders like that."

But Jesus refused to back down. Eyeball to eyeball, inhaling second-hand, fetid breath, Jesus stood His ground, remarking, "Age does not always bring wisdom.

You asked for my Father's help. Do you want it or not?"

Confused, the bum retreated to the park bench. Attempting to focus his thoughts, he stammered, "I need . . . Something."

"We all need something, sometimes," said Jesus as He sat down next to the man. Then, extending His right hand in the universal gesture of friendship, He asked "What is your name?"

Perfunctorily, the bum accepted the handshake. But as he did so, he instantly felt an exhilarating force surge throughout his being. Startled, he recoiled, but Jesus held his hand firmly and did not let go.

"What is your name?" Jesus calmly repeated.

Taken aback, the bum managed to utter, "Condo Don," as Jesus relaxed His grip.

The Redeemer sat on the park bench talking with Condo Don for almost a half hour. His brothers sat motionless in the tree, but could only catch bits and pieces of the conversation that was taking place beneath them. Finally, they climbed down, announcing that it was time to leave.

"Go ahead without me," ordered Jesus.

"But what will we tell mother?" asked Esteban.

"Tell her I am spending the night with a sick friend. I'll be home before breakfast."

Esteban gathered his younger brothers, helping them to put on their coats and brush themselves off. One final glance backwards at Jesus sitting on the park bench and they dashed across the road to the Crystal Cathedral.

* * *

Condo Don didn't really trust Jesus (or anyone else). Thirty years of hard living on the streets learning the lessons of life the tough way had made him a cynic. But he had also learned not to look a gift horse in the mouth. This kid was offering to help him without any obligation on his part. It was no skin off his hind end to play it out and see what the kid had to offer.

And Condo Don was desperate for help. Thirty years of alcohol and drug abuse had aged him considerably. His skin was yellowed with jaundice and he had pussy open sores that refused to heal. Arthritis caused his joints to ratchet like the Tin Man in Wizard of Oz. He wasn't able to keep pace with the nomadic migrations the homeless must make to survive. A straggler cut of from the herd, he was easy prey for the truly evil deranged predators that roam city streets at night. Sometimes delirium tremors made him envision his own death and awaken screaming. He felt physically and mentally that the end for him was near.

And this kid was different from the other Bible thumpers that Condo Don had encountered. Jesus treated him like an equal and did not attempt to make his personal decisions for him. He had stood up to Condo Don's intimidation and had slowly backed the aging derelict down. Jesus was somebody that Condo Don could respect.

Just sitting next to Jesus was having an effect on Condo Don. His gestures were becoming more animated and his thoughts less hazy. He was slurring fewer words. It was almost as if Jesus was recharging his battery.

Jesus proved to be the consummate listener. As Condo Don rambled on, spinning tales of his travels, Jesus encouraged him to expound upon his somewhat vulgar philosophy of life, occasionally asking him to elaborate on certain points.

The time flew by and it was twilight before Condo Don realized he hadn't had a drink in hours. Reaching under the park bench, he fumbled with a plastic sack and brought forth a pint liquor bottle that had already been emptied of everything but the dregs and started to unscrew the cap.

"Is that what you want?" inquired Jesus.

"What I want is not important," scowled Condo Don. "It's what I need." With that he raised the bottle to his lips and turned it upside down, draining its contents. Just as quickly as it went down, the liquor came back up and was spat on the walkway. Condo Don's face turned a vivid flushed red and he coughed violently.

Jesus laughed. He looked at Condo Don and doubled up with laughter.

"What did you do?" Condo Don angrily demanded, "I bet you pissed in the bottle when I wasn't looking."

"Your body had a normal reaction to alcohol," said Jesus as His laughter subsided. "It has healed and is no longer dependent on chemicals. The diseases that were ravaging you are gone and your sores are no more."

Condo Don rolled up the right sleeve of his sweatshirt. Above a red tattoo of the number "13" on his forearm there had been an open sore. Nothing remained of it, not even a scab. The skin was a healthy flesh tone and all traces of jaundice had vanished.

"How did you do that?" asked an astounded Condo Don.

"Certainly not by urinating in your bottle," laughed Jesus. "You asked for God's help and He gave it to you."

Condo Don hurriedly rolled up his other sleeve and both pant legs. It was true. His afflictions had vanished. Even the purple spidery varicose veins around his knees were gone.

Giving the empty bottle a toss, Condo Don watched as it fell and shattered in a thousand pieces on the sidewalk. Once again he reached beneath the park bench. This time he removed a lump of sharp cheddar cheese from the sack. Breaking it in two unequal parts, he offered the smaller half to Jesus.

"Thank you," said Jesus as He took the cheese from Condo Don's grimy hand.

"It's me that should be giving the thanks," remarked Condo Don as tears began to well in his eyes. "I'm truly grateful to God and I will repay Him if it takes the rest of my days."

Quickly the night fell. Condo Don went to sleep on the park bench and dreamed of Christ fighting the Evil One for possession of his soul. When he awoke the next morning, Jesus was gone.

* * *

Condo Don's transformation did not go unnoticed. His friends marveled at his new found health and vitality. They were amazed by his ability to go "cold turkey" without any noticeable side effects. Besides looking ten years younger, he claimed to have been "reborn" while waiting at the threshold of death. But most of all, they were astounded by his story of the teenage "miracle worker" who had saved his life. Condo Don had a reputation for telling tall tales, but no one could refute that something strange and wonderful had changed him for the better. Overnight the dark cynicism and suspicion that had pervaded his personality departed, replaced by optimism and a new appreciation for life. It was as if an ugly outer layer had been stripped from the aging derelict, revealing a totally unexpected inner wholesomeness and freshness.

The following week when Jesus went to the park after Sunday School, He had little opportunity to play with His brothers and the other children. Several of Condo Don's skeptical friends had come to meet the young "miracle worker." They bombarded Him with questions. He chose His words carefully and tried to answer each to the best of His ability. But hardly had He finished one, when He was asked another. Finally, His brothers rescued Him by saying it was time to go.

Every Sunday thereafter Jesus returned to the park to discover the number of people waiting to see Him had grown. Condo Don tried hard to control his buddies, but with little success. They often reached out to touch Jesus without asking His permission as if He were a freak on display in a sideshow. But Jesus seemed to thrive on harsh treatment and was never offended by irrelevant or irreverent questions.

To the public it appeared that the park had been taken over by vagrants. The police swept the park one night, confiscating shopping carts and throwing the belongings of the homeless in a dumpster. They were all forced to empty their pockets and lean against a chain link fence while the cops frisked for drugs. As of the following week, the police warned, anyone found loitering in the park without visible means of support would be arrested and taken to jail.

Condo Don related the story of the police raid to Jesus the following Sunday. He also reported that many of the people coming to listen to Jesus in the park were hungry.

"Where have you been getting food?" asked Jesus.

"By panhandling and from the fruit trees that border the park, but all the fruit was picked long ago."

"Look again," said Jesus, "God's abundance is not easily depleted. I will come an hour earlier next Sunday and arrange to get you some help from the Crystal Cathedral."

After Jesus left, Condo Don and his homeless friends scoured the trees for any fruit they might have missed. Just when they thought it had all been harvested, a vigilant search would find more. Nobody went hungry all week.

Instead of attending Sunday School with His brothers the following Sunday, Jesus slipped across the street to the park. He and Condo Don set to work assembling the twenty-some bag ladies, disabled veterans, and other homeless people who were living in the park. It took the better part of an hour to get them in some sort of order. With Jesus taking the point position and Condo Don halting traffic they crossed the street to the Crystal Cathedral. Caked with dirt, dressed in rags, with pockets stuffed to overflowing with possessions, they looked like an Army of Salvation marching on a fabled temple.

Since the services had already begun, the great double doors were closed. Condo Don flung one open and held it while the others filed inside.

The congregation turned to watch as Jesus led His motley flock down the richly carpeted center aisle. With his attention focused on the television cameras, the Reverend Schiller was not initially aware of their presence. He was finishing an appeal to the congregation and his television audience for donations to help starving African children when he caught sight of the intruders. Switching off the microphone and motioning for the camera to stop, he stepped in front of the altar.

"What is the nature of this disturbance?" he demanded.

"We come to hear the word of God and beseech your charity. Please grant sanctuary to these impoverished unfortunates who are in need of food and shelter," said Jesus.

"We give only to those who deserve," announced the

Reverend Schiller in a calm, clear voice that carried unaided throughout the cathedral. "These people are clearly shiftless rabble. Unwilling to work, contemptuous of all that is holy, and lacking in self-discipline, they are prisoners of their own degradation."

"I will not waste our church's slim resources on the likes of them."

"Neither your own personal resources nor those of the Crystal Cathedral are meager," retorted Jesus. "You make millions from your televised ministries. How can you express concern for people you have never met while ignoring those who are starving before your very eyes?"

"I will not permit you to continue to disrupt these services with impunity," declared the Reverend Schiller as he signaled three beefy security guards to come out from behind a curtained backdrop. "Kindly escort these people from the Cathedral."

The cleric's curt command was answered by a rumbling noise centered directly below, miles beneath the earth's surface. From high overhead there came the sound of tinkling glass, like the rustle of the wind through chimes. As the guards moved forward, their path was suddenly blocked by falling panes of glass which exploded into myriad shards upon impacting the undulating floor.

As the quake gathered momentum and more and

more panes fell, the congregation panicked and pushed towards the exits.

Condo Don and his friends were jostled by the stampede.

"Fear not!" shouted Jesus above the pandemonium. "No one will be hurt. God seeks your assistance, not your destruction."

"Leave this place!" screamed the Reverend Schiller. "God is objecting to your foul presence in His house!"

"It is you who have desecrated God's house with your avarice" admonished Jesus. "The impure shall not glimpse my Father, though they peer through the clearest glass."

"Blasphemer!" yelled Reverend Schiller, raising a bony finger to point at Jesus. But before he could fully extend his arm, a pane of glass struck him a glancing blow, forcing it downward.

And the glass continued to crash down around the Reverend Schiller, but cut him not. In desperation he stumbled backwards and bent to pick up a sharp piece of glass which he then hurled in Jesus' direction.

But Jesus had already turned and was walking up the aisle, leading His flock to safety. Reaching the double doors, He gave a departing admonition to the Reverend Schiller: "That which you garner in my Father's name, you must distribute in His name. Hold in awe the Wonder of God, rather than the Works of Man."

Long after the shaking subsided, the Reverend Schiller stood alone amidst the wreckage. Studying the twisted beams and broken glass, he assessed the dollar value of the damage as he listened to the wail of approaching sirens. By the time a team of firemen reached him, he had finished calculating a rough estimate.

"Are you hurt?" asked a paramedic as he examined the minister for lacerations. Finding no wounds, he declared, "It's a miracle that nobody was hurt in a disaster of this magnitude."

"Yes, a miracle," the Reverend Schiller mumbled distractedly as his mind raced to compare the costs of replacement to the value of the Crystal Cathedral's insurance policy. Already he could envision a bigger and better Crystal Cathedral being built as soon as the debris could be hauled away.

Retreating to the relative safety of the park, Jesus' flock regrouped. They were scared and visibly shaken. Jesus and Condo Don circulated among them, speaking to each and alleviating their fears. A bag lady screamed hysterically until Jesus calmed her by laying the palm of His hand upon her forehead.

It was a beautiful day in the park. The sun had just began to warm the air and a light breeze rustled the tops of the tallest trees. Brimming with pinkish blossoms, the mock orchid flowers of a floss silk tree belied the spiny thorns of its trunk. Only the mangled and broken spires of the Crystal Cathedral as viewed through the trees gave evidence to the disaster that had occurred mere moments before.

Stripping some of the multiple layers of clothing they wore at night for warmth, the homeless wandered off to retrieve the trash bags that held the remnants of their belongings. Everyone froze in fear as several police cruisers drove slowly by the park.

After consulting Jesus, Condo Don summoned the flock to gather around him. There would be no immediate help from the Crystal Cathedral. He thanked them for their patience and told them not to lose faith. Following a prayer to Almighty God in gratitude that no one had been injured, Condo Don implored them to remember the miracles they had witnessed during the past few weeks. He then asked them to disperse and tell others what had happened.

After the last individual had departed, Jesus and Condo Don sat down on a picnic table. There was several minutes of silence before Jesus spoke:

"Who am I?" He asked softly.

"You are Jesus, the Messiah, the Son of God and the Savior of Man," replied Condo Don without hesitation. "You saved my life and rekindled my spirit. I have watched You perform miracles impossible for any mortal man."

"I am mortal," said Jesus, "all too soon I will be nothing but a memory."

"Let me die in your place," offered Condo Don.

"Let us not speak of death," commented Jesus as He placed a hand on Condo Don's shoulder. "Everlasting joy will triumph over sadness. Soon, I must go among the people to release mankind from the bondage of sin. You must go before Me to prepare them for my coming. Tell everyone you meet the good news."

Jesus stood, shook Condo Don's hand, and departed. Condo Don watched Him leave with tears in his eyes. "I will not fail You," he whispered.

The Reverend Robert A. Schiller was like a man possessed. For the next several months following the destruction of the Crystal Cathedral, he seemed to be everywhere doing everything at once.

Money was not a problem. Both the Crystal Cathedral and he personally owned investments worth tens of millions of dollars. Although the insurance company was raising questions concerning the structural integrity of the Crystal Cathedral (it was one of the few commercial structures to suffer damage in what had proved to be a localized quake), Reverend Schiller had little doubt that they would eventually pay the claim.

Obtaining a suitable edifice for a temporary church had been his main problem. Buildings that could seat several thousand worshippers in a single room were not easy to come by on short notice. After examining several possibilities, he chose an open air sports stadium. It had lost its team franchise and the owner was willing to lease it cheap. Open air seating would permit lavish use of zoom shots by the television crew.

Cameras, booms, and all the transmission equipment that had been lost in the quake had to be replaced immediately. Satellite time was expensive. Besides, millions of viewers in thirty-eight countries awaited his weekly sermons and solicitations. If the broadcasts stopped, the donations would also stop.

And forever boding in the back of his mind was the question of who or what had prompted a young, black twerp to lead a bunch of disheveled hooligans in the disruption of services at the very moment when his beloved Cathedral was being destroyed. Reverend Schiller suspected a conspiracy. He had made business enemies during his thirty years of competitive evangelism. Perhaps they had found a way to get even.

He decided to employ a detective agency to perform a thorough investigation. They would conduct a total surveillance of Jesus, His family, and their contacts for the next year and complete a background check. Surely this would provide some answers to the questions burning within him.

The title of Reverend Schiller's first sermon in the stadium was to be "The Miracle of the Crystal Cathedral." Not one person had suffered so much as a cut from the tons of falling glass. God had pointedly demonstrated the shortcomings of the original Cathedral. Millions of dollars in donations were needed to design and build a new, larger and safer, Crystal Cathedral.

Carlos was quite proud of his son's confrontation with the Reverend Schiller at the Crystal Cathedral. The Ortiz family had been dispossessed in Central America prior to emigration and he identified with the plight of the homeless. Many Central American refugees had received assistance from Protestant churches in the United States and this had been a major factor in his conversion from Catholicism. He viewed the mission of the church as one of charity and, unlike the majority of the congregation, he had been appalled by Reverend Schiller's display of callous indifference. Instead of attending the new church at the stadium, he chose to conduct his own services at home. On Sunday morning he had each of his sons read selected passages from the

Bible while he and his wife commented on their meaning and related them to examples drawn from everyday life. Jesus showed Himself particularly adept at interpreting the Scriptures and as time went on Carlos came to rely on His judgment.

Although he saw no reason to confront her, Carlos had always discounted Marva's assertion that Jesus was the Son of God. Yet, as he watched the Child progress and witnessed Jesus' actions, he had to admit that there was indeed an element of the Divine about Him. Could it be that Marva was telling the truth?

Several weeks after the destruction of the Crystal Cathedral, it became apparent to Carlos that he and his family were under surveillance. It scared him at first. He imagined the men keeping an eye on his home were officers of the Immigration and Naturalization Service or some other government agency. But after a while, he came to the conclusion that they were too shabbily dressed, clumsy, and ill-trained to be agents. He had only to use the backdoor to avoid them and they made scant effort to disguise their presence.

With time the stakeout in front of their home became a running joke. Several times the neighbors called the police at night and reported that suspicious people were loitering in a parked car. Esteban slipped out his second story bedroom window one night and discovered that both of the men on stakeout were asleep. They were startled awake when he shouted, “How's it going?” through the vehicle's open window.

Marva was genuinely concerned about the men on the stakeout. She often took them coffee in the morning which they accepted with gratitude. When winter came and the temperature dropped almost to freezing, she even offered to let them sleep in the living room. Although they declined, they did take some blankets. Marva would not permit her boys to tease or humiliate the men; she maintained they were simply doing their job, trying to earn an honest living.

Chapter 10

It was long past midnight when the Greyhound bus pulled into the downtown Los Angeles depot. Exiting, Condo Don walked several blocks to the Pico-Union district, known to locals as Skidrow. He found a flattened cardboard box in a dumpster behind an appliance store and dragged it across the street into the setback doorway of a boarded-up thrift store. Using the box for a makeshift mattress and the laundry bag that contained his possessions as a pillow, he slid the toes of his shoes under an edge of the improvised bed and was soon sound asleep.

Feeling a slight tug on the cardboard the next morning, Condo Don awoke in an instant to find someone trying to steal his shoes. His hand shot out and he grabbed a man's ankle, pulling him to the ground. Placing one stocking foot firmly on the thief's chest, Condo Don scrambled upright just in time to grab the man's partner by the collar of his jacket. Spinning him around, Condo Don gave the culprit a hefty heave that sent him sprawling into the doorway beside his accomplice.

When they got to their feet, the two thieves attempted to rush him, but it wasn't much of a fight. Grabbing them by the neck, he butted their heads together and tossed them back in the doorway.

Reaching down, he removed a pint bottle from the

tallest thief's coat pocket and smashed it against the brick wall, showering both with glass splinters and Muscatel. As Condo Don moved to position himself between them and the sidewalk, the duo of would-be thieves huddled together in abject fear.

From beneath his sweatshirt Condo Don produced a small, vinyl bound book and, shaking it under the short thief's nose, asked him if he recognized it.

"It's a Bible," the man stammered.

"You must be the brains of this outfit," snarled Condo Don. Snatching the Bible back, he leafed through it to Exodus 20:15. Indicating the passage with a finger, he again put the Bible in the thief's face and told him to read it.

"Thou shalt not steal," mumbled the thief.

"Louder, like you mean it!" roared Condo Don.

"Thou shalt not steal!" squealed the thief.

Condo Don put the Bible back in his sweatshirt and, leaning over, pulled the two men to their feet and made a big show of dusting them off before shoving them into the street and telling them to get lost fast. The last glimpse Condo Don had of the pair, they were running into each other as they rounded a corner a block away.

After tying his shoelaces, Condo Don took an empty trash sack from his laundry bag. Ambling down the sidewalk, he periodically stooped to retrieve aluminum cans from the gutter and place them in the plastic sack. Occasionally, he made short detours into alleys to search dumpsters for cans. Three hours of scavenging filled the sack. Taking it to a redemption center on 6th Street, he cashed in his booty for $4.87.

As he was leaving the redemption center, he encountered an old friend. His buddy told him about a burned out warehouse on Sepulveda Avenue that was being used by the homeless for temporary shelter.

Condo Don crossed the busy street to a market where he bought two loaves of wheat bread and a pound of bologna. He ate nearly a whole loaf of bread and half of the bologna in a nearby city park, feeding the crusts to a skittish stray dog who darted in and out for the crumbs. The park's restroom was locked and Condo Don was forced to defecate in some tall bushes next to a basketball court, using broad crumpled leaves for toilet paper.

It took nearly three hours for him to walk to the warehouse on Sepulveda. The sun was dipping slowly behind the rooftops when he squeezed under a cyclone fence and trotted the few remaining yards to the warehouse.

Ascending the stairs, he found six men sitting in a

circle on the second floor, passing a dark green screw top gallon jug of Red Mountain wine around. The place smelled musty and there were scorch marks on the I-beams bracing the roof. Gaping holes in the northwestern wall admitted the dying rays of an orange-red sun.

The friend he had met while cashing in his cans greeted Condo Don and invited him to take a place in the circle. Condo Don made himself comfortable, using the laundry bag for a back rest. Soon, the man on his right passed him the jug. Condo Don gave it to the man on his left without even raising it to his lips.

"I heard you got religion," ventured Condo Don's friend.

"More like it got me," said Condo Don. "I got tremendous sick and was about to croak when I latched onto this black teenager who turned out to be Jesus Christ—reincarnated in the flesh. Wasn't sure I could trust Him, but I figured He was on the level after He healed me and a few other hard cases. I watched Him shatter a big church built entirely of glass when the preacher refused to give a hand out to some down and outs. Since then, I've been going around telling folks not to give up hope—that help is on the way."

"And I suppose this Jesus fellow came here to save the likes of you," snickered the man on the right as he pointedly passed the jug around Condo Don.

"It's His job, He doesn't just mingle with saints," retorted Condo Don. "When something gets broke down here on Earth, Heaven sends Him to repair it. Don't you think the world could use some fixing?"

"Yeah, but even if Jesus has come back as a nigger, He's still got sense enough to steer clear of this shit hole. We ain't done nothing to make Him take a liking to us."

"You recycle cans, don't you?" asked Condo Don. "You don't do it 'cause you like cans. You do it 'cause it makes sense and it's profitable. Jesus recycles people. He may not particularly care for some of us or the things we have done, but it's stupid to keep putting new people on this planet if they just go bad. Jesus is here to fix things and cut down on human waste."

"I like getting wasted," chuckled the man opposite Condo Don in the circle as he took a big swig from the jug.

"Sure," glowered Condo Don as he peered into the man's eyes, "then you are really going to love the jaundice, malnutrition, and DT's that go with it. I had all those before Jesus healed me. How many of them do you got?"

The man opposite lowered his eyes from Condo Don's gaze. He declined to answer and became lost in his own sullen thoughts.

"How about the rest of you?," asked Condo Don, looking at each face in turn around the circle. "How long will you last on the street living hard like this? Ten years, maybe twenty? My pals left me on a park bench for dead when it looked like I was a goner. How do you reckon it will end for you? If it weren't for meeting up with Jesus, I'd be in the ground and the worms would be eating me right now."

"You're a real party pooper," Condo Don's friend complained. "Maybe I made a mistake inviting you here."

"Yep," agreed Condo Don, rising to his feet, "maybe you did; most people don't want to hear the truth when it's bad news." Condo Don walked over to the corner of the warehouse farthest from the gaping holes in the wall and lay down on his back, placing his laundry bag beneath his head. Although he closed his eyes, his ears strained to hear the conversation at the circle.

For a long time there was silence. Then the man who had been sitting to the left of Condo Don spoke. "You know, maybe he's got a point," he ventured.

"Shut up and pass the bottle," commanded the man on the right.

Chapter 11

The Reverend Robert A. Schiller was not pleased with the investigative report he received from the detective agency. Other than Donald Thaddeus Stearns III, aka Condo Don, the Ortiz family had no suspicious contacts. Condo Don had conveniently vanished following the destruction of the Crystal Cathedral—perhaps he had a good reason to fear prosecution. Although Reverend Schiller had never met the Stearns family, he knew they wielded heavy political clout. Maybe it all tied in some devious manner yet to be discovered.

Carlos Ortiz was an immigrant from Central America. The report pointed out numerous associations with liberal religious groups and radical clergymen of whom Reverend Schiller did not approve. Although Mr. Ortiz was a legal resident of the United States, he was not yet a citizen. A continued probe might uncover sufficient evidence to have him deported.

And there was one more curious item in the report that he could possibly use to his advantage. Data from a blood test on file at the GES National Identification & Research Center indicated that Jesus Ortiz's genetic structure was medically impossible. The preponderance of tested DNA sequences were undoubtedly of maternal origin, indicating that parthenogenesis (virgin birth) had been the incontestable source of propagation. However, parthenogenesis did not occur naturally in humans and mammals. Also, offspring conceived in such a manner were always female. The researcher who performed the analysis and wrote the evaluation speculated that parthenogenesis may have been induced artificially coupled with simultaneous stimulation of the SRY gene, resulting in a male embryo. He had recommended continued research and investigation. A note attached to the recommendations stated a follow-up investigation had been conducted by a GES agent who found the subject to be a normal healthy child. The case had been dropped.

Picking up the phone, Reverend Schiller dialed the unlisted private phone number of the Attorney General. Janet Carson's secretary answered and said that the Attorney General was not in.

Following a good deal of persuasion, she transferred the call to Carson's cellular phone, which reached her as she was exiting a meeting with senior Immigration and Naturalization Service officials. Reverend Schiller urged her to reopen the case on the Ortiz boy, stressing he had reason to believe the Child had been genetically altered as part of a plot by subversives to undermine American institutions. Janet Carson was skeptical, but ultimately agreed to have GES investigate it as a priority item and urged him to forward any pertinent information or evidence that he had in his possession to the Director, GES.

Most GES cases originated as complaints by individuals. Some were referred to GES from other agencies. A few were initiated at GES' own discretion. Rarely was a case begun or reopened at the direct behest of the Attorney General. When it was, it went directly to Carl Utz. This particular file was accompanied by a report from a private investigative agency and a yellow memo which read simply: "Fix this, J.C."

Utz scowled as he read both the file and the report. He had no intention of harassing or arresting what appeared to be a normal, healthy All-American teenager and his middle class family on the basis of a minor genetic quirk. The newspapers would have a field day with it and the department's image could be tarnished.

Orders were orders, however, and Carl knew that he couldn't just sit on this one. Something had to be done. This fellow, Donald Stearns, certainly appeared suspicious. What was he doing in a public park making secret contacts with a young boy? Why was it impossible to trace his movements? And most of all, how had he suddenly been cured of a terminal disease? Perhaps some form of genetic manipulation was involved.

Utz decided to issue an All Points Bulletin for the arrest of Donald Thaddeus Stearns III. That should satisfy the Attorney General that the department was giving the case top priority.

He kept mulling the case over in his mind. There was

something about it that bothered him; something that triggered a danger signal in the back of his well-honed analytic brain. This had all the characteristics of a political vendetta—a hatchet job as a favor to one of the Administration's biggest contributors. He couldn't ignore the matter considering the weight attached to it by the Attorney General, but he was determined to keep departmental involvement to a minimum. With luck the arrest of Donald Stearns would solve the puzzle. If not, he could always attempt to slough the case off on another agency.

There was something else. Something he couldn't quite put his finger on. Jesus was a common name among Latinos. Why did it bother him in this instance? He opened the file on his desk again and stared at the small photograph of the Ortiz youngster. Years of police work had made Carl a good judge of faces. There was something about this face, something wonderful . . .

* * *

Business had never been better for the Reverend Robert A. Schiller. The stadium seated four times as many people as the Crystal Cathedral and it was filled to capacity for Sunrise Easter Services. As the first fingers of dawn touched the top of the stadium on Easter morning, Reverend Schiller was lifted by a camouflaged hydraulic platform sixteen feet above the stage. Raising his arms towards Heaven in supplication, Reverend Schiller's solemn countenance transformed into one of joy as the sun illuminated his face and he proclaimed, "He has risen!" The congregation spontaneously stood and repeated his words.

It had been a costly presentation to produce. For a $1,000 consultation fee an astronomy professor had come to the stadium and calculated the precise time and location of the sun's first rays on Easter morning. The design and construction of the hydraulic platform had cost another $9,000. But it was money well spent. This year's Easter Sunrise Service was the finest piece of showmanship to date in Reverend Schiller's long and illustrious career.

In fact, he liked it so much that he would later arrange for a clip of his Easter Sunrise drama to be broadcast with the titles at the beginning of every subsequent sermon. He would have the sound of heralding trumpets dubbed in to coincide with the rising of the platform and the scar on his left cheek erased by digital editing.

Everyone was seated by sections and empty or partially filled sections were avoided when filming. Thus, as far as those viewing at home knew, the stadium was always filled to capacity.

Another innovation by Reverend Schiller was the use of a blimp for an aerial perspective. Although blimps had been used for years to film sporting events at stadiums, Reverend Schiller had advanced the technology to new heights. Utilizing his gift for the theatrical, he directed the video cameras to spin as they zoomed in on his sermons. The blimp also featured an electronic billboard which flashed the phone number to dial to make donations via credit card.

Televangelism had proven to be the most lucrative part of the Reverend Robert A. Schiller's ministry. His crusade to raise money for a new Crystal Cathedral had already exceeded its original goal. But he was in no rush to move his ministry from the profitable stadium. In fact, he was considering postponing construction for a year rather than risk cutting off the flow of donations to the emergency construction fund. And there was an additional reason to delay construction. He did not want to dedicate the new Cathedral until the Ortiz boy was out of the picture. Despite Schiller's considerable political influence, he had yet to succeed in getting the government to incarcerate Jesus. But he was a man of great faith and his faith in the greed of politicians led him to believe that with enough money they could be made to see the light.

* * *

One morning, when Marva took the garbage out, she encountered a bum rummaging through the trash cans. She was about to invite him to the back door for a handout when she noticed something peculiar about him. His soft hands were perfectly manicured and his nails glistened with clear nail polish. Upon detecting a faint odor of expensive cologne, Marva ran back into the house and threw the deadbolt on the door. When she peeked out the kitchen window a moment later, he had disappeared.

By the end of the week it had become obvious to the Ortiz family that they were once again under surveillance. This time, however, it was not the work of rank amateurs. At least four vehicles took part in the stakeout on a rotating basis and they never parked in the same place twice. When approached by a family member on foot, a surveillance vehicle would immediately drive away—to be replaced momentarily by another car parked at a different location.

Marva was scared. It had been three years since the first surveillance ended. She thought the threat had vanished. Who were these strange men and what was their motive? By their skill and slick professional manner, she suspected that they were government agents. But why would the government be interested in her family? From her subconscious came the answer: Jesus. Now a senior in high school, her oldest son had matured into an outspoken young man who fearlessly pursued His principles. Could it be that someone at the top of the government felt threatened by His presence?

Marva knew that Jesus was destined for greatness. The angel had told her so long ago. And he had also told her to rejoice. But Marva was concerned for her son's safety. She worried that history might repeat itself—Jesus, being the Messiah, would ultimately come to a painful death by execution. There could be no joy for her until she knew for certain her son was safe. Not even an angel could fathom the depth of the bond that joined mother and son.

What were His plans for the future? Several colleges had offered Him basketball scholarships. But the admission forms sat untouched on the desk in His room. He spent much of His time doing volunteer work for the community, helping the homeless and the destitute. Jesus had confided to her that He felt a calling from God to minister to the poor. Marva shuddered at the prospect of her eldest son returning to the world of poverty and hopelessness from which she and Carlos had escaped. She longed to shield Him even as she felt Him slipping away. Sometimes, during the day when she was home alone, her thoughts would turn to the subject and she would sit down at the dining room table and cry until her saltwater tears lay in miniature tidepools upon the tabletop's oaken surface.

* * *

When the need arose, Carl Utz could be a master procrastinator. He delayed acting against the Ortiz boy for three years while his agents searched in vain for the elusive Donald Stearns. Gradually, pressure from the

Attorney General built to do something concrete. Janet Carson demanded that Jesus be placed in GES custody prior to the dedication service for the new Crystal Cathedral. Reluctantly, Utz agreed to stage a raid on the Ortiz home in conjunction with agents from the Immigration and Naturalization Service and Alcohol, Tobacco and Firearms undercover operatives.

He finally acted on the night before the deadline. Assembling his own men and those from the other agencies, Utz briefed them on the operation. It was to be a quick, well coordinated procedure with ATF conducting a search of the house while GES took Jesus into custody and INS presented Carlos with an order to appear before a deportation hearing. If everything proceeded according to plan, it would be over in less than an hour with no leaks to the press.

Roadblocks were set up at both ends of the short residential street and six vehicles converged on the Ortiz home at one minute before midnight. As one of the ATF's operatives exited an unmarked car, his knee struck the siren toggle and its high pitched wail pierced the night. Having lost the element of surprise, Carl Utz directed his men to break in the front door.

Agents raced through the house with flashlights, dragging the Ortiz family from their beds and assembling them in the living room. Marva was handcuffed as she screamed and thrashed and Carlos was put in a chokehold when he attempted to protect her. The littlest of the Ortiz boys were crying and their older brothers were trying to calm them. Carl made his men put away their weapons to avoid frightening them any further.

Carl counted heads. Someone was missing. He looked carefully in turn at the faces of each of the older children. Jesus was not among them. He sent two agents upstairs to conduct a more thorough search. Jesus had to be somewhere in the house. The surveillance team had noted Him entering the dwelling the previous afternoon and no one had been seen exiting. Carl personally directed his men in searching the closets, cabinets and the crawl space in the attic. It was to no avail. Jesus was nowhere to be found. Carl met with stony silence when he questioned the Ortiz youngsters as to where their brother had gone. Somehow Jesus had eluded him.

* * *

Esteban and Jesus shared an upstairs bedroom. When the stakeout first began, they spent long hours thinking of ways to slip in and out of the house without being detected. Their window was on the side of the house where it could not be easily observed from the street. It was a relatively easy matter to slip through the window and climb the gentle slope of the tile roof. A large trellis that climbed the rear wall provided access to the backyard. Scaling the cinder block fence was no problem for the two oldest Ortiz brothers.

It did not take long to ascertain that Jesus was the target of the investigation. Whenever the brothers split apart, He was the one they followed. Concerned that He was causing trouble for the rest of the family, Jesus packed a backpack with essentials and hid it under the bed.

Esteban slept on the top bunk. Upon being startled awake by a siren, he looked out the window and saw armed men scurrying below. Reaching over the side of the bed, he shook Jesus awake and told Him what he had seen. Dressing quickly, Jesus grabbed the backpack and was opening the window when He heard the front door being kicked in. It only took Him a moment to slip out the window into the night. As Jesus worked his way along the roofline, He prayed for the safety of His family. It took Him almost an hour to crawl through bushes and hedges to avoid the roadblock at the foot of the street.

Dawn was still an hour away when Jesus reached the new Crystal Cathedral. The Cathedral was taller than He remembered and the top spire appeared to scrape shimmering dust from the morning star, magnifying it into a cascade of light as it fell though a thousand panes of glass. Like a gaudy, ostentatious gem that dwarfs the finger of its wearer, it transformed nearby trees into matchsticks and concrete sidewalks into thin gray lines.

Jesus was not impressed. He noted with disdain that

Reverend Schiller had learned little from their previous encounter. Sensing the presence of a malevolent spirit, He knew He would find the Reverend Schiller inside.

Swinging wide the double doors, Jesus entered. The Reverend Schiller was fidgeting with state-of-the-art special effects apparatus attached to a side wall. Jesus immediately addressed him, saying, "Why do you persist in defying God? The taller you build your Cathedral, the more you shrink from heaven."

Jesus' abrupt entrance had caught the cleric unawares. Blind, all encompassing fear short circuited his mental processes. He turned to flee, but saw Jesus blocking the open exit. There was no escape from the words that stung his soul. In desperation, his quivering hand shot to the digital carillon simulator and pressed a button on its control panel.

Reproduced electronic bells, springing from deep within the fabricated bowels of a manufactured circuit board—fully as cold and uncaring as the unmasked ecclesiastic charlatan now cringing before the Son of God—rang "Onward Christian Soldiers" in booming, rich tones from a score of THX Dolby Surround Sound speakers situated at regular intervals along the Cathedral's ceiling. But as it tolled ". . . war," a miniscule speck of dust on an internal drive prompted a laser readout to stick, repeating the same note over and over again, faster and faster, increasing in pitch and amplitude until it culminated in an unholy tone that tore at the glass panels, forcing them to resonate its demonic wail. A million unseen fingernails screeched across an invisible blackboard and were amplified a thousand times. The Reverend Schiller covered his ears with his hands but the raging sound stabbed right through, perforating his ear drums. Blood, oozing from between his fingers, trickled down his cheeks. His screams, compressed by the din, were rammed back down his throat. The piercing, horrendous torrent kept expanding, shaking the glass as if it were made of gelatin.

It shattered. And as Jesus closed the double doors behind Him, a hail of razor sharp shards descended, decapitating the Reverend Robert A. Schiller.

His bells had taken their toll.

Chapter 12

After four years of continuous proselytizing among the homeless and down and out, doubt was beginning to tug at the edges of Condo Don's faith. Often it seemed as if he was banging his head against a brick wall. Despite his evangelistic enthusiasm, he had managed to win no more than a handful of converts. Oftentimes his efforts were met with ridicule and scorn. Adding to his distress was the knowledge that he was the object of a nationwide GES manhunt. He had seen a sketch of himself on the evening news as he was watching television through the window of a discount appliance store several months before. Shaving his beard had scarcely mitigated the threat of arrest and he found himself becoming suspicious of everyone with whom he came in contact. Alerting his fellow man to the impending arrival of The Savior was becoming more difficult with each passing day.

He wondered if it was all real. Could his salvation have been just another hallucination induced by alcohol and drug abuse? No, he told himself, he had been on the verge of death and only a miracle could explain his continued presence among the living. But it was all so hard. His time with Jesus had been very short and so long ago. He could not help but wonder what had happened to Jesus in the interim.

Unintentionally, Condo Don found himself journeying back toward the site of his salvation. He had heard that the Crystal Cathedral had been rebuilt—bigger and more opulent than before. Once again it stood as a symbol of callous indifference to the plight of the poor. How could God allow this to happen? In his prayers he asked God to somehow renew his faltering faith. Perhaps returning to the place where it all began would restore his convictions . . .

Condo Don found the municipal park little changed from the way he remembered it. But opposite loomed a glass monstrosity that stretched upward as if straining to pull down the heavens—a veritable glass Tower of Babel.

As Condo Don sacked out for the night on a familiar park bench, he closed his eyes and let his thoughts drift to when the stalwart young Savior shook his hand as he departed four years ago from this very place. How the power had surged through his body! Physical and psychological addiction had instantaneously been supplanted by spiritual exhilaration. But the fire that Jesus had lit within him was now little more than glowing embers. He found himself longing for a sign from God.

Booming bells belting "Onward Christian Soldiers" startled Condo Don awake. A few notes later, they were superseded by an ear-splitting, screeching tone, escalating in pitch and amplitude like a banshee's wail—a painful, stabbing weapon of sound that cut the night like a sword. Turning to face the invisible enemy, Condo Don watched awestruck as the newly rebuilt Crystal Cathedral imploded. And there, amidst a waterfall of shattered glass, his spiritual mentor was emerging unscathed. Condo Don's heart raced in unison with his feet as he ran towards Jesus.

* * *

Jesus spent the next few months under Condo Don's tutelage, much like an apprentice, learning to survive on the streets. Since indigent wayfarers lack the money to buy the basic necessities of life, they are forced to fend for themselves in any way they can, expending every available ounce of creativity and resourcefulness to acquire the food and shelter that the affluent take for granted. Condo Don taught Jesus to scour dumpsters behind restaurants and markets for edibles and to construct a temporary shelter using cardboard boxes and plastic sheeting. His lessons ranged from caring for an open fire under windy conditions to fishing for smelt without a hook from a railway trestle using string for line and hard cheese for bait. Condo Don found Jesus to be an apt student who seldom needed to be shown anything more than once.

Surviving on the fringe of society entailed more than just food and shelter. One had to learn to address policemen and others in authority with humility. One also had to learn which areas of a city to avoid and which might provide sanctuary. And one had to learn to keep constantly on the move—for the destitute are unwanted and viewed with suspicion everywhere. Remaining too long in one location invites charges of loitering and vagrancy. Jesus quickly absorbed the ins and outs of the migratory untouchable caste of American society. Nomadic existence in a post-industrial culture was not easy. Too often His kind were viewed as surplus population rather than fellow human beings experiencing temporary difficulties. Too often they served as scapegoats for the ills of society.

Modern, post-industrial culture ignores the poor. Without an address, a telephone number, a credit card, or a driver's license, an individual ceases to exist. Those who do not take part in a census, those who do not vote, and those who file no tax returns vanish from view. Chronically unemployed individuals who have exhausted their benefits rarely appear in unemployment statistics and, having no address, the homeless have no means of receiving a welfare check in the mail. Wafting aimlessly on eddies in the backwash of a rocket propelled technocracy, they are abandoned and forgotten. Although a humble man by nature, Jesus found the descent from his former middle-class existence to be a painfully humiliating—a bolder man than myself might even say dehumanizing—experience.

In exchange for the pains and travails of homelessness, Condo Don and Jesus received one minor compensation. They were anonymous and their passing left no trail. The All Points Bulletin issued by the GES for their capture proved futile. So long as they avoided drawing attention to themselves, they escaped detection. Unemployed, homeless people wear no face and acquire no individual identity.

But anonymity was not something that Jesus actively sought. He did not fear detection and arrest. His overriding concern for our salvation was stronger than His instinct for self-preservation.

Jesus spoke with everyone He met. No one was too filthy, too disheveled, or too addled. When Jesus encountered a man mumbling to himself in incoherent monosyllables, He took the man's head in His hands and spoke to him very softly. As if awakening from a prolonged dream, the man became conscious of the world around him for the first time in ten years. His brother, who was accompanying him, declared it to be a miracle and could not heap enough praise on Jesus.

Jesus possessed a magnetism that drew those most in need of His help. As they wandered Southern California's inland rural trails, Condo Don and Jesus encountered a seemingly endless procession of people—many of whom were confused, infirm, or disturbed. Jesus met each one not as a God, but as a fellow human being, seeking parity and addressing their needs in a loving manner. When Jesus asked someone, "How are you?" it was not an idle question. He projected genuine concern which worked to surmount barriers. Oftentimes, troubled people unloaded their problems on Him. Condo Don was constantly amazed by the way in which Jesus established instant rapport with people from diverse backgrounds. Nary one left His presence untouched by His wisdom and magnanimity. With surgical precision Jesus removed life's shrapnel from the soul.

Condo Don was concerned for the Savior's security. There is an unwritten rule among the migratory homeless that they must travel in small numbers and avoid attracting unwanted attention. Increasingly, the people whom Jesus encountered were reluctant to break the bond and often followed Him for days at a time. Whenever Condo Don thought the crowd around Jesus had grown too large, he attempted to shoo them away. Jesus, however, frequently refused to cooperate and Condo Don was forced to stifle his sense of alarm. Try as he might, he was unable to impress upon Jesus the need for stealth. Condo Don's fear that they were becoming conspicuous led him to avoid populated areas and insist that they not linger more than a few days in any one location.

Although most who came to Jesus came seeking help with personal problems, some sought the meaning of life. Jesus rarely avoided controversial topics and spoke His mind on a wide variety of issues.

As Jesus walked with a small group of followers along a bicycle path paralleling a languid stream, a young man dressed in faded denim jeans and a flannel shirt asked for His opinion of divorce.

Jesus paused to look at the stream. They had reached a point where a creek descended from adjacent foothills to join the stream. Pointing to their confluence, He said:

"As these two rivers merge, so do two people marry. Their waters are indelibly joined, forming a mightier river that is deeper and swifter than either of its tributaries. Together they flow through the channel that God has cut for them. Though at times it may become turbulent, the rapids soon pass and the river once again is calm. Even when the river is swollen and floods, its destruction is short-lived. Were it not for the life-giving waters of this river, the surrounding countryside would be a parched desert.

When two people marry, they may at times argue and the argument may occasionally overflow into a fight. But the fighting is rarely more than temporary. Without marriage the community would soon wither and die. The benefits of marriage far outweigh any negative side effects."

Jesus resumed walking along the path. As He walked He taught:

"One might propose to limit the turbulence and destructiveness of the river by inserting a divider, such as an island, at some point to once again separate it into two streams. But any separation would also affect its life-giving properties. Shallow streams can eventually evaporate or may be absorbed into the ground. So too

do two people fare better in marriage than as individuals. A small degree of turbulence or an occasional flood are insufficient reasons to justify permanent separation."

Jesus and His followers had walked several hundred feet past the confluence of the two streams when He suddenly stooped beside the river and scooped up a handful of water. Raising it to His lips, He drank and then continued:

"Who can tell me of which of the two streams I drank? Can they be separated once they have united and traveled even a short distance together? Couples share memories of their lives together. Once joined they begin to affect one another in countless unseen ways. They are different and can never return to the way they were.

Can anyone tell me to whom the children born of the union between man and wife belong? If we were to divide the family, should they go to the man or to the woman? No matter how we perform the division, it is artificial. Divorce is impractical; it is impossible to separate the waters and return them to their previous state once they unite. It would be far easier to turn this river into wine."

An anxious young woman named Elizabeth interrupted, "My husband is insensitive to my needs. I want to divorce him so I can marry someone who treats me better."

Jesus replied, "Would you divorce your mother or your

father? Would you dare to divorce your grandmother or grandfather? Would you divorce your son or daughter because they are 'insensitive to your needs' or cause you problems? Would you dispose of an uncle, aunt, or cousin in order to search for a better one? You are born into a family and have no choice concerning who your relatives will be. The only relation you choose of your own volition is your spouse. Your husband should be the one member of your family with whom you are the most content. Yet you say it is not so. Who is to blame other than yourself? If you exercised poor judgment in the choice of a husband the first time, can you be certain that your judgment will improve the second or third time?"

Jesus took a step towards Elizabeth and continued softly in a voice that she alone could hear, "I realize you find your marriage difficult. Your relationship with your husband requires more work than any relationship you will form in life. If your love for him is strong, you will eventually overcome all obstacles. You must learn patience and humility. You cannot expect your husband to be sensitive to your needs unless you are sensitive to his."

Elizabeth persisted, "My husband has numerous faults. I am certain I could find someone better than him. Must I stay with a man whom I no longer love?"

Jesus peered deep within the soul of Elizabeth and said, "Ask yourself why you fell in love and married this man. Focus on his good qualities rather than those you despise. All men are flawed; God alone is perfect. If you divorced your husband and remarried, you would soon find that you had exchanged one set of faults for another. Better the set of faults you know, than those you have yet to discover. It takes work to solve life's many problems. Do not be so quick to discard the investment you have made in your spouse. You made a commitment to share the bad as well as the good. It takes work to make your life together better. Only in death should you part."

Jesus placed His hand on Elizabeth's arm and she felt soothed. Lowering his voice again to avoid embarrassing her, He whispered, "examine your own shortcomings as thoroughly as you have examined those of your husband. Happiness is achieved by correcting one's own faults. You would do well to set the example. Your marriage is not responsible for the problems you are experiencing; its dissolution would only serve to compound them."

A tall, blonde young man who had been walking beside Jesus for hours in silence now asked, "Is abortion wrong?"

Jesus halted on the path and waited a few moments for those who were straggling behind to gather around Him. In a loud, clear voice he then said, "Our Father has commanded us not to kill. A soldier who has killed an enemy in self defense during the heat and passion of battle can ask God's forgiveness. But how can a mother who has calmly sanctioned the murder of her own flesh and blood—the fruit of her womb—ever make amends?

When a mother knowingly aborts her own child, she kills a part of herself. It is a woman's natural instinct to protect and nurture her child. Only the most perverse and evil kind of selfishness could ever persuade her to do otherwise."

Nearby, a snowy egret began beating its wings upon the water. Jesus paused to watch and then continued, "All life is precious. If a mother no longer desires her child, she should give him to someone else. If she has fallen on hard times, her children must share her deprivation. In the end, this will serve to strengthen the bond between them. The taking of a life can never solve one's problems. It can only result in additional misery."

Feeling the small crowd pushing in upon Him, Jesus turned back onto the path and strode forward. As He walked, He said, "God both gives life and takes it away. Mortals must not interfere. There is no greater sin than to kill a young and innocent child, whose life God has entrusted to you. A mother may as well remove a healthy lung or kidney than to cast out the life that is growing within her. To destroy that life is to change destiny for the worse."

A teenage girl walking close to Jesus asked, "What about the doctor who performs the abortion? Does he also sin?"

Once again Jesus stopped and waited for those behind Him to close ranks. "What greater irony can there be than for someone who has sworn to protect life and minister to the sick to misuse his knowledge and power, transforming himself into an instrument of destruction? A physician who commits an abortion is no better than any other criminal who murders for profit. He is a pariah and must be treated as such. The blood of innocents will not be washed from his hands until he prostrates himself before God. He is unclean, as are all who associate with him. The weight of each unborn child he has slain presses heavily against his soul. An abortionist is a predator who preys upon the misgivings of distraught and confused mothers. He is to be cut out like a cancer."

The path twisted to the right and ascended a small hill. Jesus easily strode to the top and sat down in the short grass that bordered the trail. As the others struggled up the hill and began to sit around Jesus, a large black Labrador belonging to one of His followers approached Jesus and nuzzled His hand. Affectionately, the Son of God placed His hand on the animal's head and stroked its fur.

A man who appeared to be in his late thirties sitting to the left of Jesus asked, "Does God despise homosexuals?"

Jesus continued to stroke the dog as He answered, "God made this animal what he is. He could never become a cat. Even if he learned to purr and mimic the mannerisms of a cat, he would still be a dog. Though but a beast, he intuitively realizes this. Likewise, a man can never become a woman nor can a woman become a man. People cannot change their gender any more than this dog can change his species."

The dog lay down and put his enormous head in Our Lord's lap. Jesus went on, "Life has dealt you certain cards. Although you might have chosen other cards, you have no choice but to play what you have been dealt. If you complain, it only betrays that you have a bad hand. Sometimes even the worst cards can win in the end. Only by accepting the sex you were born with can you discover why God has made you that way. Have faith and God will not forsake you."

Closing its eyes, the dog fell asleep. Jesus twisted slowly so as to look at each person seated in the circle around Him without disturbing the Labrador. He again spoke, "This dog sleeps peacefully because he has pleased his master. He naturally knows right from wrong and does not question the things he cannot change. There is no guilt to disturb his sleep. You possess more intelligence than this dog. But if you should misuse that intelligence to challenge the natural order of things, you displease God and become less worthy in His eyes than this poor animal. Sodomy is an abomination. Any pleasure one may obtain from it will be short-lived. As God was angered by the ancient Sodomites, so is He angered by their successors. Those who do not repent shall share the fate of Sodom. Why would any intelligent man or woman risk eternal damnation for fleeting sexual pleasure? God has set the order of the universe. To oppose it is madness and can only result in pain and suffering. God asks so little. Why do people persist in breaking His rules?"

The black Labrador stirred and lifted his head. Someone had filled a plastic jug at the river and was passing it around. Jesus poured some water into the palm of His cupped hand for the dog to drink.

* * *

Several weeks later Jesus and Condo Don encamped in a county wilderness park. It rained for two days and most of the people who had been traveling with them left. Condo Don constructed a large tent from polypropylene sheet plastic for the few who remained.

The rain temporarily abated and now only a light drizzle fell. Venturing outside to dig a shallow drainage trench around the tent, Jesus, not having a shovel, used a bowl to scoop the mud. A young man who was assisting Him asked, "Are you really the Savior?"

Jesus laughed, "If you have shared my shelter for the past two days and do not know, you may never know. What more must I do to convince you? Would you have me magically transform this bowl into a backhoe? Must I stop the rain and cause the sun to shine? No matter what I do there will still be disbelievers—scoffers who require yet another miracle to dispel their doubts. The answer you seek cannot be found with your mind. Only by opening your heart can you truly know me. What you need is faith."

The young man whose name was Thomas then asked, "Are you the same Jesus who came to us two thousand years ago?"

Bending a bit further at the waist to better scoop the soft mud, Jesus laughed again before answering, "Do you doubt my age because you see no wrinkles? Have you searched in vain for wounds from the crucifixion? I have been reborn just as all shall be who accept me as their Savior. For some the passage of time brings only a dreaded deterioration of the flesh, but for those who have come to know the Creator time is meaningless. They will have eternity."

For Thomas there were still doubts. He put down his bowl, stood up straight, and said, I have heard it prophesied that the Second Coming will signal mankind's annihilation. Have you come to destroy us?"

"Do I sound like a crazed killer?" replied Jesus. For the past few minutes the rain had been steadily increasing in tempo and was now a downpour. "God created us; Our Father seeks only what is best for His children. All who can be saved will be saved and only those who are beyond redemption will be destroyed. I have come to silence false prophets, end confusion, and guide you to God."

"Then the end is not near?" asked Thomas incredulously.

"It may soon end in a flood for the two of us," said Jesus, "if you do not pick up your bowl and help finish this trench."

Outdoors life agreed with Jesus. Despite a less than adequate diet consisting chiefly of scrounged foods, eight months of life on the road had matured His boyish features into those of a man.

Condo Don never ceased to be amazed by the number of people who were drawn to Jesus. Even when they were traveling through remote, sparsely populated regions, a crowd followed them. No sooner did one follower depart, then two more took his place.

Although constantly bombarded with questions that ranged from complex theological enigmas to the mundane, His arsenal of answers showed no sign of depletion. One day, as He was picking His way along a rubble strewn path in a narrow canyon, a thin lad from the East Coast asked, "Which counts for more, physical prowess or intelligence?"

"God expects you to develop both to the best of your ability," Jesus replied. "Pure musculature, uncontrolled or undirected, can degenerate into destructive brute force. Likewise, pure and noble ideas are wasted if a person does not possess the physical ability to transform his thoughts into actions. If you are to realize your full potential and accomplish your mission in life, both mind and body must be healthy."

Jesus paused to help several people negotiate their way between two boulders that partially blocked the trail. Upon finishing, He again spoke to the slender northeasterner, "Those who stuff themselves to the point of corpulence or who abuse drugs or alcohol will find themselves severely hampered in achieving the goals which God has set for them. An addled mind or a neglected physique can hinder your accomplishments. You are the instrument of God's will. How effective you are at what you do is a factor of the physical and mental condition in which you maintain yourself."

The Son of God walked for several minutes in silence next to the easterner before continuing, "Man is at best an imperfect copy of God. He must constantly strive to correct his inherent flaws. A person who permits his mental or physical condition to deteriorate is like a tool that has become dulled or broken. He has lost his utility. God can no longer use him to accomplish His purpose and must necessarily discard him. Otherwise this person would become a burden to family and society. What choice has he left Our Father? Man often accuses God of having forsaken him. But I tell you that Man forsakes himself. The path of life is as rough as the path between these canyon walls. Continued survival depends on your mental and physical fitness."

Approximately a mile past the rim of the canyon, the narrow footpath crossed a major highway. Several people departed at this point to return home. Jesus and those going onward crossed the busy asphalt ribbon during a lull in the traffic. Resuming their journey on the other side, a russet haired lady sporting a leather backpack asked Jesus, "Does wealth denote success in life?"

Speaking so that all those with Him might hear, Jesus said, "Though you pile your treasures higher than the pyramids of the ancient pharaohs, you cannot bribe your way into Heaven. The possessions that you value in this life are as so much deadweight burdening your journey to the next. Gold is not scarce in Heaven and diamonds are as common as the stones beneath your feet. Kindness is the currency of God's kingdom and with that shall your success in life be measured."

Rolling aside a thorny tumbleweed that had blown onto the path, He continued, "Since you cannot take your wealth into Heaven, you are but a caretaker on earth. That which you do not use, you preserve for others. As it is sinful to covet material possessions for their own sake rather than for the utility that may be derived from them, so is it sinful to squander, waste, or destroy things to make them of no use to anyone else. Be frugal in your ways and do not hesitate to share. The kindness which you freely give in this life will be returned with interest in the next."

The russet haired lady lost her footing on some loose gravel. Steadying her with His hand, Jesus prevented her fall. Regaining her balance, she asked, "Are rich people evil?"

Jesus replied, "It is of little significance whether a cup is made of brass or gold. What matters is the clarity of the water it contains. Do not judge people by wealth or social status, but by their character and actions. By allowing yourself to be distracted by shiny baubles and glittering metals, you may miss the glorious pageant of life that surrounds you. Be careful that your possessions do not come to own you."

Pausing for a moment, He stooped to pick a wild golden poppy and then went on, "God's works have more value than those of Man. Why pay a fortune for a painting of a flower by an artist when you can see the actual flower for free? How much beauty is contained within a single petal? Make certain that greed does not warp your values or cause you to ignore those treasures that are beyond price."

The footpath descended an erosion-pocked ravine. Jesus half walked, half slid to the bottom and waited to catch each of the others as they came down. After the last person had safely negotiated the difficult slope and they had all gathered in a group at the bottom, an elderly man with thinning, silver hair asked, "How would God have us organize His church?"

Jesus replied, "God hears the humblest prayers of the least among you. Reject the mumbo jumbo of silken shamans who propose to act as an intermediary between you and God. God's commandments are so plain and simple that anyone can understand them. For the most part you will not need someone else to interpret them for you. Let those who are pastors, priests, deacons, bishops, cardinals, or who are bestowed with some other title renounce the privileges of rank and live as common parishioners. Their authority is delegated by God and may not be abused or misused for personal enrichment. Each person must take his own separate path to Heaven. Beware of false prophets who seek to shunt everyone onto the same highway."

A jackrabbit exited his burrow and stood motionless in front of the Son of God for a brief second, his nose twitching rapidly, before scampering away. Jesus continued, "The rudest shack will be equal to the most ornate temple when you meet within it to praise God. Take care when building a cathedral that it stands as a monument to the glory of God rather than your own frail achievement. Celebrate the goodness of the Holy Spirit and do not allow Our Father's house to be sullied by corruption. Any edifice that has been used for business, gambling, government, or other mundane purposes must be consecrated prior to being designated a house of worship."

A hawk's shriek pierced the air as it snared a field mouse in its talons. Jesus paused to watch and then said, "You will be held accountable at the Gates of Heaven for any funds raised in the name of God. All money collected is to be used to spread His word or to benefit the poor and the hungry. God does not desire His church to amass vast quantities of wealth in His name. The penny that comes from the purse of the pauper to assist the penniless will be as a fortune unto God. And the hand that is lent by a poor man to assist his impoverished brethren has more value than a golden altar."

Late in the afternoon as the sun shrank and made its way toward the horizon, they stopped at a campsite Condo Don had chosen at the base of a small hill. Here there was an assortment of wildflowers and a copse of black oaks. Condo Don scooped a fire pit from the soft earth and ringed it with stones. Most of the others were busy gathering firewood. Jesus went to the spring to wash His face.

Drawing near the spring, He noticed a young lady kneeling beside it, crying. He went to her and gently put His hand upon her shoulder. "May I help?" He asked.

"Nobody can help," she replied. "My mother is dying. A cancer is slowly consuming her body. The doctors say there is no hope. She is in great pain and says that if I truly love her, I must help her to end her life. I'm confused and I don't know what to do."

"You are doing the right thing," said Jesus. "You have

shared your mother's pain. Her misery has been your misery. My Father has heard your prayers and has answered them. Go to your mother now; she is recovering and wishes for you to share her joy. Give no more thought to death as she will live many more years."

The young woman looked incredulously at Jesus. In His eyes she saw the truth of His words and a great weight lifted from her heart. Still sobbing, but now with tears of joy, she stood and hugged Jesus. He wiped her tears with His hand. After kissing it, she set out running down the trail in the direction from whence she came.

Following the evening meal, Jesus and His followers sat around the campfire. Someone threw an armful of wood on the fire and it popped and hissed as sparks pierced the blackness of night. Jesus had answered questions from several of His followers and now He had a question for them:

"Who can tell me whether euthanasia is right or wrong?" He asked.

A portly man in a dark knit watchcap sitting beside Condo Don spoke, "God has commanded us not to kill."

"And He has never made any exceptions to this commandment," stated Jesus. "God alone determines the length of our lifespan. Pain is something we must all endure. Often, it is God's method of testing us. Even in the darkest hour we must not give up hope. Though the clouds may gather and form a shroud for the sun, only God knows with certainty when it will rain. Do not anticipate His judgment."

Chapter 13

Officer Owens could have driven the highway blindfolded. He knew every curve, hairpin turn, soft shoulder, and pothole on this stretch of State Route 33. As a California Highway Patrol Officer, he had been patrolling it for the past eight years and had got to know and like most of the people who lived along it.

One of those people was John Baork, a local rancher. Officer Owens had stopped by his place for a cup of coffee yesterday morning and Baork had complained about a group of hikers who had tramped through one of his pastures. As far as Baork knew, they had done no damage. Still, they looked too grubby to be sightseers and he thought that Officer Owens should check them out.

Baork had described the leader of the bunch as a middle-aged graybeard, athletically built, dressed in a sweatshirt and jeans. Now, as Officer Owens rounded a curve just beyond the Stauffer turnoff, he spotted a number of hikers strung out along the right shoulder. Near the front was a man who fit the description given to him by John Baork. Pulling over in front of them, Officer Owens radioed his location and stepped out of the cruiser.

"Good morning," said Officer Owens, addressing

Condo Don. "You folks from around here?"

"No," said Condo Don, "we're just passing through."

"Where you headed?" asked Officer Owens.

"No place in particular."

"Uh huh. Please step over to the other side of the car with me. I'd like to see some identification."

Condo Don went around the car with the officer and pulled out his wallet. He handed Officer Owens a tattered library card.

"This library card is from out of state. Got anything with your picture on it?"

"I know who I am," replied Condo Don somewhat testily. "Why would I need identification?"

"Move over to the patrol car," ordered Officer Owens. "Now lean forward and spread your hands wide apart on the trunk." As Condo Don complied, Officer Owens warned the others, "You all just stand quiet like where you are. Don't any of you come on this side of the vehicle."

After kicking Condo Don's legs apart, Officer Owens began to pat him down. Finding only a tarnished pocket harmonica and a small jackknife, he placed the items on the trunk. "You remain like that," he instructed Condo

Don, "and I'll be back shortly."

Without taking his eyes off Condo Don, Officer Owens sidled to the front of the cruiser and opened the door. Leaning forward into the patrol car, he tapped several keys on a computer console mounted below the dashboard, but the monitor remained blank. He picked up the microphone and keyed the "send" button on its right side. There was no sound whatsoever—not even static. Reaching down, he turned up the volume control—still nothing. The radio was dead. Next, he tried turning the key in the ignition. Nada, not even a click.

Another dead battery, he thought. They always assigned the clunkers to the guys who patrolled the rural areas. The traffic officers on the expressway got all the latest, supercharged cruisers.

No telephone on this stretch of road for miles in either direction. The dispatcher would send another patrol car to check on him in an hour or so when he failed to contact the station. Until then, he'd just have to wait. But he didn't intend to babysit this bunch. He had nothing on them except suspicion of trespassing. Walking to the rear of the vehicle, he informed Condo Don that he was free to go.

Condo Don and the others lost no time in leaving. Making a turn at the next gravel road branching off the main highway, they continued walking for several hours before taking a break.

"It was a miracle that he didn't arrest me," said Condo Don.

"It was no miracle," attested Jesus.

"I can't figure out why he didn't arrest me. The library card I gave him had my real name on it."

"His radio wouldn't work," said Jesus smiling. "While he was frisking you, I rolled under the front of the patrol car, wedged myself between the tierods, and felt along the wall of the engine compartment until I found the battery. Then I pushed the battery cable off one of the terminals."

Condo Don began to laugh. His laughter rumbled up from deep inside him like rolling thunder. It was contagious and soon all the others, including Jesus, were laughing uncontrollably.

They continued walking long past dark, putting as much distance as possible between themselves and the CHP. Somehow, Condo Don did not think that the policeman, once he discovered Jesus' joke, would find it humorous.

Chapter 14

Although no one had greater faith in the existence of Heaven and the immortality of the soul, Condo Don nevertheless felt that the primal instinct—that of self-preservation—was necessarily of paramount importance to all living creatures and had long been in the habit of governing his life accordingly. As far as he was concerned, only fools sought martyrdom. Besides, it was his duty to protect his divine traveling companion. Why draw attention to themselves? So, when Jesus proposed journeying to a nearby city, Condo Don balked.

"You know that there are warrants out for our arrest," argued Condo Don, "yet you want to go into town so you can tell everyone who you are. Ever heard of common sense?"

"Nobody wants to die, yet everyone most certainly will, irrespective of our actions. I am mortal and my time here is limited. Would you have me waste it, cowering like an animal in fear of everyone who opposes my father? Would you have me abandon my mission?"

"All I am asking is for you to take a bit more care with your personal safety. You cannot be replaced. It's not right for you to continually expose yourself to danger."

"I, and I alone will decide what is right and what is

wrong," snapped Jesus. "You lack faith in my judgment. Many people lack spiritual nourishment and hunger for my guidance. Would you have me disappoint them?"

Condo Don could see that Jesus had already made His decision and could not be swayed. Still, he felt it to be a prescription for disaster: the way things were going the mission would almost certainly end with arrest and imprisonment. But he feared neither. What he dread most was the prospect of being separated from Jesus.

Jesus sensed Condo Don's foreboding. Seeking to comfort him, He said, "Do not be so concerned with the future that you fail to enjoy the present. I am with you now and yet you do not rejoice. Do not clutch at me in desperation. Although we may be parted, I promise you we shall spend eternity together."

Tears welled in Condo Don's eyes. Jesus turned away to avoid embarrassing him.

That night by the flickering light of the campfire Condo Don sketched a rough map in the dirt. If they continued pursuing their present course, they would reach Los Angeles in three days. Were it not for continued prodding on the part of Jesus, he would have preferred to delay what he considered to be the inevitable tragic consequences of their mission by taking a more circuitous route.

Condo Don did not sleep well that night. Everything seemed to be coming to an end. The past months with Jesus had been the best in his life; never had he known such joy. Simply to be near the young Savior was both exhilarating and rejuvenating. Fear of separation from Jesus commandeered his dreams and herded them through dark, subconscious regions where he had no desire to go.

On the third and final day of their journey to Los Angeles, Jesus and Condo Don walked within the stark concrete chasm of the lower Los Angeles River where nary a tree grew and birds were all too few. The river which had until recently been a riverine paradise now lay crushed beneath giant slabs of reinforced concrete lining the bed and banks, leaving only thin lines of expansion joints to the hardiest of weeds. Wide as a six lane expressway, the riverbed stretched on and on in ceaseless man-made uniformity channeling a faint trickle of polluted water destined to evaporate long before it could reach the Pacific Ocean. An occasional graffito spray painted on its thirty degree sloping banks served to break the monotony. All was silent within, but from without came the insane clamor of the bustling metropolis. Named Our Lady, the Queen of the Angels, by the Spanish explorer, Gaspar de Potola, and subsequently inhabited by millions of lesser mortals, the city surrounded them on all sides but, due to their position at the bottom of a concrete embankment, could not yet see or touch them.

As they neared Los Angeles, their flock had grown. Condo Don and Jesus were now leading twenty-six people. While Jesus busied Himself saving souls, Condo Don worried about security.

"Are you sure of these people," he whispered to Jesus. "One of them might be a government agent."

"If so, he is welcome," replied Jesus. "Government agents have souls, too. I will turn no one away."

"But you could be arrested," pleaded Condo Don.

"What we are doing is worth the risk. Before long, you and I will risk more than imprisonment. Let your faith give you courage. He who has found nothing worth dying for has yet to find a reason to live."

Condo Don walked on in silence, pondering Jesus' words. He thought about the crucifixion and the early Christians who had been fed to the lions for refusing to renounce their faith. How could ordinary men possess such strength and courage? Looking inescapable death squarely in the eye was one thing, opting for martyrdom when presented with a choice was quite another.

Jesus sensed Condo Don's uneasiness. Turning towards him, He said, "Do not dwell on doubt. When bravery is needed, it shall come forth. God knows no fear. Place your trust in Him."

They continued on. Jesus began singing a song to brighten their spirits. Everyone joined in with gusto.

The river channel was bordered on both sides by an eight-foot chain link cyclone fence topped by four strands of barbed wire. An elevated freeway ran to the west of the river. At irregular intervals congested surface streets passed beneath the freeway and bridged the river. And at each crossing an asphalt ramp ascended the western bank, terminating in a gate in the fence.

Reaching Rosecrans Avenue, they climbed the ramp but found the gate locked. Fortunately, the fence was cut nearby and they were all able to scramble through it. Exiting into a realtor's back parking lot, they could see and hear the traffic whizzing by on the busy street in front. Brick and stucco buildings fought for space along both sides of the roadway. Ahead, an unbroken grid sprawled farther than the eye could see or the mind could imagine. They were now within the city's grasp.

Condo Don cursed himself. He had led them along the riverbed far too long and they had exited far south of the central city in an area that was unfamiliar to him. Now they would have to traverse a maze of congested streets to reach their destination.

They considered boarding one of the Rapid Transit District's buses that passed by. But nobody was certain which route to take or when to transfer. Besides, they could ill afford the luxury of a bus ride.

Condo Don left the group and walked to a corner gasoline filling station to ask directions. He found a municipal street map taped to a window of the service bay. After studying it for a while, he regained his bearings.

The going was slow. Everyone who is anyone in Los Angeles commutes by car and pedestrians who joust with them invariably lose.

At midday they stopped to eat a meager lunch in Athens Park. A thin young man in a Pendleton shirt produced four rounds of cheese from his backpack and they shared them along with a box of saltines that someone else had brought. It wasn't much, divided among twenty-eight people, but they praised God for what they had.

The light was beginning to fade in the western sky by the time they reached MacArthur Park. It was a surrealistic sunset, tinged with the outlandish shades of magenta and violet that are unique to the polluted atmosphere of Southern California. The soapbox orators, chess players, and retired people who frequented the park in the daytime had already departed and the greedy ducks and geese who lived in the small lake at the southern edge of the park were venturing onto the grounds in search of tidbits left by picnickers.

Condo Don chuckled as he watched several of his friends chase the waterfowls. At the very moment they attempted to grab a duck, it would hop or fly away and they would find themselves face down in the dirt without even a handful of feathers to show for their troubles. After a few minutes of this frivolity, Condo Don showed them how to construct a snare using twigs and string. He baited the trap with bread crumbs. Soon they had enough ducks for a fine dinner. Condo Don had to wring their necks as the others were too squeamish. When he slit their bellies to remove the entrails, one young man fainted.

None were too squeamish to eat, however. Condo Don built a large fire in one of the barbecue pits and buried the ducks in the glowing coals when the flames died down. After peeling off the charred feathers and skin, they were delicious.

Following their meal, Condo Don wrapped the entrails in newspaper, intending to save them for bait to catch crawdads at the lake the next morning. A hard life on the road had taught him to waste nothing.

MacArthur Park was ten times larger than the small park where Condo Don had first met Jesus. The trees were older and taller. Even the turf was coarser and thicker, but its lack of spring and brown tinge evidenced need of a good watering. Garish graffiti marking territory claimed by Mara Salvatrucha, a gang composed of recent immigrants from El Salvador, defaced restroom walls and lampposts. Both buildings and grounds were in sorry condition.

In a bygone era petticoated maidens had been rowed about the lake by bow-tied beaus and uniformed brass bands had entertained large gatherings. Emitting an aura of faded elegance, MacArthur Park was but a shabby specter of its former self.

MacArthur Park was one of the few remaining green refuges in the commercial center of Los Angeles. Wilshire Boulevard, the downtown business district's main thoroughfare, bisected the park. As the number of vehicles utilizing the busy boulevard had grown in the latter half of the 20th Century, the number of families utilizing the park had shrunk. A statue dedicated to

General Douglas MacArthur, the park's namesake, appeared to be leading the onslaught of vehicles, foreshadowing some not-so-far-in-the-smoggy-future date when the internal combustion engine would achieve total victory over the park.

Now, as Jesus and his weary followers set up camp for the night, they seemed as Christian soldiers: a ragtag regiment manning the sylvan bastion's final defenses. Like burning cordite on a battlefield, vehicular emissions stung their eyes and threatened them with asphyxiation.

Nobody could sleep. They were overwhelmed by the honking of horns and the constant drone of overloaded diesels. A police helicopter circled overhead, the beat of its rotors synchronizing with that of their own hearts. Headlights of vehicles and lights from nearby businesses created an eerie, artificial gray twilight which absorbed the stars and paled the moon.

Condo Don was drifting into the world of dreams when a goose bit him on the arm. Even through several layers of insulating clothing it hurt. Ranting and raving, he jumped from his bedroll and began to chase the goose. Soon everyone was up and laughing.

A ponytailed youth with a woolen blanket wrapped around his shoulders began to play a concertina. They all sang "Oh My, Bye and Bye" and other songs to a zydeco accompaniment. One person slapped rhythm on a tree trunk while the rest clapped their hands. They sang for hours until they exhausted the concertina player's repertoire.

It was well past midnight before they lay down again. Condo Don tossed and turned and rubbed the bruise on his arm. Then he remembered the night many years before when he had lain on a park bench near death with Jesus at his side and he lapsed into a blissful slumber.

* * *

Morning dawned with a chilling mist in the air. Despite the cold, several of Jesus' flock expressed a desire to bathe in the lake. Noting numerous posted "No Swimming" signs and not wishing to draw attention from the authorities, Condo Don suggested they make do with a spritz bath in the public restroom.

When everyone assembled after breakfast, Condo Don dictated the rules that would govern the group's conduct during their stay at the park:

1. *No panhandling.*
2. *All trash is to be deposited in the proper receptacles.*
3. *No swimming or bathing in the lake.*
4. *No tents or other conspicuous shelters.*
5. *No sleeping on park benches.*
6. *No one is permitted more belongings than they can carry.*
7. *All park regulations and park officials are to be*

obeyed.

8. *No defecating or urinating in the bushes.*

Condo Don stressed that the rules were necessary to ensure safety and avoid becoming a public nuisance. Anyone who disregarded the rules risked expulsion.

Assorted moans and groans greeted Condo Don from the assembly. A blonde lady named Louisa who had been with the group more than a month spoke, "I went on the road to live free. Who elected Condo Don king?"

"An absence of rules leads to anarchy, not freedom," cautioned Jesus. "We gather to praise God as civilized men, thankful that God has given us commandments to temper the beast within. Condo Don has more experience in temporal affairs than anyone else. Who among you is better qualified to advise, lead, and formulate our rules of behavior?"

Louisa and a male companion made an obscene gesture and left in disgust. Neither Jesus nor Condo Don attempted to call them back.

The mist had burned off. Many removed their outer garments. Joggers had taken command of the sidewalks and the chess players were setting up their pieces. It looked like it was going to be a beautiful day.

Southern California with its temperate climate tends to attract those who have become debilitated by loss of job, family, and/or home. From everywhere they come, by bus, plane, and foot, hoping against hope to rebuild shattered lives. Transients, fazed and dazed, they are the walking wounded in the economic war for survival. And a goodly number of them hobbled, shuffled, and stumbled into MacArthur Park each day seeking temporary sanctuary from the battles which raged in their heads.

Jesus was there to minister to their needs. He was there to listen, there to advise, and, most of all, there to care. Many had lost their faith in addition to their material possessions. Some had even lost their minds. Jesus examined their souls to determine the source of their misery. Often, He would place His soothing hand upon their foreheads and cast out the demon within them. None who came were turned away.

Condo Don knew them all. Although he may not have personally made their acquaintance, he had come to know many like them in his travels. They were the surplus population, men and women who lacked the education, skills, and drive to successfully compete in an increasingly complex world. Having fallen in the battle to succeed, many had surrendered to the forces of evil. Condo Don understood, for he had fallen farthest of all into a living hell saturated with alcohol and drugs. They bore similar scars to his and he regarded them as comrades-in-arms. Only Jesus could save them, as He had saved Condo Don in another park years before.

Word of mouth kept their numbers increasing daily. Someone who had seen Jesus would tell many others until the crowd threatened to smother Him. Condo Don attempted to organize them, but often to little or no avail. Although he pushed them back, they again pressed inward, attempting to touch the young man who had worked so many wonders before their eyes. Finally, Jesus climbed onto the lowermost branch of a stately oak where He could continue His ministry without being mauled.

At night there were now hundreds of people camping with Jesus in the park. They did not have a camping permit and Condo Don feared that the police would expel them. He also worried about logistics. Never in his life had he been responsible for so many people. The task seemed gargantuan. Although there was always just enough food to go around, Condo Don worried that they would soon run out. But when he conveyed his doubts, Jesus told him not to fret. Had not God always provided? God would continue to provide.

* * *

Otis Chandler was a well known name around Los Angeles. His was an Horatio Alger story. He had come as a penniless immigrant to Southern California between the wars and now was one of the nation's richest industrialists—in popular parlance "a winner."

But Otis Chandler was losing the fight to a cancer that was all too quickly metastasizing within him. His doctors had discovered it too late and could do little more than prolong the inevitable.

As Otis was receiving his bi-weekly chemotherapy treatment, he overheard two nurses discussing a young faith healer who was evangelizing at MacArthur Park. They snickered about desperate people being easily fooled.

Otis Chandler had not amassed millions by failing to check out long shots. Upon leaving the hospital, he told his driver to take 6th Street to MacArthur Park. As the limo cruised the park, Otis spotted a young black man encircled by a crowd and bid his driver to stop.

As Otis walked across the grass towards the crowd, he thought to himself how ridiculous this was. Here he was wasting precious minutes of his dwindling life mixing with fools and charlatans.

Jesus noticed Otis Chandler immediately. His lack of hair (chemotherapy had rendered him bald), his advanced age, and his immaculate pin-striped suit would have made him stand out in any crowd. Jumping to the ground, Jesus went to him and, looking him straight in the eyes, asked him if he believed in God.

"I did once, many years ago," replied Otis, straining to

recall his youth.

"Although you may have forgotten God," said Jesus, "He has not forgotten you." And Jesus reached out and grasped Otis by an emaciated arm.

Suddenly, Otis felt a field of energy envelop his frail body. As he felt the disease and the chemicals drain away, he realized that he was cured. Taking out his wallet, he removed two thousand dollars and attempted to give it to Jesus.

Jesus refused the money.

Condo Don groaned loudly.

Next, Otis promised that he would drive his limousine into the lake, give all he had to the poor, and follow Jesus to the end of his days.

Jesus reminded Otis that he already had an important mission in life. Thousands of people depended on him for employment and his first responsibility was to them.

Otis left the park reluctantly. Later that night he called a catering service and had them deliver 220 meals to MacArthur Park. They were told to send the bill to the *Los Angeles Times,* Otis Chandler, CEO.

* * *

On the seventh morning before daybreak a phalanx of officers from the LAPD raided the encampment. Stabbing the night with powerful beams from their four cell, baton-like flashlights and restraining snarling German Shepherds, the policemen rousted the sleeping campers. A detective brandishing a bullhorn ordered them to disperse and leave the park immediately.

The policemen wore Levis and dark blue jackets with "POLICE" emblazoned in yellow on the back. They looked more like inner city gang members wearing their colors than officers of the law. Some of Jesus' followers, still groggy with sleep, were confused as to what was happening. Condo Don circulated among them urging everyone to cooperate and leave the park peacefully.

In the haste to depart, many forgot their belongings. The police had brought a large yellow city garbage truck with them and they began loading it with clothing, backpacks, sleeping bags, and anything else left behind. In less than fifteen minutes nothing remained to indicate that the group had ever been in the park.

Jesus and Condo Don stood aside in a clump of shrubbery and watched as the garbage truck noisily compacted its booty. The officers had begun to relax; smoking and joking about their easy victory.

Condo Don motioned to Jesus and they both turned to leave. As they walked, Condo Don whispered, "We were lucky they didn't arrest us."

"If they'd done their jobs properly and checked us for warrants, we'd both be dead meat," growled Condo Don.

"Some lost everything they had," said Jesus in astonishment.

"Why did they rush in with shotguns and dogs? We were asleep and unarmed."

"They fear that which they do not understand and want to destroy everyone and everything that is not like them. Ignorance begets intolerance," lamented Jesus, turning away from the senseless destruction.

As they retreated past the large statue of General Douglas A. MacArthur, Condo Don shouted, "I shall return!" The powers that be and their forces had won this particular battle thought Condo Don, but they would lose the war. Neither Condo Don nor Jesus would ever surrender. Although their troops had been routed, he was confident they would soon regroup to fight on other fronts. It would be like guerrilla warfare; they would appear and then disperse to reappear where they were least expected. In MacArthur Park Condo Don had seen how the people adored Jesus. He realized now for the first time that Jesus could not be defeated.

They exited the park onto 6th Street. Condo Don reached into his sweatshirt and brought out a hard roll left over from the previous night's catered meal. Tearing it apart, he gave half to Jesus. Here they were again, thought Condo Don, just the two of them journeying to an unknown destination. Condo Don was happier than he had been in weeks.

Condo Don and Jesus followed 6th Street through the downtown district, past the public library and Pershing Square, back to the Los Angeles River, unaware that they had passed within two blocks of the Savior's birthplace. Continuing south along the dry riverbed, they reached the Pacific Ocean around noon. A slight breeze coming off the water had dispersed the smog and the sharp peaks of Catalina Island could be seen clearly in the distance. Both marveled at the wonder of God's vast creation.

Removing their boots and socks, they walked along the white beach, sand splaying between their toes. Breakers washed brown translucent bundles of kelp upon the beach while children played in the surf. Silhouetted against the horizon, oriental cargo vessels plied their way towards the port of San Pedro.

At twilight the breeze blowing from the ocean turned cold and Condo Don insisted that they be on their way. Following Ocean Boulevard, it was almost midnight before they reached Huntington Beach and the mouth of the Santa Ana River where they made their camp for the night under the protection of a concrete overpass. They got little sleep, however, for the sand fleas gave them no quarter.

Morning came all too soon. Still drowsy, they made

breakfast from some sourdough bread and a green apple from Jesus' backpack.

As they ate, Jesus watched several bicycles pass by on a narrow asphalt strip that paralleled the riverbed on its eastern bank. Condo Don explained that it was the Imperial Woods Trail. He proposed they follow it inland and Jesus agreed.

Several miles later they met two hikers by the side of the trail who invited them to share some beef jerky. After talking with them for a few minutes, Jesus discovered that the taller of the two, a robust fellow of mixed heritage, had attended Sunday School with Him at the Crystal Cathedral. Since they were going in the same direction, they decided to travel together.

Unlike the Los Angeles River, the Santa Ana River was not a concrete wasteland. Trees grew along its banks and a wide stream flowed along its bed. An occasional snowy egret stood on match stick legs in the slow moving shallows and tiny wrens darted over the waters in search of insects. If it were not for the manicured nature of the grass bordering both sides of the asphalt trail and concrete bridges spanning the river at regular intervals, it might have passed for wilderness. Man had learned to live in harmony with the Santa Ana River. Even Condo Don was in a good mood.

As the four men hiked the meandering asphalt ribbon, Jesus spoke of God's covenant and His own role in the salvation of Man. Condo Don and one of the other men listened in rapt consensus. But the man who had known Jesus as a youth was skeptical and made no attempt to hide his disbelief. Although the Savior's words found their way to his heart, his mind could not accept that a contemporary could be the Redeemer. When they halted for a break, he asked Jesus, "If you truly are the Son of God, why did you return?"

"I never left," replied Jesus. "My spirit and my word were always with you. However, people's memories faded with time and some, jealous of The Almighty's divine powers, declared me and My Father to be dead. That is why I now manifest myself to you. If you see me with your own eyes, but still choose not to believe, what hope can there be for you? Redemption can be yours for the asking, it won't cost you a single cent. What impedes your soul from seeking its salvation? Is it a false sense of pride? I am here now before you. Touch me, feel me with your own hands and satisfy yourself that I am real. What more must I do to reach you?"

And the man, whose name was Tom, studied Jesus' face. And although His face was of the darkest ebony, Tom saw in it a light. Pressing his hand to Jesus' forehead, he felt a powerful current surge throughout his body that was unlike anything he had known before. And in that very moment, his spirit gained mastery over his mind. Bowing on one knee, he pleaded, "Forgive me, I do believe."

Jesus fell on both knees and, after embracing, the two arose as one. Standing next to Jesus, Tom asked, "What would you have me do?"

"Go to my mother, who has not heard from me for many months, and assure her that I am well. Tell everyone that you have seen me. Let them know what happened to you here today."

They walked in silence for a short time to a junction with another path that led to a nearby road. Removing a thin silver ring from his little finger, Jesus handed it to Tom, saying, "Give this to my mother, so she will know I have sent you."

Tom and his friend turned down the path and soon disappeared around a bend. Condo Don and Jesus stood for a long time staring at where the two had disappeared before continuing their journey.

Jesus' eyes were wet. Condo Don didn't say anything, he was thinking of his own mother. It had been many years since he had last seen her. He wasn't even sure if she were still alive. A twinge of guilt overcame Condo Don.

The Imperial Woods Trail terminated in a regional park which served as a combination campground and nature center. Arriving early in the afternoon, Jesus visited the campsites, talking with whomever He met on topics ranging from sports to religion. Many people were inspired by both His presence and His words. When Jesus and Condo Don departed the following morning, four campers decided to join them on their journey.

In the months that followed Jesus and Condo Don continued to trek inland at a leisurely pace. Often, they would remain at a good campsite for a week or more. The number of true believers accompanying them continued to grow. It never ceased to amaze Condo Don that they encountered so many people in such a sparsely populated region.

As Jesus and Condo Don went deeper into Southern California's vast interior, the thorn bushes and chaparral gradually gave way to the Joshua trees of the desert. Early pioneers had imagined that the spiny arms of these giant yuccas, which grew only in the Holy Land and Southern California, pointed the way to paradise.

Chapter 15

By late fall Jesus and Condo Don reached the northern shore of the Salton Sea. Like the Pacific Ocean, it stretched over the horizon, far beyond view. Sea gulls spiraled overhead and the concentrated scent of saltwater permeated the air. Despite the lateness of the season, daytime temperatures often soared above one hundred degrees. Vast sand dunes along the languid shoreline shimmered in the heat.

* * *

The Salton Sea is a liquid monument to the fallibility of Man. Attempting to withdraw irrigation water from the distant Colorado River at the beginning of the twentieth century, engineers failed to appreciate the swollen river's potential. It burst through their gates and cut a new channel which flowed into a desert depression known as the Salton Sink. By the time the engineers were able to divert the river back to its original channel, it had created a body of water 30 miles long and 10 miles wide. Having no natural outlet, the sea became brackish. By the dawn of the new millennium, it was already saltier than the Pacific Ocean and only marginally capable of supporting life.

In the economic boom years that followed World War II, real estate developers sought to exploit the sea's recreational potential. They stocked it with bass and corbina and built marinas along the shoreline.

But the waters refused to be tamed. They alternately surged and retreated; sometimes flooding the marinas and sometimes leaving them high and dry. Eventually the developers quit in disgust, abandoning gutted structures to be reclaimed by desert sands.

The broad asphalt avenues that crisscrossed the northwestern perimeter of the Salton Sea were relics of its heyday. For forty years they had beckoned vehicles that never came. Cracked and broken, they now served Jesus and His band of followers as they searched for a suitable campsite.

As they hiked, they came upon numerous dead waterfowl, victims of selenium in wastewater leached from the nearby lushly fertilized Coachella Valley. In places the stench from their bloated and rotted carcasses was almost unbearable.

Several hundred yards beyond a rock jetty, they found a deserted and abandoned restaurant-motel complex that Condo Don thought would serve their needs. Nothing remained of the large circular restaurant but bare studs and rafters. The boxy motel, however, was in fairly good shape considering it had not been occupied for decades. Only the doors and fixtures were missing from the two story structure and its rooms, which were painted garish shades of rose and turquoise, would provide excellent shelter. Vandals had burned the palm trees bordering its main drive. Almost every exterior wall was covered in spray-painted graffiti and posters from bygone elections. A dry debris-filled swimming pool dominated the center of the complex, its crumbling gunnite having decomposed to the point where, in several spots, it exposed the rusting rebar skeleton underneath.

Condo Don commented that the place was spooky enough to be a set from a 1950's horror movie. He immediately set everyone to work gathering up the trash that littered the area. When they finished an hour later, Condo Don pronounced the site livable, although he expressed doubts that it would ever be nominated for an award from *Better Homes & Gardens*.

A flaxen haired young lady who had been accompanying them for several weeks remarked that the Salton Sea resembled the Sea of Galilee because it occupied a similar latitude and was also below sea level. Condo Don grumbled that it came closer to resembling the Dead Sea.

In the days that followed they discovered that the Salton Sea was not entirely deserted. Scattered throughout the region were a number of inhabitants. People on low fixed incomes—primarily retirees, welfare recipients, and the disabled—had gravitated to the Salton Sea to take advantage of cheap land and a slower pace of life. Many who had already rejected materialism in favor of a more spiritual existence were especially receptive to the teachings of Jesus. Even the sheriff's deputies were friendly, stopping by several times to check on the group's safety. It appeared that Jesus and His followers had at last, at least temporarily, found a home.

Soon, a viable work schedule was established. On weekdays, everyone arose early in the morning. After breakfast, they went to the jetty where Jesus stood and lectured, His spellbound flock listening attentively from the shore. White egrets often flanked the Savior as He spoke, poking amidst the rocks with their dagger like bills in search of small crustaceans. On the horizon, an aqua sea melted into an azure sky, forming a stunning backdrop. When Jesus spoke, the sea immediately calmed and quiet descended as if the waters were straining to catch each word. Rippling wavelets lapped against the jetty, providing meter for His poetic speech.

Afternoons were devoted to chores. Condo Don organized work groups to clean the living quarters and take care of other day to day tasks. With him in charge everyone was always busy.

With time their numbers grew. Some came to be healed, others merely to listen. All were welcome.

Many found employment as day laborers in the date gardens and fields of nearby Coachella. Their income served to provide food and buy building materials to refurbish the complex. The former restaurant was remodeled as a communal dining hall and utilities were restored. Gang slogans and other graffiti disappeared under a fresh coat of paint. With watering, the scorched palms put on new fronds in seeming defiance of their blackened trunks. The 1950's horror movie set was gradually transformed by Condo Don's expertise into a seaside resort. That which had before stood in mute testimony to Man's folly—gutted, vandalized, desecrated, and abandoned—now proclaimed resoundingly his rejuvenation.

One day, Esteban, having learned of his brother's whereabouts from Tom, came to stay. Jesus was gratified to learn that His mother and the rest of His family were in good health. Esteban, like his father, enjoyed working with his hands and became Condo Don's enthusiastic apprentice.

Otis Chandler, fully recovered and energetic, arrived in his limousine for a week-long visit. He was brimming with ideas for the complex's improvement, offering to finance its expansion into a sprawling utopian community and seminary for religious studies. Although Condo Don argued eloquently in Chandler's behalf, Jesus rebuffed the offer, maintaining that it would be best for the new religious community to evolve along its own natural lines.

Mr. Chandler neglected to mention that he had already located the property's absentee owners, purchased the complex, and paid the back taxes. He had intended to present Jesus with the deed as a gift, but feared that He might not accept. Before returning to Los Angeles, however, he confided to Condo Don his intentions to make the new church a major beneficiary of his will.

Jesus was walking onto the jetty early one morning when a woman standing at the edge of the crowd said, "We have heard you speak against man's prideful technological monuments to himself. Would you have us destroy them?"

Removing His coat, Jesus turned to face the gathering:

"I come not as a conqueror, sword in hand, craving destruction, but as a teacher and healer to correct the social ills which threaten the economic and technological advancements of the past two millennia. Can your television, VCR, stereo, or jacuzzi give you pleasure while your children are being menaced by drugs and your community torn apart by gang violence? What good is a freeway if it brings drive-by shootings to your front door? Man has sought too long to better his condition while neglecting to better himself. Until this is remedied mankind will progress no further.

In vain you turn to your leaders seeking answers to the problems that confront you. Life will not improve until you improve. Man must cleanse himself of his bestial tendencies to make meaningful intellectual progress. The mind cannot advance independent of the spirit. Ethical and moral decay is a disease which has reached epidemic proportions. This terrible plague will consume civilization unless you renounce hedonism and turn back to God.

Each must do his or her part. Gather around you your families and form a spiritual barrier to the vermin that swarm without. Link with others to repel the scourge, driving it from your community back into the pits of the earth from which it sprang. With God's help you shall purge lawlessness, vice, and corruption and go on to build a better world.

The peace which you so desperately seek cannot be yours until you make your peace with God. Open your hearts to me and I will guide you to the serenity which only God can give. Prayer shall open the gates of Heaven.

Do not barter eternity for the pleasure of the moment. Cheap thrills last but a fleeting second while their residual effects can last a lifetime. God welcomes all who come to Him with open arms. Who but a fool would reject Him when the sole alternative is destruction and everlasting pain?

Man cannot save himself. He has tried and failed. Only God can grant salvation."

The morning chill was soon baked from the air. Faint, wispy, dry clouds floated high overhead as the first beads of perspiration appeared on Christ's forehead. He had been speaking for over an hour and was beginning to feel the warmth of the sun's rays reflecting off the tranquil sea. Condo Don, standing at the front of the gathering, passed Him a gallon jug of water that had been circulating amongst the crowd. Jesus tilted the container to His lips and passed it along to a youth with curly hair who was seated on the sand next to Condo Don. As the young man accepted the water from the hands of the Savior, he queried, "How much should I give to help the poor. "Only your heart can answer that question," replied Jesus.

"The wise men of antiquity instructed us to tithe, but this should in no way limit your generosity. Often, while traveling, I have come upon the campsites of the homeless and shared their meager meals. Following a trail of tears, they are rejected everywhere they go. If they in their ragged, tattered condition can afford to be generous, surely those of you who have been blessed with so much more can manage to do likewise. When you make a gift to the poor and the homeless, you are giving to me.

The next time you encounter a poor bedraggled soul upon your journey through life, take a close look at him. Beneath the torn shirt and grime, is his flesh not as yours? Doe he not breathe, eat, and walk the same as you? Is he not your brother? We are all as one upon this earth. There is no separate species or caste comprising the homeless and the poor. God created us alike so that we are all of one family. Our individual differences are minuscule when compared to our similarities. He who abuses the footsore and the downtrodden demeans humanity and rejects me.

You came upon this earth without a cent and you will leave the same way. Money is important only for the good that it can do. Be careful that you do not allow it to come between you and God.

There are those among you who say that the poor are a money pit and that there have always been poor and there always will be poor. I say this: no journey can begin until you have taken the first step. The gap between the rich and the poor grows ever wider and provides fertile ground for demagogues who would take from you by force all that you have. Give of your money, give of your time, and, most of all, give of yourself. In return, God will give you the most precious gift of all—Eternal Life."

With the sun approaching its zenith, Jesus stepped from the jetty onto the shore, intending to return to the complex. But as the crowd was leaving, He noticed a woman limping behind the rest. Her limbs and features had been twisted by a debilitating disease. Jesus went to her and began to straighten her arms and legs with His hands as a sculptor would mold clay. A number of people stopped to watch and one of them commented that despite the transformation rendered by Jesus, "she's still ugly."

Overhearing the unkind remark, Jesus said, "All things that are good are beautiful to God. You must learn to look deeper than superficial features in order to discover the true nature of what lies within. The body is merely a container for the soul. A pretty picture on a label may belie spoiled contents. Have you ever removed packaging and found the product to be incomplete or damaged?"

"True beauty cannot be bought in the marketplace. There is no cosmetic that will transform a whore into a virgin; no soap that will wash the blood from the hands of a murderer."

"Do not search for beauty in a slick magazine or a videotape. Such beauty is a conjurer's trick, a mirage which quickly fades and leaves you thirsting. Mortals cannot create beauty—it can solely be imparted by God."

"The beauty you seek is a transitory thing, ephemeral at best. Although the flower on a branch soon withers and dies, the fruit that follows nourishes the body. God has given you more than one sense—do not rely on your sight alone to perceive beauty. Have patience; linger, that you may savor all the goodness that beauty has to offer."

"Beauty cannot be possessed. When picked, the rose will wilt; a butterfly in a jar soon dies. Be content to witness beauty and do not attempt to extract it. Everyone has something beautiful inside himself. Nurture that beauty and it will grow and attract all that is beautiful around you. In this way and in this way only can you surround yourself with beauty."

Jesus passed His hand over the woman's face, wiping away the scars and blemishes and revealing the true radiant beauty within. Onlookers were awestruck by the transformation. Embracing Jesus, she swore that she would be forever grateful and would praise God every day of her life. When she left, no longer limping, the man who had made the unkind comment lusted after her. But she would not heed him.

As the number of people who came to hear the Savior's sermons increased, more chose to stay and the complex quickly grew into a small community. Condo Don and his assistant, Esteban, were kept busy constructing additional structures to accommodate the influx of believers.

The community needed a name. Some had begun to refer to the complex as "Great Salton." Condo Don remonstrated that "Great" was a bit pretentious, but the name stuck anyway. A pundit noted that if a shallow, briny lake in Utah deserved the appellation of "Great," than certainly there would be nothing amiss in applying it to something associated with their own vast inland sea.

Great Salton had more than its share of organizational problems. Jesus' flock came from assorted religious backgrounds. There were Mormons, Baptists, Lutherans, Episcopalians, Catholics, Presbyterians, Methodists, Unitarians, Quakers, Jews, and others. They were constantly debating the efficacy of their individual beliefs. Usually, Jesus sagaciously refused to comment or take sides. However, these debates became increasingly fractious and eventually threatened to divide the church into feuding factions. When a difference in scriptural interpretations turned ugly at a communal supper, Jesus intervened, saying, "Why must you fight? Do you not all agree that I am your Savior? You should rejoice in your similarities instead of magnifying your differences. If you quarrel like this with me present, how will you behave when I am no longer around?

Different roads can lead to the same destination. It matters little which road you traveled once you have arrived. God gives each a separate mission. Your path may cross, run parallel, or converge with others. Are you so vain that you expect everyone else to walk in your footsteps?

How many wars have been fought in God's name? Do you believe God to be so petty that He would choose sides? Do not listen to those who bid you to kill in God's name, for God is your leader and He has commanded you not to kill.

Each of you is free to worship God in his own fashion. I am here to show you the direction, but you must decide which path to take. If you feel you have chosen correctly, pay no attention to where others are going. The path which is right for them may be wrong for you.

You alone are responsible for your choices. Do not point to others and complain that they have led you astray, for God has endowed you with the ability to reason for yourself."

Chapter 16

As Great Salton grew, Condo Don's responsibilities multiplied. All the problems of supply, administration, and finances were his. In addition he personally planned and supervised the community's construction projects and served as its one man legislature and police force. He was reluctant to delegate authority despite the repeated urgings of Esteban and others to do so. Jesus relied upon him to run the community and he was determined not to fail.

Condo Don was becoming edgy. He was putting in eighteen hour days and seldom had any time to himself. On several occasions he yelled at people for trifling mistakes. Finally, Jesus was forced to admonish him not to lose his temper.

Most of the community's building materials were scavenged from nearby abandoned structures. Condo Don was in charge of a work crew dismantling one such building when an inexperienced volunteer inadvertently broke a window while attempting to remove its metal frame with a crowbar. He could feel the anger boiling within. Windows were extremely hard to come by, most having been broken by vandals.

Just as he was opening his mouth to berate the hapless young man for clumsiness, Condo Don regained control of his temper and, turning in the direction of some nearby sand dunes, began walking off his rage. The loose, drifting particles of sand tugged at his boots as if trying to drag him under. But each step was a stride towards regaining his composure and the farther he walked, the better he felt. After a long while, he collapsed on the backside of a dune, physically and emotionally exhausted.

Some moments later when he stood, intending to return to the worksite, he became disoriented and was unsure of which direction to take. A brisk breeze had erased his footprints. Climbing to the top of a dune, he slowly turned in a circle. All about there was nothing but sand—dune after dune in every direction as far as he could see. There wasn't a bush, rock, or living being in sight. He was lost in an endless sea of sand.

But Condo Don was not given to panic. He was an experienced outdoorsman and this was not the first time he had been lost in a wilderness area. Squatting in the sand, he unwrapped a biscuit that he had been carrying in a pocket and considered the situation as he ate. He could not have gone far. The important thing to do was to remain calm and continue walking until he came to something he recognized.

The blistering sand swallowed him almost to his knees as he struggled to ascend the steep dunes. Fine grit rasped its way into every exposed pore. After trudging through the sands for what seemed to be hours, he spotted something shiny in the trough of a nearby dune. Running to it, he found it was the foil wrapper from the biscuit he had eaten earlier. All this time, he had been walking in circles!

Once again, he attempted to reconnoiter his position. It was late afternoon and the sun was to his right and rather low on the horizon. That meant that if he kept his back to the sun, he would be walking towards the sea—roughly in an easterly direction. He knew that he should make some kind of adjustment for the season, but was unsure as to what it should be.

For several hours he pushed relentlessly forward until the sun melted into the sea of sand. The sunset had been spectacular, but in his trepidation Condo Don had scarcely noticed it. Twilight was short and, as Condo Don lay his aching body down in the lee of a dune, utter blackness descended. The moon had not yet risen on the horizon and he could barely make out the outlines of adjacent dunes in the dim starlight. His legs throbbed and their recurring muscle spasms kept jolting him awake. He rubbed them until the pain subsided, then drifted into sleep, only to be awakened by an even more painful cramp. Heat radiated from the sand beneath while the chill night air filled his lungs. It was as if he had been split in half from his head to his toes. His bottomside was in an oven and his topside in a refrigerator. It was the most uncomfortable night of his life.

Towards morning a fine mist descended upon the

dunes. It wasn't thick enough to be a fog, but nevertheless Condo Don could feel its moisture upon his bare skin. He was thirsty and strained to remember something an instructor in a survival class had once said about how to extract moisture from the air. Thirty years before he had been an inattentive cadet at the Air Force Academy. Now, he regretted it.

He had thought himself to be alone in the desert, but he was wrong. Periodically, small insects explored the crevices of his prone body. Once, a small lizard darted past his head. Too late, he extended his hand in a half-hearted attempt to catch it.

It was several hours past dawn before the air warmed to the point where Condo Don felt like moving. His stomach was growling and he thought longingly about the biscuit he had so thoughtlessly devoured the previous morning. But he doubted he could swallow it even if he had saved it—his mouth was parched and his tongue had begun to swell.

Now, he walked towards the sun. It shone in his eyes and reflected off the sand, blurring his vision. He tried squinting between narrowly parted eyelids, but it was of little help. Each crack in his dry lips felt like a fissure when he licked them with his thick, parched tongue.

Shimmering heat waves in the distance made the horizon resemble a lake. His mind told him that it was merely a mirage. Nevertheless, it constantly reminded him of his desperate need for water.

A warm, early morning breeze strengthened into a hot wind that moved the sand in snake-like ripples. Sand was everywhere: in his eyes, in his mouth, in his clothes, in his boots. He wanted to halt and remove his boots to dump out the sand, but feared that his blistered feet would swell and he would be unable to put them back on.

While wiping his brow, Condo Don noticed the skin was starting to peel from his face. Belatedly remembering that more fluids evaporated from the head than any other portion of the body, he removed his sweatshirt and wrapped it over his head like a turban.

His thirst had grown until it filled his mind. He thought of snow covered hillsides and cool mountain streams. Once, many years before, he had swum in the ice cold springtime waters of the American River in Northern California. The pleasant experience played over and over again in his mind like a videotape, but only served to increase his thirst.

He slept better the second night. Either his legs had stopped cramping or he was too exhausted to notice.

Well into the morning of the third day, he awoke drained and listless. His coarse-grit-sandpaper tongue scratched at the roof of a mouth that felt like someone had shoveled sand into it.

Once again he set out towards the sun. This was day

three and it seemed as if he had been in the desert forever. Everything was swimming slowly past his blurry eyes: the sun and the sky and the sand. He dropped to his knees. His self-confidence had vanished, leaving him in fear that the desert would soon become his unmarked grave. Nothing would remain to evidence his death. Silently, he began to pray, asking God to accept his unworthy soul.

But the comfort of death was not yet his. Slowly, he crawled up the next dune on his hands and knees. Reaching the summit, he tumbled down the far side. Stumbling and crawling, he drifted in and out of consciousness. Somewhere, he had lost the improvised turban and the sun was again baking his head. He thought of going back for it, but could not summon the necessary energy. It took all of his will to keep pushing forward. Somehow, he knew that if he stopped, he would die.

Looking up in the sky, he expected to see vultures circling. But there wasn't a bird in sight. Weren't dying men in the desert entitled to have the company of buzzards? He felt cheated.

Another night passed. Was it now the morning of the fourth or the fifth day? Condo Don couldn't remember. But it really didn't seem to matter. All that mattered now was death. Death would bring relief: relief from the sand; relief from the sun; relief from the torture of thirst. Had he abandoned hope or had hope abandoned him? Or was it

God who had abandoned him?

Condo Don had long since stopped moving. It was all he could manage to raise his head and look around. He lay prone in the sun like a strip of beef set out for jerking.

And then he saw him. Shimmering in the heat of the midday sun, someone was standing at the top of the next dune. Was it a mirage? Was he having delusions? Condo Don wasn't certain, but whatever or whomever it was, it was coming towards him. He tried to shout, but his throat was so swollen that no sound emerged.

The apparition advanced until it stood over him. Despite the intense heat, it was impeccably groomed and dressed in the finest designer-made evening clothes. And it was smiling at him. Was this the face of Death, Condo Don wondered?

"Water," Condo Don managed to utter in a faint whisper.

"What, are you thirsty?," the apparition asked with a cultured accent. "Aren't you the friend of Jesus, who calls himself the Son of God? Why don't you command water to flow forth from the sand?"

Condo Don made no reply.

"Where is your friend now that you need Him?" sneered the apparition. "You've been missing for days and Jesus has not sent anyone to search for you. You are of no further use to Him and He has left you here to die of thirst and exposure. In fact, He has already replaced you with His brother, Esteban."

"Liar," rasped Condo Don.

"Loyalty is a quality better suited to dogs than humans," the apparition observed. "Be smart and save yourself. Denounce Jesus and I will help you."

"No," moaned Condo Don.

"Is life of so little value to you?" queried the apparition. "You've been a bum for the past thirty years and you have probably forgotten what it is like to really live. Allow me to refresh your memory."

The apparition removed a dark, hand-rolled Cuban cigar from the breast pocket of his tailored jacket. A small flame appeared at the tip of an upwardly bent finger and he lit the panatela. After taking several puffs, he bent low and blew a swirling cloud of noxious smoke in Condo Don's direction.

Twirling curlicues of smoke wafted into Condo Don's eyes and nostrils. Coughing and choking, he writhed upon the sand. His eyes stung and he couldn't see a thing for several moments.

When the smoke cleared and his vision returned, he

discovered that the surface of the sand had turned to smooth glass. Peering through it, he saw several people in a large room. It was as if he was lying prone on the top of a gigantic crystal ball, watching a scene unfold beneath him.

He recognized the people. There was himself as a gangly teenager and his best friend, Rob. They were standing in front of the liquor cabinet in Condo Don's father's study. Rob was opening the cabinet door.

"Good old Rob!" thought Condo Don. Why, he had not seen Rob in over thirty years. Rob's lips were moving and he strained to hear what his friend was saying.

"Go ahead," said Rob. "I double dog dare you to do it."

Condo Don's younger self reached into the cabinet and removed an almost full bottle of Southern Comfort liqueur. Unscrewing the cap, he pressed the bottle to his lips. After taking a long swig, he coughed and passed the bottle to Rob.

The scene faded and the transparent glass once again turned to opaque sand. In vain Condo Don scraped at the sand, trying to get the vision to return.

"Now that's what I call fun!" exclaimed the apparition, breaking the spell.

Condo Don remembered the incident well. It was the

first time he and Rob had drunk hard liquor. They had both become sick and vomited. But that hadn't deterred Condo Don. It was his fateful first step on the downward path to alcoholism. Thirty years of his life wasted as a miserable derelict—all because he didn't have the moral courage to resist a dare.

"You . . . Scum!" groaned Condo Don.

"What, you didn't enjoy that?" asked the grinning apparition incredulously. "I find it hard to believe that a thirsty man like yourself wouldn't enjoy watching himself take a drink! But I may have miscalculated. No matter, there are many more things I can show you from your past."

And with that, the dapper apparition again bent down without disturbing the immaculate pleat in his pin-striped trousers, took a long draw on his cigar until the ash glowed orange red, and blew an even larger cloud of smoke in Condo Don's face.

Condo Don quickly turned his head, but the smoke soon overtook him. Once again it penetrated his eyes and nose as if seeking to poison his entire being.

When the billowy smoke cleared, the sand beneath Condo Don had again turned to glass. He looked downwards and saw a new scene unfolding.

There was a car: a dark yellow Pontiac hardtop sedan

with chrome trim and sweptback fins. It was parked in a turnout on a winding mountain road. Snow was falling and it was late at night. Condo Don could barely discern two figures, a man and a woman embracing, through the arcs cleared by the wipers on the windshield. The man was wearing an elegant silver-trimmed uniform . . .

And then he remembered. It was himself, Cadet Stearns, in his dress Class A uniform. The girl he was kissing was Rita Warren, his steady girl. After a formal military ball at the Academy, he had borrowed an upperclassman's car and driven to Pikes Peak. There was an almost empty fifth of Jack Daniels beside him on the seat and several plastic vials of pills on top of the dashboard. They were both under the influence and were feeling no pain.

His hands were all over her. Now, belatedly, she was trying to push him away, but it just made him come on stronger. He pawed at her and ripped her gown.

Condo Don shut his eyes. He knew what was going to happen next. He had forced himself on her and she had never spoken to him again. Two weeks later, he had tested positive for drugs and been drummed out of the Air Force Academy. He might be a general on the Joint Chiefs of Staff today, if only . . .

"Enough!" yelled Condo Don.

"What?" exclaimed the apparition, breathing heavily.

"We were just getting to the good part."

Condo Don rose to his knees and shook his head to clear his thoughts. There was something familiar about this natty, cigar smoking tormentor. Something sinister.

"Do I know you?" stammered Condo Don.

"Of course you do," replied the apparition, rolling the huge cigar from one side of his mouth to the other. "We had some great times together. We were the best of friends for years until you let that upstart 'nigger' come between us."

No sooner had the apparition uttered the derisive N-word, then Condo Don felt anger erupt from somewhere deep inside himself. He had never heard anyone call Jesus that name before. The powerful burst of righteous indignation overcame his thirst and exhaustion and he leapt and grabbed the apparition by the throat. The cigar fell from its mouth. It gasped and struggled for breath.

As Condo Don tightened his grip on the Evil One, it suddenly transformed itself into a snake. The writhing snake thrashed and hissed, but Condo Don did not let go.

This was no ordinary snake. Condo Don had come across many rattlers in his journeys, but this was the king of them all. It coiled like a hawser upon the sand, the immense number of rattles at the terminus of its tail testifying to its great age. Mottled shadings of desert browns and tans formed diamond patterns along its body, each scale a separate tile in the mosaic.

He struggled to maintain his chokehold on the snake. Beneath his grip, he could feel its writhing coldness as it attempted to squirm from his hands. The vertical slit of its eye was a window on the fiery pit of hell and Condo Don averted its hypnotic gaze lest it capture his very soul.

The viper's flattened head arced toward his own. Its gigantic jaws hinged outward as if planning to swallow him whole. Dripping venom from extended fangs, the snake almost touched Condo Don with its flickering forked tongue.

The rattler's coils gave it leverage and it managed to flip Condo Don onto the sand. Rolling and tumbling, he wrestled with the clammy serpent for what seemed to be an eternity. The tendons in his arms threatened to snap as he fought to keep the poisonous fangs from piercing his face.

Summoning all his energy for the struggle, Condo Don managed to regain his feet. Mercilessly stomping on a coil, he felt the rattlesnake squish beneath his heel. Writhing in pain, it hissed, "Nigger lover!" Enraged, Condo Don whipped the snake's tail against the sand with such force that its rattles broke off. He repeated the motion several times until the tail slammed hard onto the spot where the sand had changed to glass. It shattered and Condo Don hurled the serpent into the void beneath.

He watched it hurtle downward, twisting in midair, until the falling snake was so small that it appeared to be but an insignificant worm.

Utterly exhausted, Condo Don lay down on the sand. He slept fitfully, dreaming that he was once again having delirium tremens. Thousands of writhing snakes were chasing him around a park bench. Just as they were about to outpace him, he awoke. It was morning, but he was unsure as to how many days he had been lost.

He wondered if his battle with the Evil One had been part of the nightmare. No, the 18 inch rattle lay beside him in the sand. He clutched it to him and began to crawl up the face of the dune where the Evil One had first appeared. For every yard he gained, he slipped two feet. Reaching the top, he saw a familiar roadway. And there, nearby, was Esteban walking towards him. He tried to shout, but no sound emerged from his dry throat. In desperation, he shook the rattle.

Chapter 17

Following his ordeal in the barren wilderness of the dunes, it was fifteen days before Condo Don recovered sufficiently to resume his administrative duties. Great Salton had grown to a community of over one thousand people and his responsibilities had in no way diminished.

As he saw it, their most pressing problem was finances. Great Salton had always led a hand to mouth existence and it bothered him that there was no surplus to cover unforeseen emergencies and disasters. Jesus continued to refuse substantial donations on the grounds that the fledgling community needed to become self-reliant so that it might help others. Every time Condo Don brought up the subject, Jesus rebuked him, saying, "Has God not always provided? Haven't you, at times, made do with less?"

Nevertheless, Condo Don was constantly searching for new sources of revenue for Great Salton. He wanted to manufacture salt by building evaporative pools along the shoreline, but the community lacked the capital it would take to make the enterprise a success.

Jesus' sermons were attracting huge crowds. People came from great distances to hear Him speak. Condo Don made a suggestion that they sell refreshments to these "tourists," but Jesus vetoed it. When Condo Don joked about silk screening The Savior's likeness onto T-shirts, Jesus did not find it amusing.

One day, an entrepreneur approached Condo Don with a deal. He offered a lot of money for the right to videotape sermons. Being aware that Jesus favored separating religion from business, Condo Don was inclined to refuse outright, but the businessman was very persuasive, arguing that videotapes could reach a larger audience and were, therefore, an effective and efficient means of spreading the gospel. Reluctantly, Condo Don agreed to arrange an interview for him with Jesus.

When the entrepreneur subsequently met the Savior, he carefully repeated his earlier offer, emphasizing the potential profits, then asked Jesus to sign a contract. Jesus declined, explaining, "Once what I say leaves my mouth, I have no more claim to it than an ocean has to the marks it leaves upon the sand. For me to profit from doing my Father's bidding would be a sacrilege. You may record what you like, providing you faithfully reproduce it verbatim and in no way disturb the congregation. I neither encourage nor discourage your enterprise. My teachings are the property of all men."

After the businessman departed, Jesus went up to Condo Don and said, "This does not mean that I want to see my face on T-shirts."

* * *

Life can be hard for those who dwell in the Mojave. The harsh sun is unrelenting as it chokes the moisture from the sand. Water is the lifeblood of the desert, but it must be imported via canals from great distances and at substantial cost. Irrigated farms are often only marginally profitable. When crops fail, farmers can be forced into bankruptcy.

When one such local date grower could not meet his payroll, he offered Great Salton an older model, dilapidated 1 1/2 ton stakebed truck in lieu of the $600 in wages he owed. Although Condo Don disliked the deal, it was either that or nothing. He reluctantly accepted, reasoning that the community could put it to use hauling building materials and provisions.

At some time in the distant past the truck had been white, but rust stains, numerous dings, and an accumulation of grime now left its color open to debate. Windblown sand had pitted the windshield and exposed blotches of bare metal on the hood. Neither of the doors would budge, requiring the driver and passengers to enter and exit by crawling through the windows. Large cavities in the dank, rotting upholstery had been haphazardly filled with a motley assortment of cushions tied to the seat springs and covered by a filthy blanket. A broken speedometer cable had frozen the odometer at 99,999.9 and pegged the faded orange needle of the speedometer at 0. Condo Don immediately dubbed it "Grapes of Wrath" for its resemblance to the truck the Joad family had driven from Oklahoma to California in Steinbeck's classic novel about the Great Depression.

It wheezed, coughed, sputtered, and belched, but it ran. Although subjected to the tortures of negligent maintenance, its venerable flathead, low-compression engine had refused to die. When driven by an expert who could gauge RPM by the whine of the motor, its non-synchromesh standard transmission could be shifted without grinding the gears. Its 6-ply tires and split ring rims were indestructible. The weathered and tarnished Chevrolet cross on the grill was perhaps the best testimonial to durability that the General Motors Corporation had ever received.

Its back could not be broken. No matter how hard they tried to overload it, its jumbo leaf springs never sagged. Even when transporting a load of rock, its extra-low "granny" gear minimized strain on the engine. In time it became an accepted member of a community which judged people and machines not by how good they looked, but by how well they functioned.

Leftover paints were utilized to emblazon a rainbow across the hood. Condo Don remarked that it was an appropriate symbol, since Grapes of Wrath had obviously "weathered the storm."

* * *

Farm labor was both a bane and a salvation to Great Salton. In return for giving the community honest employment and a source of income, it demanded long, back-breaking, sweat-filled hours for minimal wages.

Each morning before dawn the labor contractor's buses would arrive at Great Salton to transport workers to fields in Coachella. Following a bumpy half hour ride, they would disembark to join the *braceros* and other migrant farm laborers in various agricultural activities ranging from ascending tall ladders in date orchards to duck walking in the furrows to pick berries and other low-growing produce.

Although crops are grown year round in the Coachella Valley, much of the work is seasonal. During harvest, more laborers are needed and twelve to fourteen hour workdays, six days a week, are not unusual.

A typical workday at harvest time began at dawn. The workers formed a line at the end of a field, one to a furrow, and began to walk down the furrow, picking ripe vegetables as they went. When his box became full, a laborer would carry it to the opposite end of the field where it was tallied by the owner or his agent and loaded onto a flatbed truck. Since most workers earned minimum wage plus a small production bonus per box, everyone worked hard to pick as much as possible. Rough leaves and spiny stalks tore at callused fingers as they reached into the plants.

By 9 or 10 AM it was already uncomfortably hot. Most laborers wore bandannas and broad-brimmed hats to shield their heads from the blazing sun. In summer the temperature sometimes reached 120 degrees and perspiration evaporated before it had a chance to form on the body.

Come noon there was an hour break for lunch. Everyone ate quickly and then sat or lay in the shade of the trucks. English mixed with Spanish, Tagalog, Arabic, and other languages as recent immigrants struggled to communicate with each other.

When the blistering fireball in the sky came to scorch the far horizon and the light began to fade, the workday ended. Everyone climbed onto the buses and sacked out on the seats and in the aisles as best they could for the long ride home. Arriving at Great Salton, it took all their remaining strength to eat dinner before falling asleep, exhausted. Next morning, long before first light, it would be time to get up and do it all over again.

Manual labor tended to toughen the community's new recruits and weed out those who lacked determination. Nevertheless, Condo Don felt their pain and longed to create an alternative means of livelihood for his brethren.

* * *

Condo Don was quite familiar with the recycling trade. For many years he had made his living from the aluminum cans and other scrap metals that he scavenged. From knowledge gained at the Air Force

Academy and conversations with fellow scavengers he knew that Great Salton was less than a hundred miles from a virtual El Dorado of scrap metals, the Chocolate Mountains Aerial Gunnery Range which lay approximately ten miles east of Salton Sea's eastern shore. It was rumored that a man could not take a single step anywhere on the range without stumbling over spent aluminum, brass, and copper ordnance.

There was only one drawback. Some of the bombs, bullets, and shells comprising the vast scrap heap were duds that had failed to explode on impact. Anyone disturbing a "live" detonator ran the risk of blowing himself and everyone in the immediate vicinity to smithereens. But Condo Don figured that by following tracks left by previous scavengers, he could minimize the danger. Besides, he reasoned, all profit involves risk, and the greater the risk, the greater the profit.

The Chocolate Mountains Aerial Gunnery Range had been leased by the Air Force at the beginning of World War II. In an age prior to the advent of smart bombs and sophisticated electronic guidance systems vast amounts of real estate had been required to compensate for navigational errors. The perimeter of the Aerial Gunnery Range formed an imperfect ellipse approximately 50 miles long by 10 miles wide—an area over 1 1/2 times larger than the Salton Sea. Although the range fell into disuse after the war, the Air Force was reluctant to decommission it because it was cheaper to maintain the lease than to restore the property to its original condition.

The way Condo Don saw it, anyone who removed the scrap metal would be doing the federal government a favor.

War is by far the most wasteful of human endeavors. It greedily consumes a nation's natural resources and generates nothing but destruction in return. Shells and bombs that take many man-hours to manufacture explode in a fraction of a second. Airplanes and tanks representing the cutting edge of technology quickly become outdated and are left to rust as worthless junk. Condo Don had a gut feeling that the immense ordnance graveyard was beckoning him to recycle into positive uses military hardware and former weapons. Had not God through the Prophet Isaiah said that men would "beat their swords into plowshares?"

Condo Don anticipated that Jesus might have some reservations about approving any such scheme, so he rehearsed his presentation, mentally outlining the points he should make. It would take three days at the most for him and two helpers to load Grapes of Wrath full of scrap and return. Besides being their own bosses, they would earn many times the wage paid to farm laborers. Considering the huge size of the Aerial Gunnery Range, the supply of scrap metal was practically limitless. Condo Don envisioned his project supplying full employment to Great Salton for many years to come.

Two days later, Condo Don presented the proposal to Jesus with the flair and acumen of a professional huckster. Jesus listened politely and, as predicted, was somewhat concerned with the danger involved. However, Condo Don argued eloquently on the project's behalf, quoting scripture until he made it sound like a Mission from God. When he finished, Jesus, seeing that Condo Don was not to be dissuaded, said, "Be careful that any mistakes you make are not fatal. Some people learn best through experience."

Condo Don took this to be approval, albeit reluctant, and was surprised by the easy victory. He had expected to lose the first battle and had prepared for a long campaign.

The next morning Condo Don loaded a crowbar, two shovels, ten white plastic gallon "milk jugs" filled with drinking water, and enough provisions to last three people for one week onto Grapes of Wrath. He had chosen two recent young converts, Lyle and Simon, to accompany him, leaving Esteban behind to perform his customary duties.

Lyle was primarily selected for his enormous strength. At 6 feet 8 inches in height and 270 pounds, Lyle was a modern day Sampson—easily the strongest person at Great Salton. His slow speech and a slight lisp caused people to assess him as backward, but in actuality he was one of the few people at Great Salton who possessed a college degree.

Simon was Grapes of Wrath's regular driver. Besides

being familiar with desert roads and driving conditions, he had an uncanny sense of direction. Gregarious and outgoing, he had become one of the most popular young men in the community. His quick wit and tireless sense of humor made him an excellent traveling companion. In a desert wilderness devoid of modern electronic entertainment, his ability to play the harmonica was a highly prized skill.

Before beginning their journey, Simon checked the water and oil levels. Condo Don had recently fashioned a radiator overflow bottle for Grapes of Wrath from a sports bottle and a small length of vinyl tubing and it had reduced the aging truck's tendency to overheat. Simon also brought along several quarts of oil and a funnel in case they were needed.

Although Grapes of Wrath was certainly not the slowest vehicle to ever travel Highway 86 along the northwestern periphery of the Salton Sea, it probably ranked high in the competition. Something about long, straight desert highways transforms normally rational motorists into raving speed demons. These demons were now honking their horns and making obscene gestures as they struggled to pass Grapes of Wrath. And, although Simon drove on the extreme right of the road hugging the shoulder, he could not entirely escape their wrath.

Grapes of Wrath whined as it struggled to produce maximum RPM in fourth gear. The ancient truck's passengers had to shout to make themselves heard and before long relinquished their attempts to maintain a conversation. In desperation Condo Don switched on the truck's radio. It took almost a minute for the tubes to warm up before the speaker crackled to life. Turning the station selector, he got mostly static from the AM dial, finally settling for a Spanish language station specializing in *musica ranchero*. The accordion strains of Los Tigres Del Norte mingled with the din of the engine to produce a hybrid drone that Condo Don found relaxing. However, he soon surmised from the expression on his companions' faces that they did not share his taste in music. Reluctantly, he turned to a news station.

Despite not having listened to a newscast in months, Condo Don found that little had changed. War still raged in the Balkans and the Mideast. The Republicans were still in power and were making further cuts in aid to the poor. Pepsi still claimed to taste better than Coke and Schick still out shaved Gillette.

The only real changes were in sports. Army had beaten Navy only to be trounced by the Air Force's Falcons. The Bengals were going to the Super Bowl and the World's Cup Soccer finals were coming to the United States for the second time. Just as everyone was getting interested, the signal began to fade. Although Condo Don monkeyed with the controls and slapped the metal dashboard several times, there was nothing but garbled noise. Disgusted, he switched it off.

It was hot in the cab and Condo Don was beginning to perspire. With stinging beads of sweat trickling into his eyes, he belatedly realized why Simon always wore a bandanna tied around his forehead. He stripped to his undershirt, but was still hot. Outside, it was well above 100 degrees and not yet noon. Shimmering waves of heat consumed the asphalt highway on the horizon. They passed around a jug of water and everyone drank deep.

Upon crossing the Coachella Canal, the road deteriorated into a rock strewn unimproved track. Simon downshifted into second gear, but it was still a bone jarring ride. Each time Grapes of Wrath ran over a rock, Lyle's head bounced against the cab's hot bare-metal roof. Improvising a headliner from a towel met with little success—the towel soon fell down. Finally, Condo Don admonished Simon to slow down; he was afraid Grapes of Wrath would bust an axle.

"Chocolate" proved to be a misnomer. As they began to climb the foothills, the earth took on a reddish tint. Mesquite lined both sides of the dirt road and the occasional stunted bushes appeared to be suffering as bad as everyone else in the sweltering heat.

The perimeter of the Aerial Gunnery Range was marked with an ancient, sagging security fence topped by barbed wire. Although its gates were padlocked, Simon had no trouble driving Grapes of Wrath through it. Entire sections were missing, having been torn down by vandals, hunters, and other intruders.

The road grew rougher and Simon shifted down into first gear. Grapes of Wrath crawled along, jostling its passengers from side to side. Despite sixteen inch tires that gave Grapes of Wrath excellent ground clearance, they heard the oil pan scrape bottom several times. Swerving from left to right, Simon did his best to avoid potholes and boulders.

Condo Don was disappointed. He had expected to find the range a moonscape pocked with craters brimming with metal debris from exploded shells and bombs. Instead, both craters and scrap proved to be few and far between. He remembered an example used by a senior instructor at the Air Force Academy to explain the ineffectiveness of mass carpet bombing, "Strolling through a park stocked with well fed pigeons, the odds are good that your expensive new suit would not get sullied by pigeon droppings."

They had driven about four miles into the range when they came upon three abandoned biplanes arranged in a semicircle slightly to the left of the road. Wings and propellers were missing. Scant remained of them but wooden fuselages, tattered canvas, and a few frayed guy wires. Judging from their boxy appearance, Condo Don reckoned them to be Brewster Buffalos, early World War II vintage fighters.

Simon parked the truck and they slid out the windows. Condo Don cautioned them to avoid anything that looked like it might be an unexploded bomb as they walked to the planes. Reaching the first fighter, Condo Don climbed into the cockpit. Although most of the gauges and the control stick were missing, Condo Don closed his eyes and imagined himself soaring among the clouds.

It had been more than thirty years since he had last sat in an open cockpit. The years rolled away as he recalled his first solo flight back at the Academy. Exhilarated, he leaned back and in an amazingly sonorous baritone belted, "Off we go into the wild, blue yonder . . ."

By the time he sang "go down in flames . . .," Lyle and Simon had climbed into the cockpits of the other two biplanes and were pelting each other with small stones. Never one to be upstaged, Condo Don scooped up a handful of pebbles and, making machine gun noises, tossed them at his fellow aviators.

A mock battle ensued such as the Aerial Gunnery Range had not experienced since the Second World War. Each pilot verbally maneuvered his aircraft to gain advantage over the others. Lyle shouted, "Bandits at 12 o' clock high!" and Condo Don responded *"Achtung, Jaeger!"*

After ten minutes of dogfighting in the blazing sun, Condo Don and Simon were so worn out that they could only occasionally plink a stone in the direction of the enemy, while Lyle was only warming up. Sensing that the others were at the point of surrender, Lyle increased his rate of fire. An exceptionally large caliber stone whizzed by Condo Don's left ear and struck a rounded metal object protruding from the ground a short distance away.

A tremendous, ear-splitting boom was followed by real shrapnel tearing through all three planes. Condo Don's Brewster Buffalo was pitched into the "wild, blue yonder" of whose praises he had so eloquently sung by the force of the explosion and came to rest with its tail in the air and its nose buried in the soil. A short while later, when the smoke and dust cleared, Condo Don jumped down and joined his startled friends. Miraculously, they had emerged unscathed.

Spying a shiny foil fragment on the ground, Condo Don stooped to pick it up. With a snappy salute he then "pinned" it to Lyle's pocket, proclaiming, "I, Air Marshal Donald Thaddeus Stearns III, in my capacity as supreme commander of Chocolate Mountains Fighter Command, Royal Salton Air Force, do hereby award the Distinguished Flying Cross to Air Cadet Lyle, who in his first combat engagement bravely cleansed the sky of a superior enemy force using primitive missiles and surplus ordnance." Having honorably winged their way through the impromptu ceremony, the valiant trio gingerly made their way back to the truck, carefully retracing as near as possible their original footsteps.

Simon drove on, stopping periodically for Lyle and Condo Don to dismount and retrieve a crumpled aluminum tail fin from a bomb or a tarnished brass shell casing. By the time they reached the shelter of an abandoned mine where Condo Don intended to make camp for the night, the smoldering sun was threatening to ignite a peak on the horizon.

Lyle and Simon gathered mesquite for firewood while Condo Don lit a campfire inside the entrance to the mine. Flickering flames cast strange shadows on the tunnel walls. Here and there a quartz outcropping caught the fire's reflection and glistened with a red glow.

Following a hot meal of rice and beef franks, Simon played the harmonica while Lyle and Condo Don sang along. Unfortunately, neither could carry a tune and the sound of their off-key voices reverberating down the tunnel put an untimely end to their musical endeavor.

As the night wore on, conversation turned to their past lives. Simon asked Condo Don if he had ever flown a biplane. His answer was in the negative—such antediluvian aerodynamics were before his time. Missing the point, they both innocently encouraged him to tell them about the "olden days."

Condo Don took a long drink of water from a plastic gallon jug and commenced, "When I was your age, this nation was an industrial giant. There were factories from coast to coast. Anyone willing to work could get a full-time job with health insurance and fringe benefits. People worked overtime and got paid time and a half for it. You even got paid for holidays you didn't work. There was no such thing as homeless people back then.

Everyone could afford to own their own home. Most families had two cars. Ordinary folks ate steak and roast beef for dinner. We were producing more goods than we consumed and made far more money than we spent. Marriages lasted a lifetime and families stuck together. Drugs, gangs, and crime weren't the problems they are now. Almost everyone read the Bible and went to church on Sundays."

"Gosh, what happened?" asked Lyle.

"We blew it," answered Condo Don. "We mocked our puritanical ancestors and lost our work ethic. We traded our high standard of living for drugs, sex, and cheap thrills. Parents became too self-centered to properly supervise their children. When we lost touch with God, we lost discipline and respect for authority, our social structure crumbled, and the institutions that our forefathers had so lovingly labored to build began to fall apart."

"Now we are out here trying to pick up the pieces?" ventured Simon.

"That's right," replied Condo Don. "Our nation needs to rediscover morals and ethics. We have to return to the faith that made us strong. People have to realize that their wicked ways are hurting everyone, themselves included. Change or perish; everyone must be reborn in Jesus Christ. Jesus is the Great Recycler. Only He can make it right."

The fire burned low and they all spread their bedrolls on the tunnel floor. Before lapsing into sleep, Condo Don thought about what he had said. Something had gone wrong with his own life and Jesus had recycled him. Jesus was here. There was still hope for the world.

* * *

When Simon turned the key in the ignition to start the truck the next morning, nothing happened. The only sound was the faint click of the solenoid. Lyle and Condo Don climbed out the window and pushed. Once Grapes of Wrath began to roll, Simon popped the clutch and the engine sparked to life.

It took them the rest of the day to get a full load of scrap. Since scrap steel and iron would fetch next to nothing, they took only brass, copper, and aluminum. By the time they finished, it was getting dark and they hurried back to the mine to spend the night. Simon parked Grapes of Wrath on an incline so it would be easier to push start in the morning.

Leaving the Chocolate Mountains the following day proved far easier than getting there. Since it was mostly downhill, it put little strain on the engine. Upon reaching the paved highway, they figured the worst was over. They were wrong.

Only on rare occasions does it rain in the Mojave Desert. The surrounding mountain ranges normally catch the clouds and wring them of their moisture. None but the largest thunderstorms manage to reach the Salton Sea and they can brew up in a matter of minutes.

Simon was the first to see the angry black clouds clearing the mountaintops in the distance. As they got nearer, lightning zigzagged across the heavens. Condo Don counted the intervals between flash and thunder and estimated that the storm was moving towards them rapidly. Thunderclaps burst in their ears.

It began to rain. At first there were only a few drops. Then came the deluge. Since Grapes of Wrath's windshield wipers were powered by vacuum from the engine, the only way to increase their speed was to increase RPM's. Although Simon was forced to slow to a crawl, he frequently engaged the clutch and raced the engine in order to clear the windshield. They shivered as the temperature plunged.

A half hour passed and Condo Don noticed a grayish blue mass rushing towards them. It was a solid wall of frothing water more than two feet high and was on them before Simon could pull to the side of the road. A small European car, riding the waters like a surfboard, shot past them. When the wall of water broke against Grapes of Wrath, the truck shuddered as if it had been hit head-on by a big rig. But Grapes of Wrath was quite heavy with its load of scrap and would not be budged by the raging flood. It was over in seconds. By the time Condo Don finished a prayer thanking God for their deliverance, the storm had already disappeared over the horizon moving towards Mexico and the thirsty sands had swallowed all traces of the flash flood.

* * *

As Grapes of Wrath ascended the gravel driveway leading to the junkyard, Condo Don was busy estimating the worth of their haul. He calculated that they had salvaged approximately 1,000 pounds of aluminum, another 500 pounds of copper, plus 200 pounds of brass. They should clear nearly $1,000—not bad for two days of labor! With $750 of that money they could buy another old truck and haul twice as much the next time. Within six months, as he figured it, Great Salton would achieve full employment and be well on its way towards becoming a prosperous desert community rivaling Las Vegas and Palm Springs.

Inside a rusting corrugated iron fence, the junkyard was bustling with activity. Forklifts flitted about carrying massive dumpsters full of scrap, crushing machines pressed cans into aluminum blocks, and giant electromagnets hanging from cranes separated steel and iron from non-ferrous materials.

Simon backed Grapes of Wrath up to a bevy of empty dumpsters. Then all three climbed into the truck's bed and began to sort the scrap into the waiting dumpsters. When one was filled, a forklift shuttled it to a large scale for weighing. After subtracting the weight of the dumpster, the forklift driver entered the total on a bill of lading.

When they were finished, the yard foreman handed Condo Don the bill of lading on a clipboard for his signature. Glancing at the totals, Condo Don was elated—they exceeded his estimate. He quickly scrawled his name at the bottom and returned the clipboard to the foreman.

"Source of materials?" questioned the foreman.

"Military hardware," stated Condo Don, mainly shells, bombs, and similar stuff."

The foreman wrote something across the bill of lading, tore off a copy and gave it to Condo Don. "Take this to the cashier," he said and turned to walk away.

"Wait a minute," said Condo Don, what does 'contaminated' mean?

"It means your scrap is contaminated with residue from high explosives and has to be cleaned with solvents before it can be processed. We pay only one quarter of the regular price for contaminated materials."

"Oh," Condo Don uttered dejectedly.

There was nothing he could do but to go to the cashier's cage and collect the money. It barely covered the cost of the venture when Condo Don took into consideration the price of a new battery for Grapes of Wrath. Gone were Condo Don's entrepreneurial visions. The prospect of getting rich quick had lost its allure. They push started Grapes of Wrath and drove home in silence.

* * *

Despite Condo Don's misgivings, Great Salton was flourishing. By the time Jesus walked to the jetty every morning, an enormous crowd had already formed along the shoreline. They parted just enough to let Him squeeze through. Outstretched arms struggled to touch the Savior. People shoved crippled and diseased relatives in His path, besieging Him to cure them. Anyone but Jesus would have sent them all away.

A sudden hush fell over the crowd when Jesus began to speak. His voice was soft, yet it carried to everyone gathered on the beach. Several small boats stood off the jetty within the sound of His voice. The multitudes were never disappointed. His words touched everyone and many returned day after day.

Still, Jesus was not satisfied. He often told Condo Don that it was His responsibility to take God's message to the people, rather than wait for them to come to Him. Jesus wanted to go on the road again and He especially desired to travel to the larger cities.

Condo Don was vehemently against the idea. He felt it

was not safe for Jesus to expose Himself in such a manner and worried about there being a warrant for His arrest. Great Salton was safe and secure—Condo Don could see no motive to leave.

Jesus was adamant, however, and, as often was the case, Condo Don found argument to be of little use. The community no longer required their presence to survive. To Jesus Great Salton was not the end, but a beginning. They had laid a foundation—now it was time to go forward and build.

But Condo Don still remembered how near they had come to being arrested in Los Angeles. He was concerned for the Savior's safety and wanted to go in advance, as he had done before, to prepare the way. Not wishing to get in an argument, he decided to stretch the truth and say he was going on a business trip to buy concordances, hymnals, and similar materials for the church.

Simon drove Condo Don to the bus terminal. It would take the Greyhound two days to reach its destination. Condo Don planned to use the time to study the Holy Bible, a gift from Esteban, that he always carried with him. Up until now, he had absorbed more of it by osmosis than by reading. Having almost made it through the Old Testament, he could hardly wait to start reading the New Testament so that he could finally find out what it was all about. With Jesus as his tutor, he had confidence in his ability to eventually learn what he needed to know.

PART THREE

CONDO DON, THE MESSENGER

". . . my messenger. . . shall prepare thy way. . ." Mark 1:2

"A cult is a religion with no political power."

- Thomas Wolfe, *In Our Time*

Chapter 18

As Condo Don exited the bus at the Chicago terminal, two young men in business suits with "high and tight" haircuts approached him. One stood firmly in front of him blocking his path. "Donald Thaddeus Stearns III?" he asked. "Yes," Condo Don replied. The word had no sooner left his lips than he felt the other man slip something cold around his right wrist.

"You are under arrest for violation of Section 4 of the National Eugenics Act," declared the first man, flashing what appeared to be a badge before Condo Don's face. As he finished, the second man secured the other manacle to Condo Don's left wrist and they led him away.

Two days later, Condo Don boarded a commercial flight from O'Hare Airport to Dulles International near Washington D.C. He sat in first class between two GES agents who wore sunglasses, attempting to determine the color of their eyes. Try as he might, he could see nothing but his own reflection in the mirrored lenses. Was there a chance that the glass was opaque and the agents had no eyes? They simply sat there, stiff and sullen, with nothing but their breathing to betray that they were alive.

After a short while, he turned his attention to more pleasant matters. His seat was soft, contoured to fit his body, and richly upholstered. The steward was friendly and offered him a magazine (his Holy Bible had been confiscated as evidence at the Federal Building in Chicago).

For dinner he was given his choice of entrees: Marinated Chicken Breast or Beef Stroganoff. His two traveling companions declined to eat. When the steward brought his meal, the agent on his right reached over and unlocked his handcuffs, enabling him to eat. The chicken was excellent and the boysenberry pastry dessert was an especial delight. As the smiling steward removed his empty tray, Condo Don contemplated the irony that he had seldom traveled in such luxury as a free man.

When he had to use the restroom, the agent who accompanied him insisted on also going inside. It was quite cramped and Condo Don had trouble relieving himself with someone watching. The scowling agent prodded him to "hurry up." What was the man afraid of? He could hardly escape from a lavatory with only one exit in a DC-10 cruising at 30,000 feet.

Disembarking at Dulles International, the agents ushered Condo Don into the back seat of a sedan. They drove in silence to the rear entrance of the new seven story GES Building on Pennsylvania Avenue. The GES had come a long way from its origins in a rented one-room upstairs office in the Adams-Morgan District.

* * *

Carl Utz was bored. Most of his duties as the Director of the Genetic Enforcement Service were administrative in nature: administering personnel changes, signing documents, and managing the agency's budget—not the sort of things that piqued the interest of a man who had spent thirty-two years investigating homicides. However, occasionally a case came across his desk that rekindled the spark. That was why he had decided to personally interrogate Condo Don.

Condo Don was ushered into the Director's spacious seventh floor office by two burly agents. Through a large picture window that dominated the far wall, he could see the dome of the Capitol. One of the agents shoved Condo Don into a wooden chair. Carl Utz did not bother to look up from the file he was studying at his desk.

"Donald Thaddeus Stearns III," he read, "also known as Condom Don. Do you fancy yourself an expert on prophylactics?"

"Condo is short for condominiums, not condoms," replied Condo Don. He had already made up his mind that he did not like Carl Utz.

"Strange, you don't look like an architect. You look more like the kind of pervert who arranges liaisons with young boys in public parks after dark."

Condo Don's temper boiled. He sprang forward, but the brawny arm of an agent flung him forcibly back into the chair.

"And you are violent," the Director stated in a deliberate matter-of-fact tone.

"What do you want from me?" demanded Condo Don.

"Nothing much," replied Utz with a smile. "I wanted to question you about some genetic abnormalities in one of your cult members, Mister Jesus Ortiz. However, after examining your file, making your acquaintance, and assessing your capabilities, I have decided to waive GES jurisdiction in this matter."

"Does that mean I'm free to go?" asked Condo Don somewhat incredulously.

"Not quite. The FBI wants to question you concerning your part in a conspiracy to extort money and services from the Crystal Cathedral. The State of California has also issued a warrant for your arrest for the murder of the Reverend Robert A. Schiller. I don't imagine you will be free to go anywhere for what remains of your life."

Carl Utz made a hand motion and the two agents grabbed Condo Don and hustled him from the office. They shackled his wrists and feet, causing him to frequently stumble as he negotiated the seven flights of stairs.

Reaching the bottom, he was escorted through a rear

exit and thrown into the back of a van. It was only a few blocks to the FBI Building, but to Condo Don, who sat alone in the darkness contemplating his fate, the drive seemed much longer.

The Federal Bureau of Investigation had a million and one questions for Condo Don. And every question was repeated over and over again in grueling marathon interrogation sessions. Whenever the subject of the questioning became Jesus or the "cult," Condo Don pleaded a lapse of memory.

Confronted with the affidavits of two homeless friends placing him at the park shortly before Reverend Schiller's demise, Condo Don maintained that he never crossed the street that night to the Crystal Cathedral. Nor had he seen anyone that night other than the two friends.

Not being satisfied with his responses, the agents wired him to a polygraph machine and asked him the same questions in varying order several more times. Finally, he pulled off the wires and refused to answer any more questions.

Condo Don was exhausted, but the agents had not finished with him. First, he was fingerprinted. Then, hair, blood, and urine samples were taken. Anonymous technicians in white lab attire subjected him to relentless probing, treating him as if he was a laboratory animal.

He became disoriented and lost track of time. There

were no windows in the interrogation rooms, no way of telling night from day. Once, he got a good look at an agent's watch, but was unsure as to whether it meant AM or PM. When they at long last locked him in a small cell, he slept fitfully. It seemed like less than an hour passed before they were shaking him awake for yet another interrogation session.

The agents worked in shifts. Except during the polygraph exam, there were never less than three agents in the minuscule interrogation rooms with him at any given time. All wore similar dark business suits and white shirts. All had close cropped hair. Often, one would shoot a question at him and another would answer it for him. Sometimes, they did not bother to wait for an answer before asking another question. It was all very confusing. Faces and voices began to merge. Closing his eyes, he imagined himself among the dunes being questioned by the Evil One.

They had it all on tape. Whenever he said something that his inquisitor thought differed from an earlier response, the agent would replay his original answer and ask him the question again. Condo Don began to doubt himself as well as his answers. He was uncertain as to what was real. Were the events of the past few years merely an hallucination? Amid the ongoing confusion, he struggled to retain his sanity.

Chapter 19

Several weeks later Condo Don was extradited to California. This time he traveled economy class from Washington National Airport to Ontario International. He fervently hoped that this was an indication that his value as a prisoner had diminished.

Condo Don appeared in Superior Court for arraignment trussed like an animal. The cold steel shackles on his wrists and ankles were attached by chains to his waist. As he shuffled forward to stand before the judge, he couldn't help but wonder if any person who looked like he did in his orange prison jumpsuit and chains could hope to have credibility with the court. And if the answer was yes, then why were all the lawyers present wearing expensive designer-label suits and silk ties?

Charged with murder by the District Attorney, he entered a plea of "Not Guilty." The judge, absorbed with something on his computer's monitor, appeared not to have heard. Condo Don waited politely for almost a minute and then, to gain the magistrate's attention, shouted, "NOT GUILTY, YOUR HONOR!" Whirling in his swivel chair, the judge faced Condo Don and admonished, "One more outburst and I will have you removed from this courtroom."

There was to be no bail. Since he had no money, Condo Don had not expected to be able to post bail anyway. However, he was grateful to the court for having assigned him an attorney upon learning of his indigence.

His gratitude was short lived. When Condo Don first met his attorney, Marvin Dusslemore, the next afternoon in his cell, he was struck by the man's youth and inexperience. Marvin had never heard of the Salton Sea, seemed only vaguely aware that the Mojave Desert was part of Southern California, and insisted on referring to the residents of Great Salton as "the cult." Expressing doubt as to his client's innocence, he initially suggested that it might be to Condo Don's advantage to plea bargain and claim diminished capacity. It was his fixed opinion that the police did not arrest people who weren't guilty.

Marvin was short, timid, and bookish—not the type of man who Condo Don would have chosen to defend him in a battle that could cost him his life. Yet Marvin was all he had. Instinctively, he knew that his survival depended on his ability to transform Marvin from a milksop into a gladiator. And doing that, he surmised, would be about as hard as instilling backbone into a jellyfish.

Nonetheless, Marvin Dusslemore was not entirely worthless. He promised to bring Condo Don a Bible on his next visit and arranged for the use of a phone. Condo Don thought seriously about calling Great Salton or Otis Chandler. Not wanting to involve Jesus, he phoned his family instead. It proved a waste of time. His cousin refused to accept the charges.

The Los Angeles Times' headline read "CULT

LEADER TO BE TRIED FOR MURDER." Condo Don didn't bother to read the article. He had already seen himself through his attorney's eyes and could guess its content: fugitive cult leader, an alcoholic and former drug addict, will stand trial for the gruesome decapitation of Reverend Robert A. Schiller, a well-thought-of, nationally prominent evangelist and theologian. . . The FBI had already painted their portrait of Condo Don for public consumption; a cheap, flawed copy of the Charles Manson original. He could expect no sympathy from the media.

The Reverend Schiller had died by an Act of God from the sins of pride and greed. But there was no way that Condo Don could explain that to the court without implicating Jesus. Nothing could ever persuade him to divulge what had actually happened that night. If necessary, he was determined to take the secret with him to the grave. Condo Don owed Jesus more than his life; he owed Him his soul. Whenever anyone broached the subject of Jesus or Great Salton, his memory became hazy. When pressed to answer, he dismissed the others as "mere followers," and implied that they were easily duped.

His second interview with Marvin Dusslemore proved even less productive than the first. There was, however, one consolation. If his own attorney was convinced that he was guilty and had acted alone, it stood to reason that no one would be searching for an accomplice.

Jury selection was the next topic on the court's

agenda. When Condo Don was brought into the courtroom, he noticed five persons seated at the prosecution's table. "Which one is the Prosecutor?" he asked his attorney.

"They all are," replied Marvin, "they are a team."

"Five to one," said Condo Don, "that's not fair."

"The law allows them to field a team," lectured Marvin, "and it accords you the same privilege."

"But they only assigned me you," protested Condo Don.

"It is not the State of California's fault that you are an indigent."

Condo Don was righteously indignant. This wasn't even remotely sporting. The other team was fielding five experienced, well-paid professional heavy hitters in a match against his single bush league second stringer. No referee or official of any sport would consider allowing such a lopsided contest to take place.

A slaughter of this magnitude had not been staged since the Coliseum bouts in which the early Christians were pitted against sword-wielding, heavily armored gladiators. He was convinced that he was about to be fed to the lions in the modern version of a Roman blood fest.

In truth he would prefer trial by combat. At least he would then have a fighting chance. As it was, his champion, Marvin Dusslemore, was admitting defeat prior to entering the arena.

It was obvious to him that nobody was interested in truth or justice. Society and the judicial system had already tried and convicted him of the crime of poverty, a capital offense.

Nonetheless, the selection of those who would vote "thumbs up" or "thumbs down" continued. Each prospective juror was grilled by the prosecution concerning his or her background and beliefs. Any juror who admitted to ever having problems with drugs or alcohol was dismissed. So were those who were agnostics or who were not from mainstream denominations. One lady was not impaneled because she was a social worker. Condo Don could only watch in horror as the prosecution systematically disqualified every juror who stood even a remote chance of sympathizing with his plight.

In contrast Marvin Dusslemore seemed to like everyone in the prospective pool of jurors. He asked an occasional question, but he never rejected anyone.

The jury, as it came to be impaneled, consisted of two men and ten women with four women serving as alternates. Condo Don was puzzled by the jury's final composition and asked Marvin why he had failed to challenge the appointment of so many women.

"That would be sexual discrimination," replied Marvin tartly, "and sexual discrimination of any kind is prohibited by the 19th Amendment and various civil rights acts."

"Which of the amendments prohibit economic discrimination?" queried Condo Don.

"None of them," Marvin retorted. "That would be silly."

Following jury selection, Condo Don was escorted back to his cell to await trial. The days passed slowly as he paced up and down the narrow confines of his cell. His sole solace came from reading the Bible.

Esteban and Simon came to visit him. Since Condo Don suspected that there was still a warrant extant for the Savior's arrest, he made them promise that they would never visit him again or bring Jesus.

"Jesus knows no fear," said Simon, "how can we discourage Him from coming?"

"Tell Him you spoke to me and heard me renounce Him," replied Condo Don as he fought to hold back the tears that were welling in his eyes. "It is the only way."

In its opening statement the prosecution accused Condo Don of almost every conceivable sin. They labeled him an alcoholic, a drug addict, a pedophile, an extortionist, an impostor, a con man, a derelict, a blasphemer, and a cold blooded killer. According to his detractors, he was so vile that his own family had abandoned him.

As the prosecution droned on and on, Condo Don scrutinized the jurors' faces. They hardened whenever they glanced his way. Not a kind smile or a warm look in the entire bunch. They seemed to be swallowing all the bad things that were being said about him.

Two hours later, it was Marvin's turn to deliver an opening statement to the jury. In his soft, whining voice Marvin depicted Condo Don as a victim of circumstances, an aimless drifter who was unfortunate enough to be in the wrong place at the wrong time. If Condo Don was waiting to hear Marvin call the prosecution liars or say something good on his behalf, he waited in vain. The only thing that Condo Don liked about Marvin's opening statement was its brevity.

Condo Don wondered if he had made a mistake in allowing Marvin to act as his attorney. Maybe he would be better off dismissing Marvin and representing himself. It was tempting. But Condo Don knew next to nothing about the law. Undoubtedly, the prosecution would make short work of him. Some help, however ineffective, was better than none at all.

The prosecution called its first witness, a homicide

detective who described Reverend Schiller's death in graphic detail. Blood stained shards of glass were entered as exhibits. There were gory color enlarged photographs of the Reverend Schiller's decapitated body that made the jurors gasp. Describing the murder scene, he attributed the shattered glass to "sympathetic vibration" produced by a sabotaged carillon.

"Objection!," interrupted Marvin. "The witness's expertise in electronics has not been established. It is far more likely that the instrument merely malfunctioned."

"Objection sustained," concurred the judge.

But the prosecutor was not deterred. He immediately entered as evidence a report relating tests performed by the carillons manufacturer which attested to the reliability of its solid state digital technology.

Concluding its questioning of the detective, the Team of Five turned its witness over to the defense for cross-examination. Marvin remained seated at the table as he squeaked, "No questions for the witness at this time, your Honor.

It was 5 PM. Court was adjourned until the following day.

When the court reconvened at 9 AM the next morning, Prosecutor #1 summoned Colonel Thomas Lang, United States Air Force, Retired, to the stand. The Colonel was a balding, thin man in his late seventies who, despite his advanced age, still carried himself with military bearing. He looked vaguely familiar to Condo Don, but, try as he might, he could not recollect where he had seen him before.

"Do you know the defendant, Donald Stearns?" queried Prosecutor #2.

"He was a cadet in a Physics class I taught at the Air Force Academy 34 years ago," replied Colonel Lang.

"Please point him out for the benefit of the court," continued Prosecutor #2.

"That's him, sitting there," said the Colonel, pointing toward Condo Don.

"Did your course in Physics include the study of Acoustics?"

"We spent several weeks on the subject."

"And was one of the course requirements a lab experiment that involved shattering a pane of glass by means of sound waves—a phenomenon commonly referred to as resonance or sympathetic vibration."

"Yes, it was."

"Was Mr. Stearns a good student?"

"Tolerable, as I recall."

Condo Don had hated Physics. He had found the plethora of formulas and the advanced mathematics it entailed to be mind boggling. Despite the assistance of a tutor, he had barely managed a passing grade in the class. He jumped to his feet and shouted, "Objection!"

"Counsel for the defense will instruct his client to make no further outbursts," admonished the judge as Marvin struggled to pull Condo Don back into his seat. "Does the defense wish to voice an objection?"

"No, your Honor," declared Marvin as he and Condo Don exchanged burning glances.

During the melee, Prosecutor #2 had quietly taken his seat. Prosecutor #3 now resumed the questioning of Colonel Lang:

"To the best of your knowledge, did the Academy's curriculum at that time include courses in Electronics that emphasized hands on practical experience in wiring?"

"Most definitely."

"Your witness," concluded Prosecutor #3 as he turned towards the defense.

"No questions at this time," murmured Marvin.

Prosecutor #4 proceeded to call a number of witnesses, all of whom testified that they had been among the congregation in the Crystal Cathedral on the Sunday it had been destroyed by an earthquake. Each in turn identified Condo Don as one of the intruders who had attempted to extort money, food, and shelter from the late Reverend Schiller. Following the fourth witness' testimony, Marvin stipulated that Condo Don had indeed been present at that time.

Next up for the prosecution was Arnold "Stony" Williams. At one time Stony and Condo Don had been drinking buddies, having shared numerous bottles of muscatel together over the years. Now, Stony appeared aged and haggard as he took the stand. Eyes fixed on the floor, he never once glanced at Condo Don as he hesitantly answered the questions put to him by Prosecutor #2. He spoke in such hushed tones that the court stenographer found it necessary to prompt him repeatedly to "speak up." Condo Don felt sorry for Stony. The withered individual who sat shaking and cringing in the witness' seat was not the Stony he remembered from earlier years.

Stony claimed to have seen Condo Don in the park across from the Crystal Cathedral on the night of Reverend Schiller's demise. Although Condo Don had no memory of having seen Stony that night, he urged Marvin not to cross-examine him. Condo Don was afraid that Stony might recall having seen Jesus. Besides, he thought, Stony had already suffered enough. But Condo

Don need not have worried, for Marvin had no intentions of prolonging the trial by cross examining witnesses.

Throughout the trial, Prosecutor #5 had exhibited an annoying trait of intermittently scratching his right ear. Whenever the trial had become too technical or boring for Condo Don to follow, he had amused himself by attempting to predict when the prosecutor would next go for his ear.

As Prosecutor #5 rose to call the next witness, he again put his hand to his ear. On an impulse Condo Don decided to render him some assistance. Taking careful aim with a rubber band, he stretched it taut and then released it.

Like David confronting the Philistines, Condo Don struck his target. Whirling, the legal Goliath turned to confront his tormentor. For an instant Prosecutor #5 just stood there, bewildered, staring at Condo Don in total disbelief that anyone would do such a thing in a solemn court of law. Then, recovering his acumen, he threw himself upon the floor, clutching his ear. Writhing and thrashing, he screamed and howled in exaggerated agony.

The bailiff yanked Condo Don from his seat and hurled him face first to the floor. Trailing blood from a broken nose, Condo Don was dragged from the courtroom.

Condo Don spent the remainder of the trial listening to

the proceedings via intercom while sequestered in an anteroom adjoining the court. Although his nose hurt and he had problems breathing, he was not sorry for having disturbed the hearing. In his opinion the trial was a travesty of justice. Denying them his presence had been his sole means of protest.

He did not have to wait for long. Marvin Dusslemore rested his defense without calling a single witness. It took the jury less than two hours to reach a verdict.

Chained, shackled, and flanked by two brawny bailiffs, Condo Don hobbled back into the courtroom to await the jury's verdict. Standing in front of the bench, Condo Don watched as the jurors returned to their seats. Their grim, sober appearance foreshadowed his fate.

His gaze was fixed on the mahogany paneled wall before him. Mounted near the ceiling was a large brass disk, approximately three feet in diameter, bearing the legend "Great Seal of the State of California." Condo Don counted and recounted the stars that stood out in bas-relief along its perimeter, assuring himself that they totaled thirty-one. He wondered if he ever again would be permitted to lie in a bedroll beneath God's twinkling nighttime pageantry and count the stars.

The bailiff called the court to order and a hush descended, broken only by the sound of the air conditioner as it attempted to circulate air in the densely packed courtroom.

"Has the jury reached a verdict?" asked the judge.

Slowly rising to his feet, the foreman answered, "We have, your Honor. We find the defendant, Donald Thaddeus Stearns III, guilty of murder in the first degree."

Applause erupted from the spectators. Pounding his gavel, the judge shouted for order. When the din subsided, he thanked each juror individually for his or her diligence and remanded Condo Don to the custody of the Department of Corrections.

As he emerged through the courtroom's double doors, Condo Don met with an angry crowd. Several people held placards aloft that read "**BURN IN HELL**." An elderly woman spat in his face. Several reporters thrust microphones in front of him but, before he could comment, his guards thrust him beyond their reach. The corridor seemed to stretch forever as he ran the unyielding gauntlet of bystanders' recrimination.

Three days later, Condo Don was returned to the courtroom for sentencing. Since California law permits capital punishment only under "special circumstances," i.e. use of a gun in the commission of a felony, he was instead sentenced to life in prison without the possibility of parole. He was not relieved. Having spent the majority of his life on the road as his own master, Condo Don had no desire to squander the years that remained in captivity. He would have preferred a quick death to a slow one.

In examining his case, the Department of Corrections focused on Condo Don's association with a "cult." The official who reviewed the file exercised his personal prejudices, equating cult membership with membership in a gang, and he concluded that Condo Don would make a poor candidate for rehabilitation. Accordingly, he recommended that the prisoner be incarcerated with hardened career criminals in the Security Housing Unit (SHU) at Pelican Bay State Prison. For Condo Don it was to prove a fateful error.

Chapter 20

Pelican Bay State Prison is situated amidst old growth redwood forests near Fort Dick on California's extreme northern shoreline, barely thirty miles from the Oregon border. The few locals who don't work for the Department of Corrections call it a pristine paradise; the rest refer to it as living hell. To get to Pelican Bay, Condo Don would have to travel more than a thousand miles.

Since his first class flight to Washington D.C., the quality of Condo Don's transportation at the expense of the taxpayers had been steadily declining. It was about to hit an all time low.

Along with other prisoners, he was herded aboard an already crowded Department of Corrections bus for the inter-prison run up the California coast. At one time in the distant past the ancient bus had delivered children to a suburban school. After becoming scarred and weather beaten, the school district had sold it to the Department of Corrections, who had repainted it white. But the white paint had peeled, exposing in places the yellow-orange paint beneath. The faded black naugahyde vinyl seats were patched with gray duct tape and the handles on the emergency exits had been removed. One guard served as the driver and another sat in the rear.

Talking was prohibited. This was probably for the best

since Condo Don had little in common with the rapists, muggers, and drug pushers who were his traveling companions. Forty minutes into the journey, one of the prisoners told the guard he urgently needed to relieve himself. The guard advised him to either "hang it out the window or tie a string around it." And just in case the prisoners had failed to get his point, he proceeded to describe in similarly salient language how little he, the Department of Corrections, and the State of California cared about their needs. There would be no unscheduled stops.

The bus paused briefly at the California Men's Colony (see map) near San Luis Obispo and the Avenal State Prison to drop off paperwork. No one got on or off. At the Coalinga facility they changed drivers and were allowed to use the restroom facilities. On the way back to the bus, they had to walk past a courtyard where some resident inmates were lifting weights. The weights clanked to the ground and the inmates began to hoot and whistle. Shouts of "new meat" and similar taunts were interspersed with blown kisses and obscene gestures. Although Condo Don had seen many sickening, disgusting sights in his years on the streets, there were none that compared with this. Putting men in cages caused them to revert to animals. This was life at its lowest. But he refused to let his mind dwell on it and instead silently recited a passage from the 23rd Psalm, ". . . I shall fear no evil."

As the bus labored its way up US 101, it passed some

of North America's most spectacular scenery. Surf pounded against towering cliffs and gnarled pines clung to precipitous slopes. Squirrels, deer, and jackrabbits frolicked within sight of the highway. But it was all a waste, since the filthy windows were covered with thick wire mesh that obscured the view.

By the time they reached San Quentin, it was dark and the bus was half empty. Condo Don attempted to stretch out on the seat, but the guard made him sit upright.

Sometime during the night Condo Don dozed off. When he awoke, it was daylight and only a handful of prisoners remained on the bus. In the distance loomed the guard towers and slate gray concrete walls of Pelican Bay State Prison. Narrow vertical slit windows were arranged in pairs on the buildings like the eyes of the Evil One. Numerous strands of barbed wire reminded him of cattle enclosures he had seen in his travels.

Condo Don's new home was nothing like he had imagined. The grim faced, shotgun toting guards of Hollywood's prison movies had been replaced by state-of-the-art electronic technology. Buried beneath the grounds were sensitive devices that triggered an alarm at the touch of a human foot. Motion sensors and closed circuit television cameras monitored movement along the corridors. Cell doors were opened by remote control.

During the trial, Condo Don had been confined in a

noisy, crowded county holding facility that stank of sweat and urine. By comparison his new cell was the Taj Mahal. It was much larger (he estimated it to be 8 by 10 feet), freshly painted, and he did not have to share it with other inmates. Clean almost to the point of being sterile, the faint odor of pine oil cleanser lingered in the air. The stainless steel toilet shined almost as bright as the metal mirror. At first Condo Don hesitated to touch anything for fear of sullying it.

And there were amenities. A television set was mounted on one wall. Condo Don looked for the "on-off" button, but couldn't find it. Next, he searched the entire cell for a remote control. As he was about to give up, the screen suddenly flickered and came to life. He sat on the edge of his bunk and watched as a portly well groomed man introduced himself as the Assistant Warden, explained the regulations, and welcomed him to Pelican Bay State Prison. As soon as the Assistant Warden finished what he had to say, the television went dead.

Although rather bland, the food was plentiful. Three times a day a slot in the wall opened and a meal appeared. Since his cell was windowless and Condo Don had no watch, he reckoned the time of day by the arrival of his meals.

His happiness with his new surroundings was short-lived. Life in the Security Housing Unit settled into a boring routine. He had no job and there were no activities. Once a day he was taken to a small yard without weights or other equipment where he could exercise alone for ninety minutes. Three times a week he left his cell to shower. Rarely did he see other inmates. Face-to-face contact with guards was minimal. The silence closed around him until he could hear his own breathing. Suffering from sensory deprivation, he longed for meaningful contact with another human being.

He asked for a Bible. The guard answered that he could visit the law library once a week. Condo Don explained that he was not interested in the law and merely desired a Bible. A bit confused, the guard managed to stammer, "I'll see what I can do." Two weeks later, after asking three more guards, he was finally brought a Bible. It was the same one that he had received as a parting gift from Esteban. He had not seen it since it had been confiscated in Chicago.

One morning Condo Don noticed a small brown spider in a corner near the ceiling. Never before had a bug managed to penetrate the sterile environment. One of the spider's eight legs was a mere stub. Over the next few weeks, the leg regenerated. And as the leg grew, so too did its web. First, it attached lines to the wall to form an outer perimeter. Next, working outward from the central hub, it connected a series of radials to the outer perimeter. Finally, the nimble arachnid covered the entire net with a spiral of webbing. By the time its leg was whole, so was the web. Was the synchronization of the two events coincidental? The gossamer structure was a masterpiece of engineering. Condo Don marveled that a mere spider could build such a complex lattice. It made his own skills seem trivial. He was humbled by the experience.

Since there weren't any insects in his cell, he wondered what the spider would eat. He crawled on his hands and knees during an exercise period looking for an insect until a guard ordered him to stand. The spider completely ignored a grain of rice that he put in its web. Finally, in desperation, Condo Don carefully wrapped the spider in toilet paper and released him in the exercise yard. Watching the minuscule arachnid scurry away, he felt as if a dear friend were departing.

Several months later a guard escorted him to the infirmary for "inoculations." He was made to undress and lay upon a cold, bare stainless steel gurney. Soon, a dour-faced bearded man in a white lab coat entered and, without introducing himself, began to poke and probe Condo Don's flesh. Following a quarter hour of this, he wearied of being treated like a specimen and decided to break the silence.

"What kind of shot are you going to give me?" inquired Condo Don.

"I'm not here to shoot you," replied the Beard.

"Then what are you doing?"

"Nobody told you?"

The Beard explained that he was conducting biological research under a grant from the GES. The FBI laboratory had notified GES that Condo Don's tissue samples had demonstrated regeneration at an accelerated rate thought to be impossible in humans. The Beard wanted to perform some experiments on Condo Don and was prepared to make a deal. If Condo Don would sign a waiver authorizing experimentation, the GES would arrange for him to be transferred to the California Men's Colony at San Luis Obispo where there was an opening for a Chaplain's Assistant. In return for his willing cooperation, a reduction in sentence might also be arranged.

Condo Don mulled the offer for a long time. The memory of a vivisection he had seen performed on a monkey in a PBS television documentary dominated his thoughts. He also worried that the GES might eventually trace the source of the phenomenon to his contact with Jesus. Reluctantly, he declined.

"No problem," said the smiling Beard. "My offer will remain in effect indefinitely. Should conditions change, you may wish to reconsider. Sooner or later, I'm certain that you will decide to cooperate."

Upon returning to his cell, Condo Don found it to be unusually warm. Over the next few hours the temperature continued to rise until he was perspiring heavily. He complained to a guard that it was too hot in his cell, but the guard only shrugged and said it was a maintenance problem.

Taking a do-it-yourself approach, Condo Don traced the difficulty to a duct through which hot air was blowing into his cell. Removing his shirt, he stuffed it into the grate. In less than a minute, the guard reappeared and angrily demanded that he put back on his shirt.

Condo Don was starting to suspect that his activities within his cell were being monitored. He searched for a hidden camera or a microphone. Despite a minute examination of every square inch of the walls, floor, and ceiling, he found nothing. If there was such a device, it was sophisticated enough to escape detection.

Although it was uncomfortably warm, Condo Don had endured far greater heat at Great Salton. He took a stoic view of the matter and decided that such a minor inconvenience was not worth a major confrontation with his jailors.

A week passed and the heating system continued to malfunction. He awoke each morning drenched in sweat, his mattress sopping wet. Within minutes of returning from the shower, he felt sticky again.

It was difficult for him to suffer in silence, knowing that he did not commit the crime nor deserve the punishment. Whenever the anger and frustration became too much to bear, he opened his Bible to 1 Peter 3:17 and read, "For it is better, if the will of God be so, that ye suffer for well doing, than for evil doing."

A guard came to escort him to see a visitor. As he left the hot confines of his cell and followed the guard through the long, cool corridors, Condo Don speculated as to who his visitor might be. Could Esteban, Simon, or Jesus have ignored his warnings? After passing though several checkpoints, they came to a large, steel door. Opening it, the guard pushed Condo Don inside and closed the door behind him.

Sitting at a rectangular table against the far wall of the narrow room was Condo Don's "visitor." The Beard, dressed in a business suit, greeted Condo Don and motioned for him to take a seat at the table. As Condo Don warily sat, the beard placed a cold can of Pepsi-Cola on the table in front of him.

"You look hot," observed the Beard.

Condo Don did not answer. Instead, he stared into the Beard's pale, watery eyes.

Diverting his eyes from Condo Don's gaze, the Beard continued, "My offer still stands. I really can make life better for you. In a place like this you could use a friend like me."

Condo Don continued to stare at the Beard in silence.

Several drops of perspiration formed on the Beard's forehead. Taking a handkerchief from his breast pocket, he wiped his brow. He coughed several times while waiting for Condo Don to reply.

Condo Don continued to sit in silence.

"You would be helping humanity," the Beard reasoned. "I am convinced that the secret to everlasting life lies in accelerated tissue regeneration. Out of thousands of samples I've examined, yours alone displayed the desired characteristics. Together we can achieve immortality. We can become gods!"

Condo Don lifted the ring on the can of Pepsi. Putting the can to his lips, he drained its contents.

"Thanks for the drink," Condo Don said as he stood and walked to the door. He knocked once on the door, it opened, and the guard took him back to his cell.

After being in the cool corridors, the cell seemed an inferno. He went to the sink, intending to run some cold water on his head, but when he turned on the tap, nary a drop emerged.

Catching the attention of a nearby guard, he asked why had the water to his cell been shut off?

"It must be a maintenance problem," replied the guard,

"I'll put in a work order."

The water remained off for several days. When he complained about the stench emanating from the toilet, a guard brought him a bucket of water with which to flush it. He had no sooner finished flushing the toilet than the water came back on. Had it been shut off for maintenance or as punishment?

He soaked a towel in the sink and draped it over the grate. Adding moisture to the air seemed to cool it a bit. At least it provided a brief respite from the suffocating heat.

Three days later, the heating problem ended as mysteriously as it had begun. No repairman came. No announcement was made. One minute a blazing sirocco was blowing out the duct and the next it was circulating cool, fresh air.

He had scant time to rejoice. Suddenly, the lights went out and Condo Don's windowless cell was plunged into darkness. A guard explained that it was a "maintenance problem" that would be fixed "as soon as possible."

"As soon as possible" stretched into several weeks. Unable to read his Bible, he sat on his bunk and replayed in his mind's eye his journeys with Jesus.

The darkness was disorienting. He sometimes fell

asleep in the middle of the day. Only the regular arrival of his meals through the slot in the wall heralded the passage of time and prevented him from slipping into nirvana.

The exercise periods stopped. Nobody came anymore to take him to the showers. He compensated by doing pushups on the floor and taking spritz baths in the sink.

He could not see what he was eating. The food, always bland at best, now tasted like cardboard and he lost his appetite. Listlessness and depression followed. Motivating himself to do anything became a chore.

Then the lights came back on, making him squint in the sudden brightness. Before his eyes could fully adjust, the cell door opened and a guard took him to the exercise yard. It was very cold and raining, but Condo Don was grateful to be outdoors. Running in circles, he caught raindrops with his tongue. When he could run no more, he fell to his knees and gave a prayer of thanks to God. For the first time in weeks he felt alive and a part of creation. The rain thickened into a deluge. He hardly noticed and remained on his knees praying until it was time to return to his cell.

* * *

There were still the weekly visits with the Beard. Condo Don came to pity the man. Like many men with large egos, the Beard was obsessed with his personal achievements. Condo Don suspected that the Beard was a godless man who had no honor. Once he obtained what he wanted, he would forget any promises he had made. For men such as the Beard, the ends always justified the means.

Nevertheless, Condo Don worried about the Beard's soul. But whenever he mentioned religion, the Beard denied the existence of God and claimed that science, and science alone, had the power to save mankind. Condo Don rejoined that Divine intervention, not science, was responsible for the miraculous healing powers that the Beard referred to as "highly accelerated tissue regeneration."

Scoffing at Condo Don's naiveté, the Beard launched into a lecture concerning evolution and man's preeminence. Man, through science, had come to dominate the universe. Now, with Condo Don's assistance, the Beard intended to make man immortal. Only a fool would refuse. Condo Don's unwillingness to cooperate constituted criminal behavior and justified harsh solitary confinement within the Security Housing Unit. As Condo Don sowed, so would he reap.

Chapter 21

When his cell door opened one afternoon, Condo Don got a pleasant surprise. The guard who was there to escort him to the exercise yard was none other than the ponytailed youth who had played the concertina long ago at MacArthur Park—now in uniform and sans ponytail. They both stood dumbfounded for an instant, staring at each other, until the guard put a finger to his lips to indicate that the hallway was possibly under remote surveillance. Condo Don nodded and accompanied him to the exercise yard in silence.

The uninitiated who have never heard the hollow, forlorn clank of a prison gate as it shuts out the joyful world of free men are apt to believe that there could be no more extreme opposites than a guard and his prisoner. But prison walls do not discriminate and have a way of wreaking their devilish effect on both parties. For if the truth be known, both guard and prisoner are incarcerated—one by the criminal justice system and the other (though to a lesser degree) by economic circumstances. Few, if any, become jailors in fulfillment of boyhood ambition; most are motivated by a paycheck to endure the harsh circumstances of prison life. It is a pseudo-macho, brutal life, devoid of the softening influences of the fairer sex, a life that stifles kindness, generosity, and all the best parts of human nature. And in their place, it substitutes man's most primitive instincts:

anger and lust. All that survives is base and perverse—art is the tattoo of a naked lady on a burly arm; literature is graffiti scrawled on a cellblock wall; and camaraderie is a shared needle. Indeed, all who enter such a vile place are lost and the inmates more often than not receive their paroles before the guards receive their pensions.

Is it any wonder, therefore, that Condo Don and the guard he had known under more pleasant circumstances on the outside soon discovered themselves to be soul mates and spent the entire hour allotted for exercise talking about their shared experiences with Jesus? And does it surprise anyone that the guard returned to Condo Don's cell at the end of his shift bearing gifts of chocolate and writing paper?

It was then that the guard begged Condo Don to baptize him. Condo Don refused, saying that he was not worthy. Condo Don claimed to be neither a saint nor a prophet. Although he knew Jesus, he had served Him merely as a messenger and an advisor on secular matters and feared that he had poorly performed his duties. He suggested that the guard journey to Great Salton where he could be baptized by Jesus in the Holy Spirit.

It had taken Condo Don more than a year to make his first friend at Pelican Bay State Prison. He had never known such intense loneliness. Before he fell asleep, he thanked God for having sent him someone in whom he could confide.

Condo Don's troubles were not over. In the middle of the night the television blurted to life with a self-help show featuring a round table discussion with several prominent psychologists. He could neither change the channel nor lower the volume. Resisting a nagging urge to break the tube, he sat upright on his bunk for an hour until the credits appeared and the screen went blank. His thoughts turned to a book, *1984*, that he had read for an English assignment in high school. It was now several decades past 1984 and even a futurist like George Orwell could never have imagined the sophisticated tortures that Big Brother would ultimately develop.

As he drifted into slumber, the spider that had so recently shared his cell crept into his dreams. Its gossamer webbing was so transparent as to make it appear to be hovering in mid-air. Levitation was indeed the answer; and as his sleep deepened, Condo Don's soul floated over the prison walls to join Jesus at Great Salton. Escape was sweet, albeit only ephemeral.

Chapter 22

The Beard was becoming adamant. During his visits, no longer cloaked with the guise of friendship, he made increasing use of "hard sell" tactics by which he attempted to intimidate, cajole, and threaten Condo Don into consenting to experimentation. Whenever Condo Don became offended and tried to leave, the Beard would curtly advise him to remain seated until dismissed.

According to the Beard, Condo Don lacked a sense of social responsibility. He was using religion as subterfuge for his criminal lack of concern for his fellow man. The Beard hinted darkly that if he did not change his mind soon, a way would be found to conduct the experimentation without his consent.

Confinement was taking its toll on Condo Don. He could feel his self control slipping away. During a routine cell search, he spoke harshly to a guard and was shackled to the toilet. Several hours later, upon seeing his lunch arrive through the slot, he yelled for someone to unshackle him, but nobody came. In frustration he beat his right manacle against the stainless steel toilet, making a tremendous racket.

Inmates in other cells began to bang on their toilets as well. Soon, the entire cell block was reverberating with the clash of metal upon metal.

The cell door opened. A guard holding a Taser gun stood in the doorway. Suddenly, a barb trailing two thin wires hurtled through the air. Penetrating his shirt, the barb lodged in the upper portion of Condo Don's left bicep, pumping its voltage into his nervous system and causing him to convulse violently before losing consciousness.

When he regained his senses, Condo Don was still shackled to the toilet, lying in a pool of his own vomit. Blood oozed from beneath the manacle that had torn his right wrist as he had writhed from the electrical shock. Anger consumed him and once again he beat the manacle against the toilet.

This time four guards entered his cell. Three restrained him while the fourth guard unlocked his shackles. They pulled him to his feet and hurled him against a wall. While two of them held his hands behind his back, the other two took turns punching him in the gut until he stopped resisting and slumped forward.

One of the guards then left the cell and returned shortly with a length of cord which he used to bind Condo Don's hands behind his back. Next, he laid the cord twice around the neck, then passed it across the shoulders and tied the ends to the hands at the height of the hips in such a manner that any attempt to lower the arms would cause the cord to tighten around the neck. Strangulation would result from the slightest downward motion. Condo Don was trussed tighter than a rodeo calf.

But his righteous indignation would not subside. As soon as the guards departed, he shuffled over to the television. Sliding his hands as far as humanly possible up his back, he bent forward and, smashing his forehead against the tube, shattered the screen into fragments. Ignoring the blood streaming from his head, he calmly sat on the floor in a lotus position, careful to keep his hands above his hips. Leaning backwards, his fingers grasped a shard of glass which he utilized to saw through the cord.

When the guards returned, he was ready for them. As the cell door opened, Condo Don leaped into the corridor, bowling over a guard. His momentum carried him forward into a second guard whom he tackled at the legs.

Howls of encouragement issued from the other cells along the corridor. Inmates beat on toilets and sinks until a klaxon sounded its alarm.

A stream of guards came rushing towards Condo Don. Realizing the hopelessness of his position, Condo Don retreated into his cell and attempted to slide the door shut. It would not budge.

Condo Don caught the first guard to come across the cell's threshold and threw him against the metal sink. While they struggled, another guard came from behind with a raised wooden baton. Condo Don shifted slightly and the blow, which had been aimed at his head, descended on his left shoulder with a loud crack, breaking both baton and shoulder. Reaching around with his right hand, Condo Don wrested the sharply splintered stub of the baton from the startled guard's grasp and stabbed another guard with it.

Although Condo Don fought like a cornered animal, it was to little avail. A solid mass of guards pummeled him to the concrete floor. He rolled into a protective fetal position as clubs struck him from every direction. Screaming in agony, he tried to raise himself from the floor, but his injured left arm would not bear his weight. A truncheon was slipped underneath his chin and the guard who was holding it pulled with both hands until Condo Don choked and lost consciousness.

When Condo Don came out of it, he was in a different cell. His entire body ached and there was throbbing pain coming from the socket of his left shoulder. Although his forehead was wrapped in a gauze bandage, blood still trickled from the wound. He stumbled to the sink, intending to rinse his face, but when he turned on the spigot, nary a drop emerged.

Condo Don sat down on the thin mattress. He was angry with himself. Although he was in intense physical pain, what hurt most was that he had once again allowed himself to be provoked into losing his temper. Tears flowed freely as he begged God for forgiveness.

Unlike God, the prison administrators at Pelican Bay State Prison were not in the business of granting forgiveness to repentant sinners. Rehabilitation, a concept spearheaded by reformers in the first half of the twentieth century, had lost credence with both penal authorities and the public. The high rate of recidivism—55 percent for parolees of California's maximum security institutions—and a swelling prison population had led to a reevaluation of penal philosophy. Pelican Bay State Prison offered prisoners no jobs, no activities, few self-help programs, and nothing to stimulate the mind. The prison system was designed for one purpose and one purpose only—to warehouse inmates at the cheapest possible cost to the taxpayers.

Prisoners who cooperated with the system and exhibited no violent behavior were usually not molested by the guards. But Condo Don had demonstrated a lack of cooperation by rebuffing the Beard's offer. Much worse, he had injured several correctional officers. He was now viewed as a "hard case" and was subjected to the full range of "correctional" measures that the prison staff had at its disposal.

At random intervals Condo Don was moved to different cells. He was neither given prior warning nor allowed to take any personal belongings with him. Sometimes he went months without a Bible.

Showers became a privilege. He often went a week or more without one. Occasionally, a guard would order him to get out of the shower before he could rinse off.

Meal delivery no longer followed a regular schedule. Sometimes he received his breakfast at dinnertime. This was especially disconcerting since Condo Don had always relied upon the arrival of his meals to calculate the passage of time.

At any moment of the day or night the television was liable to flicker into life. The closed circuit transmissions consisted primarily of announcements and propaganda. Often the volume was so loud that Condo Don could still hear it clearly with his head buried beneath a pillow.

Visits to the tiny exercise yard became increasingly rare. When he was allowed to use the yard, it was almost always at night or during inclement weather.

He no longer received haircuts and was not permitted to shave. Since he had no comb, he attempted to remove the tangles from his hair with his fingers. His gray hair grew long and his beard became matted, causing his jailors to jokingly refer to him as "The Prophet."

All too often, Condo Don's cell resembled a furnace, but he learned to ignore the extreme heat and did not remove his shirt regardless of how hot it got.

Condo Don also learned to suffer verbal abuse in silence. He no longer bickered with the Beard or the guards. Although all might be chaos around him, he retained an inner peace and felt he was finally becoming the man that God wanted him to be.

Although the State could imprison his body, they could not bind Condo Don's mind. Rejecting the stark reality of his surroundings and the demeaning circumstances of his undeserved incarceration, his thoughts turned inward. He analyzed the numerous mistakes he had made in life and vowed to make amends.

In his dreams Condo Don relived pleasanter times and talks with Jesus.

A year later, primarily due to unanticipated budgetary constraints, correctional supervision decided to remove Condo Don from the Security Housing Unit and allowed him to mix with the general prison population. He immediately began to proselytize, exhorting his fellow inmates to renounce violence and seek redemption through Jesus. At first, they laughed at him. Many thought that the long years of solitary confinement had affected his mind.

One day in the exercise yard, a muscular inmate known for his short temper declared that he was tired of listening to Condo Don's preaching and attempted to silence him with a blow to the head. Instinctively, Condo Don ducked and knocked the man down with a single, well-placed punch. Shocked by his own behavior, Condo Don knelt in the dirt beside his unconscious opponent and begged forgiveness.

Gradually, Condo Don made headway with his ministry. He taught that God was well aware of the imperfect nature of Man and asked only that he acknowledge his sins and strive to do better. If Jesus could save a hardened, confirmed sinner like himself, he reasoned, then there was hope for everyone.

It was sincerity rather than prowess with words that won Condo Don converts. Since he had obviously learned life's lessons the hard way, many saw in him an older, wiser version of themselves. Although not all inmates agreed with him, the majority eventually came to respect him. The enormous strength of his convictions rendered him fearless and he never hesitated to speak his mind.

By traditional standards, he still could not qualify as a candidate for sainthood. However, his occasional use of course language, irascible nature, and rough manner only served to endear him to fellow convicts. Having one of their own genuinely concerned about their welfare and the fate of their immortal souls was a novelty that required a degree of adjustment. Here was a Christian who accepted men for what they were and passed no judgment; here was a Christian who had withstood the ultimate test of faith; here, in the very midst of living hell, was Good that was not afraid to do battle with Evil—here was someone in whom they could confide; someone they could trust; someone who actually cared. Condo Don might not be an authentic bottled-in-bond saint, but they were in no position to be choosy and they would just have to make do with him until someone better came along.

Chapter 23

Igor Kurchatov, the scientist-enigma known to Condo Don as "the Beard" due to his most prominent and conspicuous physical feature, was a native Georgian—not the American Georgia of the Piedmont and the Okefenokee Swamp, but the former Soviet republic of the Caucasus and the Black Sea. The Kartvelians, as Georgians call themselves, are a vigorous people among whom lifespans of 100 years or greater are not uncommon. In fact, Igor was only mildly aware of human mortality until a 43 year old Biology professor, his mentor as a young undergraduate at the Medvedev Institute in Leningrad, suddenly collapsed and died in the midst of a laboratory presentation. The incident had a profound impact on young Igor, causing him to ponder the factors governing longevity and fueling an interest (later to become an obsession) in genetics.

But science, like everything else under Communist rule, was subject to state control. Igor found his graduate studies restricted by the policies of Soviet agronomist Trofim Lysenko who, with the endorsement of first Stalin and later Kruschev, denounced genetics as bourgeois and contrary to the principles of dialectical materialism and the interests of state managed agriculture. Research in classic Mendelian genetics (the study of heredity in both plants and animals) had become a political crime punishable by death.

An international conference in Helsinki provided Igor a gateway to freedom. He simply walked into the Canadian Embassy and told the official at the front desk that he desired to defect to the West. Following several days of intense interrogation, he was granted political asylum and whisked aboard a commercial airliner bound for Montreal. Less than a year later, he won acceptance to the graduate program in genetics at Princeton. Several months after earning a doctorate degree he swore an oath of allegiance and became an American citizen. Naturalization, he reasoned, had removed the last political obstacle from his scientific path. At last he was free to pursue knowledge for its own sake; to investigate the mystery of life; to search for the elusive Fountain of Youth. He was a modern Ponce de León eager to claim uncharted territory in the name of Holy Science, a conquistador determined to slay any heathen who might dare to interfere with his quest.

In 1961, American biologists Paul Moorhead and Leonard Hayflick had discovered that human fibroblasts, or connective tissue cells, could duplicate themselves a maximum of 50 times before dying. Cells from older donors perished after significantly fewer than 50 times, indicating that people are born with a preset number of times that their cells can replace themselves. Once this number is reached the body wears out and dies. They subsequently found that when they removed the nucleus of a young cell and put it in an old cell and vice versa, the old cell would live longer than the young one.

Obviously, the mechanism that determined an individual's lifespan—his "biological clock"—was located somewhere within the nuclei of his cells.

Could the aging process be delayed by resetting the biological clock? Igor had a hunch that the answer was yes. By 1992, research had identified talomere decay as a precursor in the aging process. Situated on the ends of the chromosomes that are found within the nucleus of each of the trillions of cells that compose the human body, talomeres are composed of long chains of repeating DNA sequences. Talomeres are protective of chromosomes in much the same way as a hard plastic tip prevents a shoelace from unraveling. Every time a cell divides, its talomeres shorten until eventually the shielding effect deteriorates to the point that the chromosomes become worn and cell death occurs. If Igor could find a way to restore an elderly individual's talomeres to their original condition, he was certain that he could make man immortal.

Somewhere deep within the darkest recesses of Igor's soul lurked the conviction that Holy Science, a creation of mortal man, would someday reward its creators by transforming them into immortal gods. It was the closest that poor Igor's mind, tutored as it had been by the atheist Soviet state, could approach the concept of religion.

Because the rate of aging varies throughout the population, Igor theorized that some people's talomeres must wear down slower than others. It might even be possible that the process could reverse itself under certain conditions. If he could gain access to enough tissue samples taken at various times in people's lives, he could make comparisons and perhaps discover the secret of eternal youth.

The largest single depository of human tissue cultures in the world is housed in a refrigerated sub-basement laboratory of the GES headquarters in Washington, D.C. The GES is also the federal agency with the most experience in DNA analysis. It's hardly surprising that Igor applied to the GES for a grant or that they approved his research.

For months Igor laboriously analyzed tissue samples and pored over reams of statistical data. The work was tedious and the results were discouraging. In nature, it appeared, talomeres only decayed; he hadn't found a single instance of regeneration. Had he taken a wrong turn somewhere and come to a dead end?

If Sir Isaac Newton hadn't fallen asleep beneath an apple tree, gravity might never have bonked him on the head. Likewise, if Igor Kurchatov hadn't run out of paper towels in the men's room while working alone late one night, he might never have been able to validate his theories concerning cell regeneration. Cursing the janitor who had forgotten to replenish the paper towel dispenser as he exited the restroom, he scooped up a pile of papers on the nearest desk and used them to wipe his hands.

As he was about to toss them in a waste basket, he noticed an FBI request for analysis and evaluation of various inconsistencies found in tissue samples taken from a prisoner, Donald Thaddeus Stearns III, incarcerated at Pelican Bay. As Igor's eyes eagerly scanned the computer printout accompanying the request, he reached for a telephone and frantically dialed Dulles International Airport to arrange booking on a redeye flight to San Francisco.

Whenever a laboratory technician performs a routine test on a specimen and gets results that are not within established parameters, standard operating procedure dictates that he check his methods and equipment. Should everything prove to be in order, he would next suspect contamination and obtain a new sample. And if the results still aroused suspicion, he would seek independent confirmation of his findings. Thus, the FBI Laboratory had refused to accept its own results—which, according to their computer printout, indicated an almost total lack of glycosylation of DNA (glycosylation is damage that increases with age and would be expected to be quite advanced in a man of Condo Don's age)—resulting in an interagency request to GES for evaluation and possible retesting. By chance, or perhaps by fate, the computer printout had wound up in the hands of Igor Kurchatov—the one individual most likely to comprehend its implications and be inclined to exploit them. If the printout was to be believed—and Igor placed as much faith in computers and science as other men place in God, then Condo Don's biological clock had either come to a halt or was running in reverse. It was Igor Kurchatov's bounden duty as a socially responsible scientist to discover the how and why of it.

* * *

Igor had witnessed countless experiments performed on unwilling zeks (political prisoners) in the Soviet Union. He had come to regard them as human guinea pigs and was quite dismayed to learn that American prisoners had civil rights. After Condo Don refused to sign an authorization document, Igor, with the assistance of correctional administrators, cunningly devised a plan to convince him to cooperate.

But Condo Don proved to be an exceptionally stubborn zek. Neither psychological torture nor the enticement of parole were able to persuade him to yield. Having exhausted both the carrot and the stick, Igor tried appealing to Condo Don's social conscience. When nothing seemed to work, Igor lost patience and began to regard Condo Don as Evil incarnate—a demon opposed to Holy Science.

Although delayed, Igor was determined not to be deterred. Under the pretext of preventative medicine, he took frequent tissue samples. DNA analysis led him to conclude that Condo Don wasn't growing any older; whether this strange phenomenon was of temporary or permanent duration remained to be seen. Nor could he effectively run experiments to ascertain the cause of the phenomenon on the minuscule skin scrapings he was permitted to obtain. He longed to surgically remove a sizable chunk of the prisoner's flesh. It was frustrating to sit across the table from Condo Don, yet to be unable to remove some tender morsel that would satisfy his ravenous hunger. Occasionally, he entertained the thought of arranging an accident by which the prisoner might lose some part of his body, preferably an arm or a leg. However, there were too many "if's" involved. What if the limb became mangled? What if the shock was too much for the prisoner's heart? And, worst of all, what if Igot got caught in the act?

There had to be another route which could ultimately reveal what had induced the changes in the prisoner's DNA and had bestowed upon that unworthy creature a seemingly unlimited potential for cell regeneration. Perhaps the zek himself unwittingly held the key! Igor devoted more and more of his time to interrogation. Had Condo Don ever been exposed to radiation? Did he have a history of drug abuse? Were his father and mother still alive? How old were his grandparents at the time of their death? Had he experienced any unusual allergic reactions? Was he ever exposed to toxic chemicals or biological agents? Could he remember having felt a sensation of rejuvenation surging throughout his being?

The idiot zek either gave guarded answers or refused to respond. No topic other than religion seemed to interest him. And Igor knew that there was nothing to be gained by discussing the infinite with a man who was not his intellectual equal. Yet Condo Don could not be dissuaded from speaking on the subject. It was all a waste of time; man occupied the top rung on the evolutionary ladder and beyond that was not heaven, but only the vacuum of space. Igor was unsure as to the nature of the mechanism that had either reversed or retarded the glycosylation of Condo Don's DNA. Only one thing was certain: it wasn't the handiwork of an imaginary Supreme Being.

Igor treated Condo Don like he would a chimpanzee or any other laboratory animal. The few instances of cooperation were rewarded. However, the stubbornness and rebellion which the zek more often exhibited triggered prompt psychological punishment. Igor arranged to have the guards reset the thermostat that controlled the temperature in Condo Don's cell, cut off water and electricity, and do similar things to aggravate the zek. And as the months amassed into years, Igor's creativity at devising new tortures grew in proportion to his impatience.

Condo Don was not Igor's only test subject. Nor was this his sole research project. The zek was consuming an inordinate amount of time. Although strongly tempted to turn Condo Don over to one of his eager young graduate research assistants, Igor could not bring himself to admit defeat. Besides, of all of his many research activities, this one was the most promising, albeit frustrating. Discovering the means by which biological clocks could be slowed would be an achievement worthy of the Nobel Prize.

But time had run out for Igor Kurchatov. Delay had cost him the game of chess he had been playing. That which he thought could at worst end in stalemate had surprisingly become checkmate or, perhaps more appropriately, *zekmate*. The latest tissue samples taken from Condo Don showed an increased rate of glycosylation. The metamorphosis in the prisoner's DNA was, although of long duration, alas was not of a permanent nature; perhaps it had been simply a freak occurrence. Whatever had caused the alteration in DNA structure had ceased for some unknown reason to exercise its effect. Nothing short of an autopsy could now reveal the secret of eternal youth and even that might prove fruitless. The stubborn zek was worthless!

Igor was too angry to walk away without a parting shot. Sportsmanlike conduct was, to his way of thinking, a decadent Western custom unworthy of assimilation. Yes, he would exact revenge. The zek had impeded his mission, had blasphemed Holy Science, and refused to repent. There was no doubt in his mind that Condo Don deserved eternal damnation.

Igor had heard of a hellhole named Corcoran where bone-dry, cellblocks without air conditioning often reach 120 degrees and higher, a place where tempers swelter, riots are frequent and violence is a daily occurrence. There, fights between inmates, often with racial or gang overtones, are routinely orchestrated for the benefit and amusement of the staff. Before departing for

Pennsylvania and Princeton, Igor Kurchatov surreptitiously arranged to have the impudent zek transferred to Corcoran State Prison with fervent hopes that Condo Don's life sentence would prove to be of short duration due to an untimely demise.

Chapter 24

Late September 2010

No drug had ever given Condo Don the exhilaration he had felt when he was with Jesus. It was a lasting high that didn't leave needle marks or cloud his consciousness like the chemical exuberance that had previously fueled his life. Containing a magical ingredient, hope, that was missing from both bottle and syringe, it had rejuvenated his being and given him a purpose in life.

That purpose was not his, but God's. He found strength in obeying God's will; strength that enabled him to survive and flourish in a hellhole where evil feeds on the weak and the meek. For if ever there was a Den of Iniquity, it is a prison. What motivates society to concentrate all of its worst elements—rapists, muggers, serial killers and perpetrators of heinous crimes that defy the imagination—within an infernal crucible and label it a correctional facility? Correction necessitates change—substituting something right for whatever is wrong—and it is difficult to imagine a place with worse role models on which to base positive change than a prison. Indeed, it is the most vile and vicious predators who soar in the putrid atmosphere of fear and violence that pervades most penal institutions. They are the ones with the outside connections; the ones that steal and intimidate; the ones that provide protection in exchange for unnatural sexual favors. One is the lowest possible common denominator in a penal setting: one either victimizes others or is himself victimized.

Condo Don was not surprised when one afternoon shortly after the midday meal the Assistant Warden came to his cell and told him he was being transferred to Corcoran State Prison. It was thoughtful of him to say that Corcoran had superior medical facilities for the care of older inmates, but Condo Don knew without saying that the real reason for the transfer was that he had stepped on too many toes at Pelican Bay. The Beard wasn't the only person he had angered. Two weeks before, Condo Don had forced an inmate drug dealer to strip in the exercise yard and empty in the dirt several plastic baggies of cocaine that were taped to his torso. Only yesterday he had kicked a trustee in the groin whom he had come upon sodomizing a young inmate. Word had gone out via the prison grapevine that Condo Don was a marked man.

Actually, Condo Don welcomed the change. Corcoran would be a fresh challenge for accomplishing the Lord's work. From what he had heard about it, it needed his presence even more than Pelican Bay did. And it was closer to Salton Sea—closer to Jesus. Perhaps the Beard would not follow him and he could receive visitors without involving them in an investigation. He fervently prayed that night that he would be allowed to see Jesus one final time.

Before sunrise the next morning he boarded the interprison bus. It was the same decrepit transport that had borne him to Pelican Bay so many years before. A feeble attempt had been made to mask the rust and peeled paint with spot painting. The dabs of fresh paint stood bright against a faded background. Condo Don remarked to himself that the bus resembled an aging trollop who had hurriedly applied a touch of rouge prior to answering a knock on the door. The old girl would have done far better to have simply splashed some water on her filthy face.

If inner beauty redeems a weathered exterior, then this bus was definitely not headed for Redemption. A viscous wad of freshly expectorated gum attached itself to the sole of Condo Don's left shoe as he gained the topmost step of the stairwell. Likewise, the accumulated stench of decades of blood, sweat, and tears that might have satiated Winston Churchill in his finest hour greeted Condo Don's nostrils. The ribbed black vinyl strip that ran the length of the aisle had worn down to the bare metal in numerous places. Above his head some long gone passenger had etched into the enamel of the arched steel ceiling a grotesque rendering of the lower portion of the female anatomy with an undue emphasis given to the pubic region.

Pausing to remove the sticky mess from the sole of his shoe was a mistake. As he stood precariously perched flamingo-like on one leg, a shove from the driver sent him reeling down the aisle. Hurtling headlong, he grabbed at the back of a seat to regain his balance and inadvertently ripped its leatherette covering. Storming up from the rear of the bus, the guard struck him across the back of the neck with an open-handed blow. Having no desire to further provoke the guard, Condo Don slumped into the seat and cast his eyes submissively downward. After a minute or so of berating him for his clumsiness, the guard exhausted his anger and returned to his post at the rear of the bus. Although seething on the inside, Condo Don maintained a calm demeanor. Years behind bars had taught him the folly of reacting rashly when being disciplined by those in authority.

He was sitting next to an emergency exit. The handle was missing but he still tried his weight against it. It wouldn't budge. Surmising that it had been welded shut from the outside, he next tried each corner in turn to test for give. Just as he thought he felt it move a fraction of an inch, the guard at the rear, who unbeknownst to him had stood up for a better view, caught sight of what he was doing and ordered the last prisoner boarding the bus to sit between Condo Don and the exit.

If Condo Don had not had his mind on more pressing matters, he might have thought it odd that a penal system that prided itself on high tech gadgetry such as motion sensors and closed circuit television hadn't bothered to upgrade transportation on the inter-prison route. There simply was no incentive to buy new buses. Although the

California legislature had many years before passed strict safety regulations governing maintenance of school buses and public transportation, it had specifically exempted farm labor and correctional buses. School children and John Q. Citizen have political clout, farm laborers and inmates don't.

Although Condo Don didn't know his seat mate well, he recognized him as a pedophile whom everyone called Chatty Cathy. Child molesters were the pariahs of prison life—most got the silent treatment or worse from both guards and inmates. Condo Don correctly guessed that the man was being transferred for his own safety.

Chatty Cathy lived up to his name. From the time the driver let out the clutch and the ancient bus lurched forward in first gear to the time it pulled into the gates of the Lassen County facility some six hours later, he never once closed his mouth. Since talking was prohibited, Chatty Cathy looked straight ahead and talked in a low whisper out the side of his mouth. At first Condo Don was sympathetic. But the man had a garbage mouth and a brain to match. And although Condo Don was no prude (his own language was a bit too salty for refined tastes), he resented the man's quick familiarity and gross sexual imagery. When he tried to steer the conversation to anything other than sex, Chatty Cathy pretended not to notice and continued to drone. Changing seats was not permitted, so Condo Don was a captive audience. Mile after mile it went on and on. When they made their second stop at Folsom the following morning, Condo Don had neither had a chance to sleep nor to read the Bible he clutched in his right hand.

For the next two hours Condo Don didn't say a word. In fact, he didn't even look in Cathy's direction so as not to encourage him. But nothing seemed to work. Finally, in desperation he leaned towards Cathy and said, slowly and distinctly, "Shut up."

"You feeling sick, man, what got into you?"

"I can't sleep and listen to you at the same time."

"Well, why didn't you just say so then? No reason to be so all fired touchy. I mean we bein' from the same sty and havin' wallowed in the same filth and all, you and me is good bro's and not like those godforsaken buddy mucker bimbos that's got no respect. I tell you, you and me, we are a pair—like friggin' Batman and Robin—we get off together and that's just what we're goin' to freakin' do as soon as we blow this joint! You know what I mean? I mean we're a team an' there ain't nuthin' . . ."

"Shut up," Condo Don interrupted.

"Sure, I'll shut up. You ain't gotta tell me twice. I know when to keep quiet. Why, I remember a time at frigid Folsom: Folsom!, now there's a pisser for you, not some diddly squat puddle of muck like the Bay. Home boys fight tough at the Big F. They shove it in hard and ream it till you feel it ."

Condo Don had heard enough. The rage that had been brewing inside of him for hours was now thundering so loud that he no longer heard what Cathy was saying. His attention focused on Cathy's potty mouth and he clenched his Bible tighter as he watched the vile lips, moist with venom, form words that had no sound.

Suddenly, without having willed it, his right hand flashed forth and the Bible smote Cathy's left cheek.

It was but a tap—scarcely strong enough to leave a welt. But it burned as if set afire. Writhing in agony, Cathy emitted a curdling wail that quickly summoned the guard.

Grabbing Condo Don by his gray hair, the guard pulled him off the seat and kicked him repeatedly in the abdomen. In vain, he attempted to roll away. Cursing, the guard reached down and got a choke hold on him, lifting him high in the air before dropping him, gasping for breath, back into his seat. All the while, Cathy continued to scream in a piercing falsetto that enraged the guard and would have resulted in more blows had not the brakes been suddenly applied, causing the guard to lurch forward and direct his wrath towards the driver.

When at long last the bus resumed its journey, silence reigned. Exhausted, Condo Don slumped in the seat, leaning his chin on his chest, and fell into a fitful slumber. When he awoke, his kidneys were throbbing from the beating he had taken and Chatty Cathy was mumbling something about "ungrateful bastard." It was dark and the bus, half-empty when he dozed off, was now nearly full.

Where were they? How long had he been asleep? They must have made a stop somewhere because there was now a sack lunch on his lap. Opening it, he found a cold burrito, some carrot sticks and a pint carton of milk. Despite feeling queasy, he managed to choke it all down. Soon afterwards, the low pitched hum of the engine, laboring as they ascended a steep grade, lulled him into a blissful dream.

* * *

Condo Don was running towards Jesus in the middle of a desert. Hot sand sucked at his feet. Someone was chasing him, but he wasn't afraid. Prophets were tumbling from a rip in a hazy blue sky; he recognized Moses and Elijah. But they weren't the stern men he had imagined them to be: they were laughing and motioning to him to quicken his pace. He was so close now that he could see the sunlight glistening on the little beads of perspiration that were forming on Jesus' ebony brow. It was blazing hot, but angels were descending to cool Him with their wings. A television reporter was running alongside, thrusting a microphone in his face and cursing.

Popcorn balls were flying everywhere . . .

One hit Condo Don in the back of the neck and

startled him awake. But it wasn't a popcorn ball, it was a piece of paper crumpled into a ball. Examining it a bit closer, he saw that it was a page from a book. No, not just a book, but a Bible. As he spread it smooth on his lap, his vision focused on the phrase "let us go three days journey into the desert." Why, it was a page from Exodus!

Unbeknownst to Condo Don, Chatty Cathy had taken revenge on him by ripping pages from his Bible while he was sleeping. Noticing that the guard at the rear was also nodding, Cathy had attempted to dispose of the torn pages by wadding them up and tossing them into the aisle. But Cathy's hand shackles spoiled an otherwise excellent aim and one of the balls sideswiped a particularly mean looking fellow's handlebar mustache as it flew past. But instead of cursing, as Cathy expected, the prisoner had stooped down, picked up the ball, and playfully batted it back. Soon, the desecrated scriptures were flying everywhere and Cathy had become the center of attention. For the first time in years, Cathy had won acceptance and was having a great time.

But Cathy's fun was destined to be short-lived. As soon as he realized what was happening, Condo Don hastily liberated the Holy Word of God from Cathy's contaminative grasp. Rage, like surf surging in a sudden squall, swept through his nervous system and flooded his reasoning. Raising his hands as if to strike a blow, he barely managed to gain control of his temper and avert violent action.

Cathy, who had been cringing with fear, misinterpreted his hesitation as a sign of weakness. Glancing at the other prisoners as if seeking their support, Cathy managed to muster enough courage to confront Condo Don. "Don't wimp out; go ahead and hit me," the pathetic creature squeaked, "take your best shot. You don't scare me, you or your butch God. Friggin' take your god awful stupefyin' holier-than-thou religion and **shove it**!"

Not being one to ignore excellent advice, Condo Don instantly obeyed. The defiled Bible, shorn of a quarter of its content, shoved nicely between Cathy's blasphemous lips. In fact, it made such an excellent fit that Condo Don was loath to stop shoving. He shoved so hard that, if Cathy had swallowed, new meaning would have been given to accepting the Word of God.

Pandemonium ensued. Some prisoners applauded; some smashed windows with their manacles; two ripped a seat, bolts and all, from the floor and heaved it at the driver. Howling inmates overpowered the groggy guard before he could get to his feet.

The interprison bus weaved into oncoming traffic as the guard/driver struggled to fend off rioting convicts. As luck would have it, there weren't many cars on the highway at that hour and they narrowly missed an ambulance that darted by with siren wailing and headlights flashing. The out-of-control bus had slowed to less than 35 miles per hour when the left front tire strayed off the shoulder and hit a patch of sand.

Whereas a car in a similar situation would most likely have skidded to a halt, massive inertia, combined with a high center of gravity, caused the bus to roll. As it righted itself following the second roll, the emergency door flew open, hurling Chatty Cathy and Condo Don into a shallow roadside gully.

If Condo Don had been aware that his actions would someday appear in print, or if he had cultivated a taste for dramatics, or if he had finished his college education, or if his body hadn't been covered with abrasions, he might have jumped up, lifted his eyes towards heaven, and shouted, in the immortal words of the late Doctor Martin Luther King, Jr., "Free at last, free at last, my God I'm free at last!" Unfortunately, however, he failed to rise to the occasion and lay there, face down in the gravel, for several moments until he was certain that no bones had been broken.

Rising to his knees, Condo Don surveyed the scene. Fifty feet away, the bus lay on its side, wheels continuing to spin. Prisoners were running every which way, with nobody in charge and nobody knowing where he was going. Other than the two lane asphalt roadway, all was scrub, mesquite and ocotillo. The sun was at its zenith—approximately midday—and beat down mercilessly despite the lateness of the season. Chatty Cathy lay next to him, insensate, making strange gurgling sounds. He pried the remnants of his Bible from Cathy's teeth, reached into the foul mouth and pulled out the tongue that had been obstructing the airway. But it did no good.

In desperation, he rolled the unconscious body onto its back, lifted the chin, pinched the nose closed, and, smothering an intense feeling of revulsion, placed his lips against those of the now silent blasphemer and gave two full breaths.

Cathy coughed thrice and, rising slowly on one elbow, puked on himself. But Condo Don hardly noticed. His attention was riveted on a Deputy Sheriff who was stepping from a black and white at the side of the road. The deputy, like the ambulance they had passed earlier, had been hurrying towards the scene of a jackknifed tractor-trailer when his attention was drawn to the overturned bus. Yelling "halt!," at some fleeing prisoners, he leveled his shotgun in the general direction of Condo Don and Cathy and let loose two rounds in lightning fast succession. Although the closest pellet missed them by more than five feet, Condo Don and Cathy quickly fled in opposite directions, their separate paths destined to never converge again either in this life or the next. Since they had been lying motionless when the deputy first fired, surrender had not seemed to be a viable option. By the time the report of the shots had ceased reverberating from nearby hills, Condo Don had slid down a steep ravine and succeeded in removing himself, at least temporarily, from the officer's line of fire.

Looking up, Condo Don could see many of the other fugitives heading for high ground. That was stupid; it was exactly where any searchers would expect them to go and they would soon be flushed by helicopters and dogs.

Besides, rock climbing was hard work even without manacles. Better time could be made traveling downhill and that was exactly what he intended to do.

A large sandy riverbed bearing a trickle of water ran parallel to the highway. After following it for a half hour, Condo Don began to recognize his surroundings. If this was the Mojave River, then the railroad tracks he spotted in the distance must be those of the Union Pacific. Fifteen or so miles down the tracks would be the junction town of Barstow.

Several freeways crossed near Barstow. Condo Don figured he could hide in the dense landscaping at the interchange until they quit searching for him. Knocking off a couple of sprinkler heads would give him a source of water and he could borrow a hacksaw blade from the maintenance truck that would eventually be dispatched to make the necessary repairs. Once he got rid of the handcuffs and the prison garb, he would be relatively safe. Perhaps then he could transverse the 150 miles between Barstow and Great Salton without being caught. By making a wide detour to the east, he thought, he might add an extra 100 miles to his journey, but he would avoid populated areas.

There was one big problem, however. Great Salton would never harbor a fugitive from justice. He ought to know—he had helped to formulate the rules and had even been charged with enforcing them. No matter, he simply wanted to see Jesus one last time. After that, he reasoned, he would turn himself in to the authorities and suffer the consequences.

PART FOUR

THE REVELATION—OUR WORLD REBORN

"...it came through the revelation of Jesus Christ." Galatians 1:12

"I am he that liveth, and was dead; and, behold, I am alive for evermore...and have the keys of hell and of death." Revelation 1:18

Chapter 25

When Esteban and Simon returned to Great Salton after visiting Condo Don in jail and told Jesus that Condo Don had renounced Him, He read in their faces that they were lying. Disappointed, He turned towards Esteban and asked, "How many grains of sand are there in the Mojave Desert?"

Esteban looked puzzled and, after giving the matter some thought, answered, "I have no idea."

"Do you suppose I know?"

"Even when we were children, I was always amazed at how much you knew—I can't remember anything you have ever not known!"

"Then rest assured that I know what has passed between you and Condo Don."

Although Esteban had always been close to Jesus, theirs was not a normal sibling relationship. Despite the proximity of their ages, Jesus had always been more of a father figure than an older brother. Moreover, there was a degree of pragmatism involved; having been the beneficiary since childhood of Jesus' excellent judgment,

Esteban had come to rely upon it. Helping Jesus with the day to day management of Great Salton was a natural extension of having assisted in the care of his younger brothers. Assuming Condo Don's responsibilities was no easy task, but he was anxious to please and felt honored to be chosen.

Esteban was less inclined to take the weight of the world upon his shoulders than Condo Don had been. He preferred to delegate authority and decisions concerning everyday affairs were often reached by consensus. Dissatisfaction, formerly suppressed by strict regimen and uncompromising discipline, now became increasingly apparent.

Some groused about harsh conditions. Communal life was short on material rewards and the work was exhaustive. All too often individuals felt their personal needs were being ignored. Although no one ever went hungry, commonplace amenities such as deodorant, razor blades and mouthwash were frequently in short supply. To deny one's self, take up the cross, and follow Jesus required commitment and superhuman effort. If occasionally someone stumbled and complained, they were to be forgiven, for, indeed, forgiveness is the very essence of Christianity.

At the dawn of the Third Millennium, the environment posed the paramount threat to the continued survival of the pious pioneers of Great Salton. The Salton Sea was an ecological disaster. Its two major tributaries, the

Alamo and the New rivers, flowed north from Mexico, receiving runoff containing selenium and other harmful toxins from irrigated farmlands along the way. With a long-standing reputation as North America's most polluted waterway, the New River trickled through Mexicali, Mexico, a city of almost a million people that dumped in industrial and slaughterhouse wastes, raw sewage, and leachate from landfills, plus a heaping visible helping of trash, phosphate detergents and dead cats. Contaminants tended to settle in the silt at the bottom of the Salton Sea where the pile worms lived. The pile worms were eaten by fish which in turn were eaten by grebes and other fish-eating birds, resulting in semi-annual die-offs of millions of fish and thousands of birds. Sometimes the stench from rotting flesh was so strong that everyone was forced to breathe through bandannas like bank robbers in a Hollywood B grade Western movie.

Having no outlet, the Salton Sea was unable to dispose of the four million tons of salt that were deposited into it annually by the Alamo and New rivers. It began life in 1905 as the largest freshwater lake in California, with rainbow trout originally tumbled into it by the rampaging Colorado River. By the close of the Twentieth Century due to neglect, it was 25 percent saltier than the Pacific Ocean and appeared destined to become a dead sea.

The body of water had long been rejected by purist environmental activist organizations as a man-made abomination (but no more so than Lake Mead and Lake Havasu) and it is perhaps ironic that those most concerned with the sea's welfare were those doing God's work. With no hope of compensation other than that of the spirit, they collected the rotting carcasses that washed up on the shore and buried them beneath the desert sand. Although the Salton Sea was increasingly becoming an unappealing wasteland, the contention by some that it was God forsaken was belied by the presence of Jesus. Biblical scholars assert that Divine Intervention usually occurs at the times and places where mankind has made such a mess of things that no other form of extrication is possible. It was not by accident or by chance that Our Lord, after many years of wandering throughout the Holy Lands of Southern California, came to found His modern church on the western shore of the Salton Sea.

One morning, while Jesus stood on the jetty addressing the multitude on the shore, an out-of-control dirt bike thundered through a portion of the crowd, scaring many, but fortunately injuring no one. After the dust settled, Jesus spoke words of reassurance and was about to resume His sermon when the wind shifted, causing a large, amalgamated mass (not unlike a floating island) of putrefying birds, fish and phytoplankton to drift towards shore. The stench was unbearable and many people, overcome with nausea, began to leave. Others complained vociferously about the foul smell. A few became unruly and had to be dispersed. One freckle faced young lady went so far as to taunt Jesus, shrieking "where is God when we need Him?"

Jesus was deeply affected by the incident. That evening, as He paced the froth-covered sand of the beach behind the communal rotunda, He thought of little else. The waters that brought life to an otherwise barren desert were dying; it was only fitting that those who dwelt beside them would seek God's assistance in their time of need.

Their prayers were about to be answered.

On that moonless night, His way lit only by the stars of the infinite universe, Jesus strode in a southerly direction, following the shoreline, for several hours until He came to a deserted cove. There, on the moist sand beside the gently rippling waters, He knelt and wept. As the salt of His tears joined the salt of the sea, the heavens could not help but weep also. Soon, a steady rain was falling.

Rising, Jesus cupped the palm of his right hand to capture a drink. Heaven's nectar refreshed Him as no other could. His body welcomed its coolness as it soaked through His garments and drenched His pores.

The unexpected rain continued unabated as Jesus resumed His journey. Dawn failed to disperse the clouds and the sun remained in hiding throughout the day. All was dismal and bleak as far as the eye could see. As Jesus grieved, so too did the desert.

Towards late afternoon, the downpour ended as rapidly as it had begun. Jesus trudged onward, His clothes soon drying upon His body. Moments before darkness fell, He caught sight of the mud geysers at the southwestern tip of the great sea.

In those days, the mud geysers were not the hot springs spa and geothermal energy production station that they are today. In fact, they were known as boiling mud pots and were largely shunned due to the unpleasant, odoriferous presence of small quantities of hydrogen sulfide gas. They stood as reminders of volcanic activity that had helped to create the vast, below sea level depression (of which both the Salton Sea and the Imperial Valley are part) that geologists term the Salton Trough.

At a point near the outermost mud pot Jesus got down on His knees in the rough sand and prayed to Our Father in Heaven, beseeching Him to take pity on the sea and to forgive mankind for having poisoned its life-giving waters.

And God, responding to His only begotten Son, caused the Earth to move. Miles beneath the Salton Trough, the viscous, superheated, molten matter of the earth's mantle exerted pressure upon a fault in the crust, causing the entire Trough to shake. But Jesus, giving His full and complete attention to His communication with the Creator, paid the temblor no heed. Nor did he notice the increased activity in the mud pots where the boiling had intensified to such a degree that mud was now spouting hundreds of feet into the air.

Far to the northeast, beyond the mouth of the Alamo River, magma pressed against the sea bottom, thrusting it upwards until it formed a narrow mesa that split the sea into two unequal parts, almost as if a dike had been constructed across its southern end. Simultaneously, much, much farther to the north in an uninhabited region of the Northern Mojave, the Amboy Crater, an ancient inactive volcano, began to issue white smoke and ash as a portent of an impending metaphysical eruption that would be of—literally—biblical proportions.

As Jesus prayed throughout the night, mighty changes were set in motion that would change Great Salton and eventually the world for the better. When Jesus arose at daybreak, it was to the Dawn of a New Age.

Chapter 26

Jesus did not walk back to Great Salton. Nor did he go by truck nor by any other form of earthly transportation. How he got there is unfathomable to us and remains one of the great mysteries of the infinite universe.

What we do know is when He got there. He arrived as the first light of dawn tinged the horizon—the exact same instant that He arose from prayer at the mud geysers. Seventy-seven people, who were gathered in the communal-rotunda-dining-hall to organize a relief effort for victims of the moderate earthquake that had struck the night before, witnessed His arrival. All have signed statements testifying to His miraculous appearance. I have personally interviewed 37 of those present and each and every one of them corroborates the others' account. They state unanimously that He did not enter through any door or window, but suddenly appeared in their midst.

"Why do you assemble here before breakfast?" Jesus asked.

Seventy-seven panicky voices attempted to answer, all speaking at once. Eventually they hushed and allowed Simon to explain that they had been awoken by a deep rumbling noise the previous night, had experienced some unnerving shaking, and had since heard reports of hills rising from the sea and intense surf conditions at other points along the shoreline. One girl, a recent immigrant from Peru, had run helter skelter through the compound shouting in Spanish that the end of the world was upon them.

"Go about your duties," Jesus ordered, "there is no need for you to be here. No one anywhere has received so much as a scratch and there has been no structural damage. You should be happy, for God has erected a barrier to the herbicides and pollutants that have been threatening the sea. Gradually, the saline content will be reduced—fish and birds will multiply. You and your children for many generations will prosper, living in a land of plenty. Praise God, for it was He who led us here and parted the waters."

Before dismissing them, Jesus led a prayer of thanksgiving from Psalm 145:10-13:

All living things shall thank you, Lord, and your people
 will bless you.
They will talk together about the glory of your kingdom
 And mention examples of your power.
They will tell about your miracles
 And about the majesty and glory of your reign.
For your kingdom never ends.
 You rule generation after generation.

After going about their normal work for the day, as

Jesus had directed them to do, they feasted that night on roast duck to celebrate their deliverance from the quake, the rejuvenation of the sea and Jesus' miraculous appearance at what has come to be called the Assemblage of the Seventy-seven. Thus, the Feast of the Appearance was born, which Christians now commemorate with a working holiday on March 15.

And all the things that Jesus promised came to pass. In the course of the next few years the entire Salton Sea experienced an incredible recovery. Selenium decreased significantly and the saline level dropped to less than that of the Pacific Ocean.

The warm waters were soon teeming with bass and corbina that attracted migratory waterfowl and sportsmen. Marinas opened, hotels were built and Great Salton continued to expand until, today, it virtually rivals Palm Springs as a desert resort community.

Although no one disputes that the sea's contaminants have become trapped behind the narrow mesa that stretches across its southern end, opinions differ as to the mechanism that brought it about. Some scientists theorize that diatomaceous caverns within the mesa act as a screen to remove chemicals from water as it slowly percolates through the barrier. Others say that the process is facilitated by slight temperature variances between the bodies of water on either side of the partitioning mesa. Regardless of how it happened, it is quite clear that the sea has been saved. At the time of this writing a treaty is being negotiated between the United States and Mexico to construct a tertiary water treatment plant on the New River at Mexicali and dig a sea level canal through the Laguna Salada in Baja California to connect the Salton Sea with the Gulf of California.

As has been earlier recounted, the Assemblage of 77 credit the sea's transformation to a miracle performed in the flesh by Our Savior, Jesus Christ, who had been reborn into this world as the fulfillment of biblical prophecy. They claim that Great Salton is the New Jerusalem shown to John in Revelations 21:1,2 and that He has made " . . . all things new (Revelations 21:5)" and restored the . . . Water of Life (Revelations 22:1)."

Indeed, they convinced many of the truth. Wise men from around the world came to talk with Jesus and sit at His feet. He welcomed them, one and all, without regard to religious affiliation.

But there were also powerful men who scoffed at reports of the Messiah's return and sought to pervert the truth. By means of media manipulation, they cunningly conspired to portray Our Savior as a fraud . . .

Chapter 27

TV Guide magazine for the week beginning Saturday, September 25, 2010, describes SCOOP as a "one hour, primetime news magazine devoted to in-depth coverage of topical issues and intriguing personalities. To Emil Velasco, investigative reporter and a frequent contributor to its individual segments, the show was a cash cow that he had milked for four sports cars, three divorce settlements, several drug rehabs at the Betty Ford Clinic, casino debts, psychoanalysis, and a posh Manhattan penthouse.

SCOOP was neither the first nor the best of its genre. It was, however, a survivor, having managed to endure twenty-three seasons. The producers and sponsors had reason to believe that the old girl was headed for the slaughterhouse, but reckoned they could ride her for one final season if they could boost the ratings during sweeps week with a bold, provocative expose. Emil was the right man for the job. Off camera, he frequently quipped to friends and acquaintances that SCOOP was a cleverly devised acronym for Sensationalism Can Ordinarily Outgun Professionalism.

There were reports of a crazy cult leader somewhere out in the California desert who was claiming to be Jesus Christ and had managed to dupe a few prominent personalities, one of whom was Otis Chandler, into assisting Him to promote His scam. The producers wanted Emil to fly to Los Angeles, put together a crew and interview everyone involved. The piece they had aired the previous season on the Virgin Mary's image being reflected from a window on the 16th Floor of the World Trade Center had been a hit. Besides, miracles were "in" this year, along with shorter hemlines and cockroach races. This Jesus impostor had somehow managed to convince a lot of otherwise intelligent people that He could heal the sick and raise the dead. Exposing how He did it might give SCOOP the boost it desperately needed.

Emil argued against the idea. He said that stories about cults that didn't involve brainwashing and sexual perversion tended to bore viewers and were of transitory value. What he was thinking (but didn't dare say) was that the desert would be hot as hell this time of year and the last time he had done a piece attacking a cult he had received numerous death threats.

But the producers were adamant and Emil soon found himself stepping off an airliner at Los Angeles Airport's Tom Bradley International Terminal in the midst of a rare summer downpour with no raincoat. On top of that, his flight had been delayed on the tarmac at JFK for several hours while a loose rivet on an aileron was being replaced and the driver that the local affiliate had sent to meet him had evidently given up and gone home.

Obtaining a cameraman and a technician proved easier than outfitting the self-contained mobile unit provided by the local network affiliate. Resembling an oversized recreational motor home with a dish antennae attached to the roof, the mobile unit had to be stocked with everything its crew of three would need for an excursion of indeterminate duration. Although Great Salton was less than 200 miles from Los Angeles, it had no broadcast facilities whatsoever and might as well have been on the opposite side of the globe. Emil had learned the hard way that one could never take along too much food, spare parts, or gasoline when filming in a remote location.

Emil took the wheel for the 3 1/2 hour drive to Great Salton. Along the way, he filled in his cameraman, Neil, a sharp-faced, balding native Angelino dressed in a gaudy paisley print shirt, Bermuda shorts, and sandals on what he had in mind:

"I want you to get the camera on Him as soon as possible. He's a twenty-something black guy, medium build—usually wears a denim shirt and jeans. Get a shot of Him out the windshield, if possible, while we are rolling up, just in case He bolts as soon as He catches sight of us."

"Didn't you call Him in advance to arrange an interview?" Neil asked incredulously.

"I don't work that way," Emil retorted. "Give some

sinister sleaze ball notice that you're after him and he'll will probably make himself scarce. Ambush journalism emphasizes the element of surprise. The only footage we have of this Jesus poseur is some low quality videotape from a couple of His sermons. Even when edited, it doesn't look promising. He's got a serene, charismatic charm about Him and a gentle, honeyed voice. We need to catch Him off-guard—preferably angry and defensive. Call Him names or whatever it takes to get under His skin—we can always edit that part out later."

"Don't we need His permission to film Him?"

"Hell, no! This scumbag is a public figure; if He can't take the heat, He has no business being in the kitchen."

Emil swerved hard to the left to avoid a backhoe traveling slowly along the shoulder. As he did so, the massive vehicle, having a high center of gravity and an over-sized body mounted on an under-sized chassis, swayed from side to side. A steady stream of curses emanated from the passenger compartment. Ed, the technician, had cut himself while splicing and was letting Emil know what he thought of his erratic driving.

Two miles beyond the village of Oasis, at the northern edge of the Salton Sea, Emil turned right down a gravel road leading to a double wide mobile home with a hand painted sign that read "Salton Sirocco" in large, seemingly wind-blown letters. Parking the mobile unit between two graceful date palms, the three men dusted themselves off before passing through the open doorway of Penny Phillips, owner, publisher, editor, and sole full-time employee of the weekly advertiser-newsletter known as the *Salton Sirocco*. Although the last three pages of the four page Sirocco were devoted exclusively to advertising, its front page contained local tidbits and gossip, qualifying it to appear in Emil's copy of Complete Guide to American Newspapers and Magazines as the primary printed news for the Salton area.

Despite the diminutive size of both her living room-office and her publication, Penny proved to be a veritable storehouse of information concerning anything and everything that had ever happened, was happening, or was supposed to happen in what she termed the "Greater Salton Basin." Not only did Emil and his crew learn that the cult's chief lieutenant was serving a life sentence for having decapitated a prominent televangelist, but they also heard that Jesus had never been seen with a woman and His followers didn't use deodorant. In between viewing photos of grandchildren and petting Penny's pampered calico cat, Emil managed to glean that most desert dwellers regarded the cult as good, clean living neighbors and that some even credited its leader with the recent turnaround in the sea's fortunes.

Three glasses of freshly squeezed lemonade and a slice of homemade double fudge cake later, Emil was back on the road driving the final miles to Great Salton. Neil was dozing in the passenger seat and Ed was cussing potholes as he attempted to thread a piece of videotape through a metal spool. Had Ed realized then how bumpy the ride would eventually become, he might have saved his curses for the rough terrain ahead.

Chapter 28

These were boom times for the "Greater Salton Basin" and its inhabitants. Rejuvenated, the warm sea waters played host to sportsmen and tourists who came to sail, fish and bask in the sun. In the course of a few years, enough resorts, marinas and related businesses opened to provide full employment for the residents of Great Salton. Many of Jesus' followers were doing so well that they were able to buy lots adjacent to the original communal compound and build proper homes for their growing families. Some even purchased cars and luxury items that had been beyond their dreams during the church's formative years.

Jesus' ministry prospered as well. Religious scholars from around the world came to hear Our Lord's words. So too, did huge crowds of everyday people—some out of sincere belief and many others from simple curiosity. All were welcome. Hundreds of rocks were assembled on the jetty and cemented together to form a platform whereupon the multitudes could better view The Savior. And children waded in the shallow waters alongside the jetty to see the Holy One without having to peer over the heads of their parents.

But prosperity proved to be a two-sided coin. Despite the installation of a public address system, sputtering motorboats and roaring jet skis occasionally interrupted services. People came with lawn chairs, ice chests and beach umbrellas and often left refuse in their wake. Solemnity disappeared as the crowds grew larger and was replaced by a semi-festive atmosphere. One insufferable wag observed that the assembled masses appeared to be more interested in spending a pleasant day at the seashore than in saving their immortal souls.

And there were sullen faced vendors who, with money in hand and eyes that neither glistened nor met those of the customers, hawked their wares along the fringes of the gathering. It was one such impious T-shirt salesman, hiding behind mirrored reflecting dark glasses, whom Jesus encountered one summer afternoon as He mingled with the faithful who had come to hear Him speak. As Jesus inadvertently brushed against the vendor's folding table, He saw that the T-shirts stacked upon it bore His likeness on the front and an advertisement for Seagram's Seven on the backside. Lifting the table above His head, Jesus hurled it and its wares far out into the sea where they sank and were never seen again. Nor was the vendor who scurried away with utmost haste to avoid the wrath of the Lord. Then, immediately thereafter, turning around with utmost calm, almost as if the incident had never happened, Jesus stooped to pickup a child.

Later that evening, following supper, Jesus walked a short distance into the desert with Esteban, Simon, and fifteen other elders from the Assemblage of the Seventy-Seven. They knelt beside a towering Joshua tree on stony ground and Jesus recited the 23rd Psalm in a sonorous voice that filled the darkness. A stillness settled about them as they remained on their knees in silence following prayer. Above them, the heavens shone in all their grandeur with the constant, unwavering, awe-inspiring light that one can properly perceive and appreciate only in the remotest regions of the desert, far removed from the artificial lights of the cities. Like untold generations of desert dwellers and nomads before them, they absorbed the beauty of the wonders of the heavens which were wrought by the Creator and testify to His Omnipotent Glory in a language that speaks not to the head, but to the soul. At the very moment that they became one with the universe, Jesus whispered, "So it was, so it is, so it ever shall be."

Rising to His feet, Jesus pointed to a barely perceptible reddish glow at the farthest edge of the northern horizon. "My time among you grows short," He said. "My Father beckons and I must follow His fire across the desert sands to a place where I will descend into a bubble beneath the surface of the earth to await the Revelation of the Secret of Creation. It will arrive in a format that can be readily assimilated by all and it will tear down the barriers of language, culture and distance that have in the past prevented us from joining in understanding, peace and fellowship to worship the One God."

"Ever since Adam bit into the forbidden fruit from the Tree of Knowledge, Man has hungered for more. He has traveled to the farthest reaches of the world and beyond to the threshold of the heavens, but has been unable to find the answers to his questions. I tell you now that the quest is almost over. In nine days' time, with the entire planet watching, Almighty God will reveal all."

"Rejoice! for you have been chosen to bear witness to the Wisdom of the Ages. Tomorrow we shall embark on a great trek—a pilgrimage of discovery—to the base of the ancient mountain on which the Flame of Creation yet burns. Guiding ourselves by a glow on the horizon at night and a thin column of white smoke by day, we shall escort three skeptical television journalists who will broadcast the Revelation unto all mankind."

"And Condo Don, who was born in a momentary flash of unholy manmade destruction, will accompany me when I go forth into the eternal, joyful brightness of the Creation. He . . ."

"But how can he join you when he is serving a life sentence without possibility of parole?" interrupted Lyle.

"He has been exonerated; the judgment was overturned by a Divine Higher Authority and Condo Don has already slipped through the prison system's clutches," promised Jesus.

"Shouldn't we find him and let him know where to meet us?" asked Simon in a voice bursting with excitement.

"That won't be necessary," Jesus advised, "since the eternal flame will burn even brighter for him than it does for others. He is no stranger to desolation, whether it be of the Mojave Desert or of the soul. Should he lose his way, he won't be able to blame it on the terrain."

And then, beneath heaven's dazzling canopy, with each star striving to outdo the next in testimony to the inextinguishable beauty of Creation, Jesus took each of His disciples in turn by the hand and embraced them. All 17 were to remain faithful and bear firsthand witness to the coming Revelation. Individually and collectively they have continued His ministry, transmitting Christ's message to the masses without benefit of remuneration. Those who communed with the Savior and received His blessing on the final night at Great Salton were: Esteban, who would later unite all Christians under one banner; Simon, who came from Los Angeles and worked as a truck driver; Jason, a laborer from San Dimas; Joe Bob, a migratory crop picker from Savannah; Sam, the mechanic from Milwaukee; Lyle, who was known for great physical strength and had at one time been employed as a teacher; Jason, who had lost an arm during the Persian Gulf Conflict; Dave, who was homeless when he was called by Jesus; Henry, also homeless; Jeff, an unemployed factory worker from Philadelphia; Steven, a file clerk from Council Bluffs; Fraser, a ranch hand from Taos, New Mexico; Norm, a salesman from Pittsburgh; Hassan, an agriculturist from Yemen; Eric, a former stockbroker and alcoholic from South Dakota; Ernie, a heavy equipment operator from Salt Lake City; and Ralph, a former stockbroker from Belfast following a long bout with rapacious greed.

On the morrow, they made preparations for their journey and left the compound in the late afternoon. After finishing their goodbyes, the disciples set out in single file along the gravel shoulder of the roadway, with a barely visible column of white smoke fixed directly ahead of them upon the horizon. They had not gone a mile when a behemoth of a vehicle, with an older man in a garish shirt holding a minicam leaning out the passenger's side window, pulled up to Dave, who was bringing up the rear.

"Hey, buddy!" Neil yelled, catching Dave's attention, "you got any idea where we can find this Jesus fellow that is running a commune someplace around here?"

"Are you the three reporters He has been expecting?"

Neil popped his head back inside the vehicle and whispered, "How did they know we were coming?"

"They didn't," Emil retorted in a low tone. "That's the way these cult guys work—he saw the network logo on the van, put two and two together and phrased it in such a way that it would lead you to think he has psychic powers."

"But he can't see Ed and he knows there are three of us."

"So, they may have been expecting the Wise Men. I could care less as long as we get our interview."

Turning away from Emil, Neil again thrust his head through the window and yelled to Dave, “We need to speak to Jesus.”

“Don‘t we all?” Dave chuckled. And then, sensing from Neil’s startled expression that a more serious answer had been expected, he added, “Please be patient and maybe something can be arranged when we stop to rest.”

For the next half hour the mobile unit crawled along in low gear behind Dave. Emil was beginning to debate racing ahead to find Jesus without Dave’s help when the road came to an end and the disciples continued to march northward through the desolate sands. Coming to an abrupt halt at the pavement’s edge, they stared in incredulous silence as the gap between them and the disciples slowly widened.

“End of the trail,” observed Ed caustically as he came forward to investigate why they had stopped. “Genuine Wise Men would have arranged to bring along camels.”

“We haven’t come this far just to turn around,” vowed Emil, shifting from Park into Drive.

“Has your brain baked?” sneered Ed as the behemoth van lurched forward, jostling him rearwards. “We are going to bog down in the sand!"

“Not with the jumbo dual tires on this monster—it’s half tank, half dune buggy—anyplace they can go, we can go in air-conditioned comfort. It's hotter than hell out there. Another mile or so and they'll be begging us for a ride."

Two hours and four miles later, as the sun inched below the far-off Santa Rosa Mountains and the white column of smoke began to fade in the dimming light, Jesus called a halt to cook their evening meal while awaiting the appearance of the northern glow to guide them onwards. As Esteban was directing the others to gather brush and dried animal droppings to prepare a fire, Emil stepped up and began to shake his hand.

"You sound like the head honcho. I'm Emil Velasco, perhaps you recognize me from television?"

"Sorry, reception is none too good out here."

"A pity. Anyway, if you would be so kind as to point me to Jesus, I would like to interview him for SCOOP. The viewing public wants to learn more about Him and your organization. One of your traveling companions told my cameraman that Jesus has been expecting us."

"Of course, all in good time. We are most honored to have an esteemed television newsman such as yourself accompany us on our pilgrimage to Creation's Holy Flame. Have patience, for Jesus will reveal everything at journey's end. Meanwhile, warm yourself by our fire. You and your associates are our guests—we welcome you and invite you to share our humble supper."

Emil felt his stomach turn as he noticed a battered skillet that a disciple had set next to a pile of brush and dried dung. Glancing furtively from face to face in the gathering darkness, he could not discern which belonged to the Savior. "Thanks, it certainly looks delicious, but my doctor has me on a restricted diet and we brought along our own grub. But, perhaps we can do you a favor and give you and your friends a lift to wherever it is that you are going. Although it might be a bit crowded, I'm fairly certain we can cram everybody in. We can take the paved roads and make your trip a lot shorter."

"How could following a highway be shorter than the straight line in which we are traveling?" asked Esteban, stomping out a stray ember from the now crackling fire with his left boot.

"I meant shorter time-wise," Emil elaborated, placing added emphasis on both syllables of the last word.

"There is no shortage of time; time is eternal. And although it must be declined, we sincerely appreciate your most generous offer. Should you require our assistance in any way during the trek, please do not hesitate to ask. You have my word that you will witness the Revelation of the Secret of Creation; that you will be free to report it in any manner you choose; and that it will be the biggest scoop of the millennium. Now, if you would be so kind as to excuse me, I have duties to perform."

Emil had been staring intently into Esteban's eyes while he was speaking. Failing to find any deception in them, he had no other viable option, at least for the time being, but to meekly acquiesce. His curiosity had been piqued; he sensed an Emmy in the offing; and he was determined to do whatever it took to get the full and complete story. If that meant trailing this bunch of weirdos to the ends of the earth, then so be it.

An hour later, after eating supper, Jesus and His disciples stomped out the campfire, shouldered their bedrolls and resumed their peregrination towards the flame in the distant hills that beckoned them ever onward. Although he drove slowly, switched the headlights to high beam and had Neil walk in front to guide the vehicle whenever they encountered rough terrain, Emil could not avoid some of the obstacles that littered the desert floor. He soon found out that the surface of the desert was not wholly flat, as he had expected it to be, but contained occasional low hills plus numerous ravines, depressions and washboard gullies. Not being designed for off-road use, the suspension creaked and groaned under the increased strain. With almost every sway and dip, cabinet doors swung open and equipment went flying. After becoming entangled in a heavy duty cable while securing a stray oscilloscope, Ed's grumbling reached a crescendo that could not be ignored: "Would you be a bit more careful: this ain't no Land Rover and we ain't filming no eagerly awaited National Geographic documentary. Mohammed or Jesus or whatever he's currently calling himself better get a new global positioning system, 'cause he's heading the wrong way to get to Mecca. Nothing in this direction but sand and lizards. Take it easy, some of this stuff breaks!"

"Shut up back there! I'm taking it at a snail's pace as it is. Do something constructive: get out and see if you can find the tailpipe we lost on that last big bump."

And so they went for hours, like some garbage truck tailing a holy procession, until an oasis unexpectedly materialized out of the darkness ahead. But this was no ordinary oasis—it was a travelers' rest area serving the eastbound lanes of Interstate 10, the expressway that cuts across the southern desert between Los Angeles and Phoenix.

Suddenly realizing that they could have reached the spot in less than twenty minutes much easier by driving on the highway, Ed, who had finally lapsed into a sullen silence for which Emil and Neil were immensely grateful, was startled into exclaiming, "Well, I'll be damned! [Ed was somewhat of an authority on the subject.] They took us all right, but not for the Three Wise Men—they've done played us for the Three Stooges!"

As the eighteen footsore, exhausted pilgrims unrolled their bedrolls on a grassy section of the rest stop, Emil scrutinized their features in an attempt to pick out Jesus. Five or six of the men fit the general description provided by Penny Phillips, but try as he might, Emil could not find Jesus.

And who among us cannot sympathize with Emil's plight? How many of us, dear brethren, have set out in search of the Savior and, for one reason or another, eventually abandoned the quest. Sometimes we must have patience. He has promised that all who seek shall find. Indeed, Emil will eventually come to know the Lord. He, and we, have only to wait . . . .

But waiting can be frustrating. Frustration is a mild term for what Ed was feeling. Fragile, expensive equipment had been (in his opinion) unnecessarily damaged by a capricious off-road romp. He said he was of a mind to awaken the sleeping pilgrims and make them divulge which one was Jesus. It made no sense to continue with the charade. Catering to the whims of wackos was not his idea of responsible journalism.

Emil was unconcerned with "responsible" journalism. He was there to get a story and one that included a hazardous trek across open desert by religious fanatics would give the viewers something they wanted much more than news: thrill-filled entertainment. Dry news served with cold, hard facts was unappetizing and too much of it, like peanut butter without jelly, made people choke.

Despite Ed's cutting reference to the Stooges, Emil Velasco was nobody's fool. Almost from the start, he had surmised that their destination was Amboy Crater, a reputedly extinct volcano that had as of late been exhibiting unmistakable signs of life. Having learned from

Penny that the cult's mysterious leader was believed by many to have had something to do with the tectonics that had saved the Salton Sea, it followed that He might now be attempting to enhance His reputation by claiming responsibility for yet another so-called Act of God. The great revelation that was supposed to occur at journey's end could conceivably be an eruption that the cult, having become obsessed with the column of white smoke and the glow on the horizon, believed to be imminent. Or Jesus might reenact Exodus by ascending to the summit of the belching crater and returning, like Moses, with several stone tablets. Whatever this person who had (presumably) usurped the Lord's name had in mind, it was bound to be good theater and Emil intended to tape it in full—including the trek across the desert.

Unfortunately, he had dropped and broken his cellular phone while attempting to steer and talk at the same time. But there was a pay phone at the rest stop and, after getting some change from Neil, he dialed the station in Los Angeles. It being near midnight, there was no one around who could authorize sending a four wheel drive vehicle without the approval of the network in New York. After being placed on hold until he ran out of coins for the phone, Emil finally had to hang up.

Several hours past noon on the following day, Jesus and His disciples resumed their northward journey with Emil and company trailing at a respectable distance. From a low-flying aircraft observing the pilgrims' progress, it must have looked as if the massive vehicle was striving to preserve the holy footprints in the sand between its humble tire tracks. Indeed, their passage was leaving its mark not only on the desert's surface, but upon the destiny of the entire world.

Shortly before dusk, the barren landscape abruptly changed. Boulders, odd-shaped rock piles and low granite hills loomed to the northwest. Layered one atop the other, the boulders seemed poised to fall should the pilgrims break their silence. Spooky, dark thorn-covered branches resembling arms bent upward at the elbow reached out to pull them into a forest of Joshua trees. Though the lengthening shadows lent their surroundings an otherworldly appearance, Neil recognized the features as part of Joshua Tree National Park—one of the Creator's more unusual wonders. Not really trees, but more like giant yuccas with trunks, religious pioneers thought that its grotesque branches resembled the arms of Joshua beckoning the Israelites to follow him into battle.

Providence led them to cross the national park in the dark. Had they done so in daylight, Emil might have had to explain to park rangers why he was cutting cross country rather than using the paved roads. As it was, however, they reached the opposite side of the park without incident shortly before dawn and slept through most of the following morning at an improvised campsite near the park's northern boundary.

Five days, two flat tires and an overheated radiator

later, the mobile unit emerged from the Bullion Mountains only to sink axle deep in a pit of soft sand. The tires spun, but would not take hold. With everyone pushing, it took the better part of a day to coax the vehicle out of the sand and onto the surface of Bristol Dry Lake where they made camp and rested until the next morning.

Gradually, the crater came into view as the weary travelers trudged onward. A thick column of white smoke, composed of ash and steam, rose thousands of feet above its red hot cinder cone and terminated in a broiling cloud that, tumbling and churning, filled the entire stratosphere. Little rivulets of lava flowed down its sides, igniting momentary puffs of flame whenever they encountered the sparse brush at the crater's base. Preparing a voice-over for the scene that Neil was shooting, Emil described it as "ominous—just short of threatening."

They were very close now and the smooth salt-encrusted lake bed would have made the last leg of their journey comparatively pleasant if it had not been for a refrigerant leak that put the mobile unit's air conditioner out of commission. Even with the windows and a door open, the temperature in the vehicle climbed until it was fully fifteen degrees hotter than the outside air. Droplets of sweat streamed down Emil's brow, stung his eyes and made the steering wheel slip in his hands.

After the air-conditioning went kaput, Ed came up front and stood behind Neil, hoping to benefit from whatever breeze might blow in through the open window. Catching a whiff of sulfur in the air, Ed made a disgusting face and proceeded to assault his companions with yet another sarcastic witticism: "This must be my lucky day—I always thought you had to die to get to hell!"

As usual, Emil and Neil ignored Ed's gibe and focused their attention on the path ahead. Although they were still nearly 5 miles from the smoldering volcano, they had come to the edge of an ancient lava flow, deposited hundreds of years before during a previous eruption. After turning on the wipers to smear some caked-on dirt from the windshield, Emil discerned what appeared to be three parked vans and an immense tent directly ahead. As they drew closer, he saw "U.S. Geological Survey, Department of the Interior" painted on the side of one of the vans and judged from the scientific paraphernalia scattered about the site that the government had set up a research station and was monitoring the awakening volcano's activities.

When the pilgrims came to a halt near the research station, Emil heard one of the disciples shout "Hallelujah!" and guessed correctly that they had arrived at their destination. Desiring some clear shots of the scientists and technicians performing their duties, Emil drove the mobile unit slowly around the tent while Neil poked the minicam out of the passenger side window. Coming to the opposite side of the tent, they were amazed to find a clone of their own mobile unit—exact in every detail except that it bore the logo of a competing network, had not lost its tailpipe and rear bumper, and was as bright and shiny as a fire truck on Sunday morning. And its crew were similar, too. But they were sitting on lawn chairs next to their vehicle, sipping lemonade.

The other news crew looked up and waved. Neil tried to say something, but coughed instead. And Ed barely managed to bring his hands together in two loud claps before collapsing in a fit of hysterical laughter.

Chapter 29

No matter how hard Condo Don tugged at the sleeves, he could not pull them over the deep cuts circling his wrists that threatened to give him away as an escaped prisoner. Although it was too small, the shirt fit the best of three that he had scavenged from a dumpster in an alley behind a thrift store in downtown Barstow. Digging deeper in the dumpster, he had also discovered a Toronto Blue Jays baseball cap which he now pulled low over his face as he walked up to an eighteen wheeler parked at an off-ramp diner and asked the driver, a ruddy complexioned fellow sporting a handlebar moustache, for a ride. "Moustache" (prisoners often substitute a person's most obvious physical feature for his given name) reckoned he could use some company on the barren stretch of Interstate 40 running east of Barstow and told Condo Don to climb aboard.

Sixty miles later, as Moustache was fast-forwarding a tape to replay Mick Jagger's "Sympathy for the Devil" for the third time, Condo Don decided it might be a good time to strike up a conversation. Pointing towards a column of dense, white smoke to the southeast, he asked, "Forest fire?"

"Hell no, there's nothing out there but empty desert. Where you been for the past two years? Don't you listen to the news? Amboy Crater is sputtering and blowing off steam."

"Any danger of it erupting?"

"Who cares? Even if it blows its stack like Mount St. Helens, it won't do much more than scorch a few lizards. It's out in the middle of nowhere, Moustache said as he ejected the Rolling Stones from the tapedeck and popped in George Thorogood.

Although it was little more than a line on the horizon, the column of white smoke held a strange fascination for Condo Don. He couldn't quite put his finger on it, but some inner instinct or sixth sense told him that he would find Jesus there. Being in the habit of trusting his feelings in such matters (without regard to their sometimes disastrous consequences), he changed his mind and opted to check out Amboy Crater before heading for Great Salton.

"Ba-a-a-a-a-d to the bone!" wailed thoroughly good George from a speaker mounted on the wall of the cab near Condo Don's right ear. Bad indeed, thought Condo Don as he reached out to turn down the volume.

Perhaps it was the tell-tale scars on his wrist; perhaps it was a fugitive poster that Moustache had seen at a post office; perhaps it was because Condo Don failed to ask permission prior to muzzling Mr. Thorogood. Who knows?, it might have even been some combination of all three. Whatever the reason, Moustache took a sudden dislike to his passenger. "Hm-m-m," he murmured as he studied Condo Don as if sizing him up. As a young boxer, Condo Don had been the recipient of many such unnerving stares from opponents when he went to touch gloves at the start of a match. The atmosphere in the cramped cab seemed to thicken. A muted George Thorogood was whimpering "ba-a-a-d," over and over again. Condo Don longed to be somewhere—anywhere—else but there was no escape from an eighteen wheeler doing 65 miles per hour on an expressway. His muscles tensed for action. Out of the corner of his eye he saw Moustache reach under the dash.

Due to a surge of adrenaline, everything appeared to move in slow motion as Moustache came up with a nickel plated .38 Smith & Wesson. There was the glint of sunlight on polished metal as Condo Don's left foot struck out and knocked the gun out of the truck driver's hand. Smashing against the tapedeck, it managed to silence George without firing a shot and dropped harmlessly onto the floor below. Disarmed, Moustache panicked and brought his foot down hard on the brake.

Grabbing hold with a vengeance, the air brakes made the rig jackknife, skidding sideways across two lanes and sideswiping a Greyhound bus, before caroming off the concrete center divider and flipping onto its side. Strewing its load of 356 cases of sliced pineapple all over the highway, it slid another 30 feet, sparks flying, before coming to a complete stop.

The overturned diesel tractor and its two trailers blocked all three lanes, bringing eastbound traffic to a halt. Several motorists got out of their vehicles and gawked at the wreckage. One, an off-duty paramedic, climbed atop the cab, shattered the passenger's side window and pulled Condo Don and the unconscious driver from the smoldering heap of twisted metal. After laying the limp body on the ground, the paramedic rendered artificial respiration while Condo Don looked for wounds. Hearing distant sirens, Condo Don slowly withdrew into the crowd of bystanders that inevitably forms at all injury accidents and made himself as inconspicuous as possible. Shortly, as a California Highway Patrol cruiser, lights flashing, came into view, he stuffed six cans of sliced pineapple into his shirt and set out at a brisk pace into the open desert.

For a while he considered doubling back and hitching a ride at another point on the highway, but rejected the idea as being too risky. He had escaped unscathed from two serious accidents in the past three weeks and had no desire to test his mortality any further. Thanking God in silent prayer for delivering him from the machinations of Moustache, he strode onward, orienting himself by the towering column of white smoke. Although he was afoot alone, he was grateful for his freedom. Blithe of spirit and heavy in the shirt, cans clanking together with every step, he was, unbeknownst and unsuspected by his pursuers, headed for a rendezvous with the Infinite that had been destined since the moment of his birth.

Chapter 30

Emil was angry. Trusting Esteban's promise of an exclusive story, he had risked the network's equipment, his own life, and the lives of his comrades in crossing the Mojave Desert—only to find that another network had beat him to the grand finale. Seeing Esteban standing off by himself with no one else around, the veteran reporter walked over to confront him.

"Enough games. How about you introducing me to Jesus, so I can get on with my job?"

"All in good time."

"Yeah, seems to me I've heard that one before. Look, how's about we speed this up with a little donation—say $2,000—to your Supreme Being? Cash, of course, and untraceable." Taking a money clip from his front pocket, he began to peel off bills: "five hundred . . . one thousand . . . two thousand" and thrust the money towards Esteban.

Esteban made no move to take the money. A scorching breeze rustled the currency in Emil's outstretched hand. Just as Emil was preparing to up the ante, Esteban, struggling not to reveal the offense he was feeling, replied slowly and distinctly, "The God I worship isn't short of cash."

Slowly the wad of money returned to its money clip and then the money clip returned to its pocket. A long silence followed during which Emil stood motionless with downcast eyes. The hot wind continued to blow between the two men. Emil, like most of those in his profession, prided himself on his ability to judge character. He was honestly ashamed at having allowed his anger to get the best of him. Recollecting the incident years later at a lifetime achievements award dinner held in his honor, Emil was to quote from Proverbs 18:12: "Pride ends in destruction; humility ends in honor."

After what seemed to be ages to Emil, but actually was mere seconds, he looked up to find that a black man of medium height and build had joined them.

"I believe it is me that you seek," said the Lord.

"Are you Jesus?" asked Emil.

"Do you require identification? I left my driver's license and social security card in my backpack."

"That won't be necessary," Emil hurriedly replied.

"Nevertheless, I sense that you are skeptical."

"Who wouldn't be after being given a cock and bull story to get us to follow you across the desert?"

"I assure you that Esteban spoke the truth."

"He promised that you would reveal the Secret of Creation."

"And so I shall."

"If this involves some kind of volcano doomsday prediction, I hope you don't expect us to wait long for the fireworks."

"What fireworks? Do you think that God would have you come all this way to inform you of imminent destruction? That would be a cruel joke unworthy of the Creator. His message is one of hope and salvation, not of death and destruction. Amboy Crater serves as a beacon to show the world the way, not an inferno with which to bury it."

"But if you are really Jesus and this is the Second Coming, then what about Armageddon?"

"That was in a vision that I gave to John over two thousand years ago. It was a 'worst case scenario' intended to show you what would happen if you didn't change your ways. As you know, nuclear war between the East and the West was narrowly averted. Does this disappoint you?"

"No, of course not." Looking somewhat perplexed, Emil felt his pockets for the small tape recorder (approximately the size and shape of a pack of gum) that he was never without. Pulling it from the pocket that held the money clip, he switched it on, only to find that its battery had died. He thought about going back to the mobile unit for Neil and his gear before continuing the interview, but, as a veteran reporter, he realized that any interruption could result in a loss of rapport. Better to rely on his memory for now; he could record it all later. Where was he? Oh yes, he remembered, something about Armageddon. He had discovered an anomaly! Clearing his throat, he reckoned it his duty to pursue the perceived discrepancy: "With Armageddon out of the picture, isn't it a whole new ballgame?"

"Precisely," said Jesus, "God has summoned us here to share His game plan."

"I assume that this mysterious 'Secret of Creation' that is supposed to change the world has some part in that plan. Would it be possible to share that secret with our viewers also—and to do it without any further delays?"

"No delay whatsoever," replied Jesus in an even tone, "it's been there, above your head, since our conversation began."

Emil's eyes shot upward. Startled, he took a step backward and almost fell over his own feet. There, slightly more than a foot above his head, was a dark cube, one yard wide by one yard long by one yard in height, suspended in mid-air. It contained absolutely nothing. In fact, it was a vacuum, an empty void, a block cut from the blue sky—as perfect and sharply defined as if God had sawed it with a cosmic blade. If the Holy City, the glorious New Jerusalem, had suddenly descended from the clouds, it would not have astounded Emil more. His normally quick mind could provide no feasible explanation for the phenomenon. It could not be, but the evidence of his own eyes told him that it was.

"What is it?" he asked, his formerly firm voice now shaken with incredulity.

"It's not; that is to say it is nothing—an absence of all things. You are witnessing how it was in the beginning, before God created the heavens and the earth. God has opened a window upon creation through which you will see what was, what is, and what shall be. Often during your journalistic career, especially at moments when you felt depressed, you have wished and prayed for a truly spectacular story. Benevolent God has answered your prayers by selecting you, Emil Velasco, to report the ***real*** Greatest Story Ever Told. You will be shown the creation and the history of mankind, not as a scientist or a philosopher might imagine it to be, but as it actually happened, full and complete down to the minutest detail."

"That is impossible," Emil declared, desperately attempting to retrieve a vestige of skepticism. "It must have taken billions of years for the universe to form and man to evolve. Something that big would have to be edited before presentation."

"Nothing is impossible for God," Jesus stated. "Take

Amboy Crater, for instance. It is but an infinitesimal spark brought to fire for an instant by the Creator. There are thousands just like it on this planet and more than can be imagined throughout the expanding universe. Yet they, and everything else in the heavens and on earth were created in less time than it takes to walk across the Mojave Desert. God made it all in just six days. It might sound improbable, but, nevertheless, it is so. What seems like billions of years to man is mere minutes to God. Time is not a constant; in the physics of creation, involving vast quantities of energy and matter, time is, as was so ably expressed by Albert Einstein, relative to the beholder. God told all this to Moses and Moses, despite being a bit unsophisticated in such affairs, described the process as best he could in the Book of Genesis. The Holy Bible is the Word of God; visual images, however, speak a universal language easier to understand than words. It is hoped that those who lack faith in what God and the prophets have been telling them will be convinced after they see it with their own eyes. The cube is currently empty space, it's screen is blank. Soon, the show will begin. What you are going to witness is not a reenactment or a staged production; it is what actually occurred."

"Go get your crew and whatever else you need," ordered the Savior. "Prepare to see the universe reborn. Esteban will give you further instructions when you return. Do you have any questions?"

"Yes," Emil ventured, "how can I set up a direct feed

broadcast, considering that a lot of the required equipment suffered damage on the journey here?"

"Perhaps if you were to share your story, the other network would share their equipment," Jesus suggested.

Emil nodded his head in agreement. He could see the wisdom in what Jesus said. Half of the awards would be better than no awards at all. In fact, he reasoned as he made his way over to the competing network's mobile unit, a deal that rendered him 85 percent would be even better.

Jesus left Esteban and walked along the hard surface of the ancient lava flow to where the other disciples were standing in a group next to the entrance to a large cavern. The cavern was actually a bubble that had been formed by escaping gases within the flow as it had cooled and solidified following a long ago eruption. Descending into the interior, they found it to be a cool refuge from the dehydrating effects of the sun and the wind.

When Emil returned, he brought both crews and a ton of equipment with him. Convincing the executives of both networks to cooperate and to authorize a direct broadcast feed had taken some doing. After borrowing a cellular phone, he had presented his case with the finesse of a Clarence Darrow. In the end, they had approved a fifteen minute preemption of regular programming on both networks and agreed to consider further interruptions of scheduled programming based on what they saw. Once again, Emil had proven himself the right man for the job.

Esteban hastily briefed them on what to expect. When wispy vapors seen through the window began coalescing at a central point, they would have five minutes to prepare for an explosion of cosmic proportions, infinitely more powerful than a hydrogen bomb. Solely the insulative aspects of the window would save them from instant annihilation. They would have to turn their backs to the explosion to protect themselves from the flash and the tripods would have to be lashed down to prevent them from toppling. When Ed asked if there was anything else he needed to do, Esteban advised him to pray.

It was three hours later on the East Coast. Tom Bryant was in the midst of a human interest story on the evening news when the screen went black and a clear, unidentified voice said, “We interrupt this program for a live news report from Amboy Crater in the Southern California desert.”

A grainy image of Emil Velasco standing stationary beside a steaming volcano appeared on the screen. Fluttering numerous times, it steadied into crispness—as sharp and clear as if it originated from a television studio in New York—after Ed made a minor adjustment to the signal being beamed to the satellite.

Taking a cue from Neil, Emil, who had been wiping the sweat from his forehead with the back of his left hand, came to rigid attention and began: “This is Emil Velasco reporting live from Amboy Crater in California's Mojave Desert. Long dormant, this volcano was thought to be extinct until it began spewing clouds of steam and ash two years ago. Scientists from the Geological Survey team charged with monitoring its activities have assured us that there is no cause for alarm. Nonetheless, we are about to witness an enormous explosion scientists refer to as the Big Bang; many times more powerful than a hydrogen bomb. It will come, not from this volcano, but . . .," pausing briefly, he and the camera swung 180 degrees before continuing, "from this cubic void—a black hole that suddenly materialized in the desert sky less than two hours ago."

"Please, do not panic. I am told that the force behind the strange phenomenon—and the tremendous explosion that everyone here is bracing themselves for—is not destructive, but creative. Out of nothing, tremendous energy is now concentrating at a central focus point. The pressure and suspense is building . . . no time to explain it in greater detail . . . excuse me, I must now duck and cover for protection from the flash and the shock wave that follows."

What happened next is best described as the Big Bang. Emil was temporarily knocked unconscious by the blast. More than 400 miles away in Sacramento, a spectacular burst of light was seen on the southern horizon, followed 33 minutes later by something that sounded like rolling thunder. Seismographs recorded a 7.8 magnitude earthquake centered at Amboy Crater in an unpopulated desert region. Suspecting a nuclear first strike by a hostile unknown foreign power, the Air Force's Strategic Air Command and NATO readied to launch their intercontinental ballistic missiles.

Television viewers saw the dark cube in the center of their screen instantaneously explode with a dazzling white brilliance that overflowed screens and lit living rooms with the intensity of lightning [Note: The Fifth Circuit Court of Appeals recently exonerated the networks in a class action seeking damages for temporary visual impairment suffered as a result of viewing the explosion on television. The court ruled the Big Bang to be an "Act of God."]. Mistaking the Creation for the End of Time, some viewers fell to their knees, repenting their sins, while others panicked and ran screaming through the streets. A lay minister in Alexandria, Virginia, said that his Great Dane "ran outdoors shaking like a leaf" when the Big Bang awoke him.

Regaining consciousness, Emil struggled to get his bearings. Formerly dark and empty, the cosmic cube was now pulsating with action. Myriads of colorful, whirling masses shot out in every direction from the center. As he stared in amazement at energy being transformed into mass, he tried to form it into words for his viewers. None came. Spellbound, he gave the microphone to Esteban, who was in tears, and could barely manage to say, "God is in His Glory—He was, is, and ever shall be. Our depleted worn out world is being reborn."

It was the beginning of the universe, Day One in replay. All regular primetime programming was preempted. Audiences were astounded. Nothing like it had ever been seen on television before. People called their relatives, neighbors, and everyone they knew and urged them to watch also. The media converged on Amboy Crater. By the following morning, the only two roads leading into the area were congested and the lava flow, according to one reporter, was beginning to resemble the parking lot at Dodger Stadium on opening day.

On the second day, as related in Genesis 1:6-8, God created the various elements. As undifferentiated particles (neutrons) continued to radiate outward from the center of the explosion, some underwent reactions by which they emitted electrons, thus leaving free protons. Each proton then captured a neutron, forming a deuteron, the nucleus of the hydrogen isotope of mass 2. Many deuterons caught another neutron, becoming tritium, the hydrogen isotope of mass 3. When these nuclei decayed and gave off an electron, they became the helium isotope of mass 3. In addition, many particles collided with various other elements and fused. By a succession of captures, decays, and fusions, God created the entire spectrum of natural elements that form the building blocks of the physical universe. Combining together, these elements spiraled ever outward, creating stars, planets, galaxies, and all the rest of the celestial bodies that dot the heavens.

It was wondrous to behold. Having exhausted his repertoire of superlatives, Emil increasingly resorted to extended pauses punctuated by “oohs” and “aahs.” Finally, recognizing his own exhaustion, he handed the microphone to another reporter and went to sleep in the mobile unit. His dreams were filled with whirling nebulae and luminous galactic clouds. In them he saw the face of God. A transformation occurred and, as he later related to a global audience, he became a true believer.

Cameras set at different angles recorded entirely different events as they happened at various locations in the rapidly expanding visible universe, providing many interesting perspectives, which, when subsequently analyzed in detail, were to provide clues toward the solution to various scientific mysteries. And, while the universe expanded, the field of vision provided by the window gradually narrowed to one galaxy.

On day three a large cloud of dust and gas was seen to form in a spiral arm near the outer edge of our Milky Way galaxy. As it condensed into a sphere, its interior pressure and heat triggered an ongoing thermonuclear reaction, releasing energy in such vast quantities that condensation ceased. The infant sun heated what remained of the cloud, driving the gases and volatile elements outward. Gravitational instabilities caused the cloud to form into planets, the third from the Sun being our Earth. “Then God said, ‘Let the waters under the heavens be gathered together into one place, and let the dry land appear‘; and it was so. And God called the dry land Earth, and the gathering of the waters He called Seas. And God [and now, through His divine assistance, mankind] saw that it was good." Genesis 1:9-10.

People were clamoring to see the Savior. A noisy crowd of reporters gathered at the entrance to the cavern. When Simon emerged at midday, they mobbed him and thrust microphones in his face. Although he patiently explained to them that Jesus was praying and would not appear until the sixth day, they did not disperse.

On the fourth day, the pull of gravity by the sun and moon, together with a gradual slowing of rotation, made our earth tilt on its axis, which brought about the seasons. And all who saw it agreed that it was good.

The Governor of California mobilized the National Guard to cordon off the crater and restore order. Since the roads were snarled with traffic, the President authorized the use of U.S. Army helicopters to bring in water and medivac those who had succumbed to the 100+ degree temperatures and sulfurous vapors.

On the fifth day, life evolved in the oceans and spread to the land. Large dinosaurs abounded; birds flew across the face of the heavens. "And God blessed them, saying, 'Be fruitful and multiply, and fill the waters in the seas, and let birds multiply on the earth.'" Genesis 1:22. And non-believers watching the broadcast were turned into believers, for they could not deny the evidence of their own eyes.

Emil came to Esteban with a problem. What little food was available to feed the multitudes that had descended on Amboy Crater was rapidly spoiling in the desert heat. Refrigeration units had arrived, but the generators needed to power them were on flatbed trucks that were hopelessly stuck in gridlock. All of the generators at Amboy Crater were already operating at full capacity. What should they do? Esteban took the problem to Jesus at the cavern. Upon returning several hours later, he advised Emil to plug the refrigeration units into any outlet he could find.

Ed, who had argued against overloading the generators, was sent to plug in the refrigerators. Upset about being overruled on a matter that fell within his field of expertise and seeking to minimize possible electrical damage while proving his point, Ed devised an electrical harness by which he hooked up 40 commercial refrigerators to one small portable generator. To his utter amazement, it worked perfectly. In fact, for the next 48 hours he continued to plug in additional equipment without experiencing a brown out. And, although no one thought to refill its 2 1/2 gallon tank, the generator never ran out of gasoline.

On the morning of the sixth day, God created mammals. And (as seen by viewers) God made the beast of the earth according to its own kind and cattle according to its kind.

Then God created man in His own image; male and

female He created them. “And God blessed them, and God said to them, ‘Be fruitful and multiply; fill the earth and subdue it; have dominion over the fish of the sea, over the birds of the air, and over every living thing that moves on the earth.’” Genesis 1:28. And, around the world, billions of awestruck, mesmerized viewers simultaneously agreed that it was indeed very good and praised God for making it so.

Over the next few hours, the entire history of man—from the Garden of Eden to the Second Coming—played itself out in fast forward on the cosmic cube. Viewers caught snippets of this and that, both famous and quotidian. Not all of it was pretty (the truth, it seems, seldom is) and some scenes were quite shocking. A lady in Duluth wrote to the New York Times that after witnessing the “cruelty and brutality committed by my ancestors, I am inclined to divorce them.” However, it should also be noted that in the same edition there appeared a letter from a man in Poughkeepsie who felt we would do well to “emulate the passion, dedication, faith, and courage of those who sacrificed their lives to make the world what it is today.”

At 2 PM, as an estimated global audience of 3.9 billion was watching the 12th Century unfold, Esteban told Emil that Jesus was ready to give him an exclusive interview. Gathering their equipment together, Emil and crew rushed to the cavern where, after pushing their way past the other reporters, they lowered a ladder and descended into the dimly lit interior.

Since the main elements of that interview are common knowledge, I will not relate it in its entirety. Suffice it to say that Our Lord revealed His imminent departure. Soon, time as seen through the Window on Creation would match that of the present day and Jesus, accompanied by Condo Don (who was expected to arrive momentarily), would depart the physical world.

"Will Condo Don sit beside your throne in heaven?" asked Emil excitedly.

"You mean that old sot, the escaped murderer?" Ed interrupted.

"I am the Beginning and the End; the First and the Last," replied the Lord. "Though once dead, I live forevermore. I hold the keys of hell and death as well as the keys to heaven and life."

"Satan has been exceeding his authority, tormenting wayward souls that are not beyond salvation. And he has attempted to destroy the world in a nuclear Armageddon. His misdeed damaged Condo Don at birth and made it easy for him to lapse into sin. When Satan came to claim his soul, I set things right by giving Condo Don the strength to defeat the Evil One and cast him into the pit."

"Condo Don will rule hell in my name. He will confine only the incorrigible and will recycle the rest. No longer will God allow those who lack willpower or who have been misguided to be consigned to eternal damnation. This was not the way that Our Heavenly Father, who is a loving God, intended it to be, so it shall be no more."

"Condo Don has, as of late, been in prison gaining an affinity with the darker side of humanity. No one has a better understanding of human weaknesses and how best to correct them. I am charging him with reforming, reorganizing, and downsizing hell so as to minimize spiritual waste. ***Rehabilitation through recycling*** shall be its motto. Those who do not get life right the first time will be made to relive their painful experiences again and again until they repent. It will be a kinder, gentler hell, a hell that challenges rather than condemns."

When the interview was over, Emil and Neil were the first to ascend the ladder. As Ed mounted the bottom rung, Jesus requested to borrow the ladder for a short while.

"Whatever for?" Ed asked, amazed that Jesus would even talk to him.

"I have to climb to the Window on Creation," Jesus replied.

"If you are truly the Son of God, then why don't you simply levitate or sprout wings like an angel and fly?" Ed retorted sarcastically.

"That would involve unnecessary theatrics and grandstanding unworthy of the Son of God."

"Suit yourself, I'll leave it here," replied Ed, climbing to the next rung.

"One last thing," said Jesus as Ed turned his back on the Savior and continued up the ladder.

"What's that?" snarled Ed.

"You'll get along swimmingly with Condo Don. You and him are very much alike."

Chapter 31

The Bristol Mountains are studded with abandoned mines—stark reminders of the desert region's turn of the century heyday when the last of the California gold rushes resulted in the boom and bust of towns with such ironic names as Klondike and Siberia. Once, rugged prospectors and miners who feared no one but God sought to get rich quick here. Few did. Hikers and naturalists occasionally stumble across the sun bleached bones of someone who didn't.

When the ore played out and the miners moved on, they left much of the heavy machinery that they couldn't carry with them behind to rust and deteriorate. For that, Condo Don was indeed grateful. At the first mine he had come across, he had found a bolt from an ore crusher which he had sharpened against a stone to fashion a crude can opener. Now, seven days later, near yet another scar on a mesquite dotted, boulder-strewn mountainside, the Blackjack Mine, Condo Don was enjoying his last remaining can of sliced pineapple as he pondered the significance of the barricaded checkpoint at the road junction below.

It was manned by troops armed with assault rifles. Surely they wouldn't call out the National Guard just to look for an escaped felon. No, they must be after something a whole lot bigger, he reasoned. Perhaps it had something to do with the tremendous explosion that had heard six days earlier.

Getting past the National Guard proved to be easier than he had expected. Most of the National Guard troops were concentrated along the roadway. The few Humvies he saw patrolling the sands passed by at regular intervals and he was able to slip between them.

Trudging on, he came to the edge of a lava flow and what at first sight appeared to be a tremendous throng gathered around the volcano to watch the fireworks. But why was everyone facing away from the volcano? People were pointing at a cube hovering in midair and the man who was climbing a ladder to reach it.

The man on the ladder was Jesus! Everyone was shouting His name.

Officer Owens had been performing crowd control for the past 14 hours. He was hot, hungry, exhausted, and right about then would have been willing to part with a day's pay for a shower. It was not easy duty. Small children were in constant danger of being trampled; he had to shout to make himself heard over the roar of the crowd; and many problems had arisen due to shortages of food, bottled water, trash dumpsters, and chemical toilets.

He had just finished writing a citation for an elderly lady who had attempted to honk her way through the crowd in her new Mercedes, when he spotted someone who looked vaguely familiar. There was something about the face: those pinned back ears and that hard, determined expression. It was Donald Stearns, the escaped murderer whom he had seen on hundreds of wanted posters and who had slipped through his hands after somehow disabling his patrol car in an embarrassing incident that, though it had happened ages ago, was burned into his memory.

"Halt!" he shouted.

Condo Don didn't stop to look over his shoulder, but went on pushing through the crowd, his eyes fixed on Jesus. Officer Owens, realizing that it would be impossible to catch up with Condo Don due to the packed crowd, unholstered his 9 millimeter service weapon and screamed for people to get down. Thumbing off the safety, Officer Owens lifted the handgun and pointed it at the sky, reaching across with his free hand to pull back the slide and jack a round into the chamber. Fully extending his arm, he brought it down in a single fluid motion while sighting across the barrel.

Less than fifteen feet remained between Condo Don and the Savior's outstretched hand. Jesus was smiling down at him from the ladder, His ebony face beaming like the Flame of Creation that had guided Condo Don across the desert. So near, yet so far. Condo Don was willing to give his life if only he could embrace the Lord one last time.

Officer Owens was an excellent marksman. At least once a week for the past seventeen years he had gone to the range to shoot at fixed and moving targets. There was no way he could miss at this range. Steady . . . careful . . . squeeze, don't jerk the trigger . . .

Jesus grabbed hold of Condo Don's hand and pulled him up. Less than a heartbeat and they would be on the heavenly side of the Window on Creation.

Officer Owens blinked twice and holstered his weapon. At that moment he could have shot Condo Don, whom he considered to be an escaped felon, without remorse but he would not and could not endanger other people's lives to do so. He could be sure of hitting Condo Don, but he was not certain that the bullet would not pass through him and injure someone else. It was a split second decision, the kind that the public trusted him to make.

Nor did it surprise Jesus. A heavenly glow emanated from the Window on Creation as the Lamb of God, clutching Condo Don tightly to His side, passed through into Eternal Bliss.

And Mother Marva, together with 4.3 billion others who had been watching the divine drama unfold, shed tears of joy.

The grace of Our Lord Jesus Christ be with you. Amen.

ACKNOWLEDGMENTS

The last place an investigative reporter like myself would expect to find a story on religion is a prison. Nevertheless, it was where I found it. Not that I was particularly looking for one at the time. While covering the Sampson criminal trial for the Sacramento Bee, I ran afoul of Judge Ito Fujikawa for refusing to reveal the source of an article I had written. He ordered me to tell how I knew that detectives had tampered with the physical evidence and I figured it was none of his business. His Honor found me in contempt of court and graciously provided me with a secluded setting, courtesy of the State of California, in which to reconsider my decision.

My cellmate at Pelican Bay State Prison, an unrepentant, grizzled murderer who went by the bizarre nickname of Condo Don, was serving a life sentence without the possibility of parole for having decapitated an internationally renowned televangelist. Guards and inmates alike uttered his name with awe that I initially mistook for fear. At the time, I suspected the authorities of having temporarily removed him from solitary confinement and placed us together expressly to intimidate me into telling them what they wanted to know. He babbled incessantly about having met Jesus—in the flesh! I thought him quite mad, but dared not tell him so as I did not wish to provoke a convicted killer. By feigning interest and encouraging him to relate his delusions, I reasoned, I was preventing him from prying information from me. Indeed, my strategy was to humor him and acquiesce to whatever he said. Soon, he had me virtually acting as his secretary; he would rave for hours about his travels with Jesus and I would dutifully jot them down. By the end of the second month, I had filled a sheaf of loose-leaf paper as thick as a phone book.

Finally, attorneys retained by the National Association of Newspaper Publishers obtained my release by negotiating a compromise with Judge Fujikawa. As I was preparing to leave, Condo Don handed me my sizable bundle of notes and requested me to turn them into a manuscript. Naturally, I said yes. I was so anxious to get on with my life that I would have agreed to anything to ensure my safety during those last frantic moments of incarceration.

Eight months later, I received a package addressed to me in care of the Sacramento Bee. In it I found more of Condo Don's preposterous imaginings, meticulously handwritten in large block letters. Reporters are notorious pack rats and never dispose of anything which might later prove useful. Since one never knows when one might be assigned to produce an article on the criminally insane, I threw the package into a file cabinet drawer alongside the earlier material.

Two years passed without anyone mentioning Condo Don. Then, as I listened to the news one day, I learned that he was at large. A prison transport bus had overturned on a desert road and he had escaped in the ensuing confusion. I feared for my life and seriously considered purchasing a handgun for protection.

Not long afterwards, Christ's Revelations at Amboy were broadcast live to an astonished world and I came to realize that I (and society) had grossly misjudged a man who will in all probability be remembered as a modern day saint. I also discovered that I was in possession of the 21st Century equivalent of the Dead Sea Scrolls. That which I had dismissed as the fantasies of a diseased mind were in reality a true eye witness account of the Second Coming. My lack of faith had cost me the greatest scoop in two millennia. I was painfully aware that further procrastination might result in the loss of my immortal soul.

The purpose of my life now appeared crystal clear. I had to fulfill my promise to Condo Don and assemble his writings, together with my notes and any other relevant material I could amass, into a lucid account of Christ's return. The world must be told the story of His rebirth; His compassion for the poor and the homeless; the persecution of so-called cultists by government and organized religion; His wanderings throughout the California desert; His teachings and miracles at Salton Sea; and the Revelations at Amboy that solved the mystery of life and revealed man's place in the universe.

I am but a humble reporter and do not know why I was chosen for this task. It was certainly not due to piety or background in theology. Perhaps my reputation for integrity made me the logical choice to present this amazing testament to the world.

In compiling *The Gospel According to Condo Don*, I have endeavored to follow Condo Don's dictations and notes as closely as possible. For the greater part, I have faithfully transcribed his testimony while deleting some street language which prudence dictates should not appear in print. However, in order to preserve a true sense of his unique character for posterity, I thought it best to let him tell his life story in his own words as they appear in an excerpt from a cover letter accompanying the parcel he sent to me in Sacramento; they now compose the Preface to this work.

It has been my pleasure to interview many of the people mentioned by Condo Don in his testimony—nary a one disputes his word. I am especially indebted to Mr. Esteban Ortiz, Mr. Otis Chandler, the community of Great Salton, and the inmates and guards at Pelican Bay State Prison for supplying valuable information which helped to corroborate, reinforce, and clarify Condo Don's extemporaneous remembrances. My heartfelt thanks go to the California Department of Corrections, the California Highway Patrol, the California Supreme Court, the Federal Bureau of Investigation, and the Genetic Enforcement Service for opening their archives to my research. Dr. Horatio N. Schwarzkopf, Professor of Theology at California Baptist College, rendered incalculable service by guiding me step by step through the Byzantine process of launching a book and faithfully offering a critique of my work that was right on target. My staff artist, Mr. Thomas Brothers, was a wizard at putting together maps that were both understandable and complete. I have not acknowledged others who assisted me in my efforts because they are too numerous. The accuracy of what I have written is, of course, my responsibility alone.

Any scholar who desires to examine the original manuscript or the material on which it is based may do so by visiting the Salton Sea Museum at Great Salton, California. Several hours of illuminating and (literally) sobering interviews on tape with various of Condo Don's early acquaintances are available at the Dr. Martin Luther King, Jr. Library on the campus of Riverside Community College in Riverside, California.

I painfully regret that skepticism prevented me from meeting Jesus in person during His brief sojourn among us. If these humble words help to guide someone to Him, then they will have accomplished their purpose.

Fred Dungan

October 30, 2012
Riverside County
California, U.S.A.

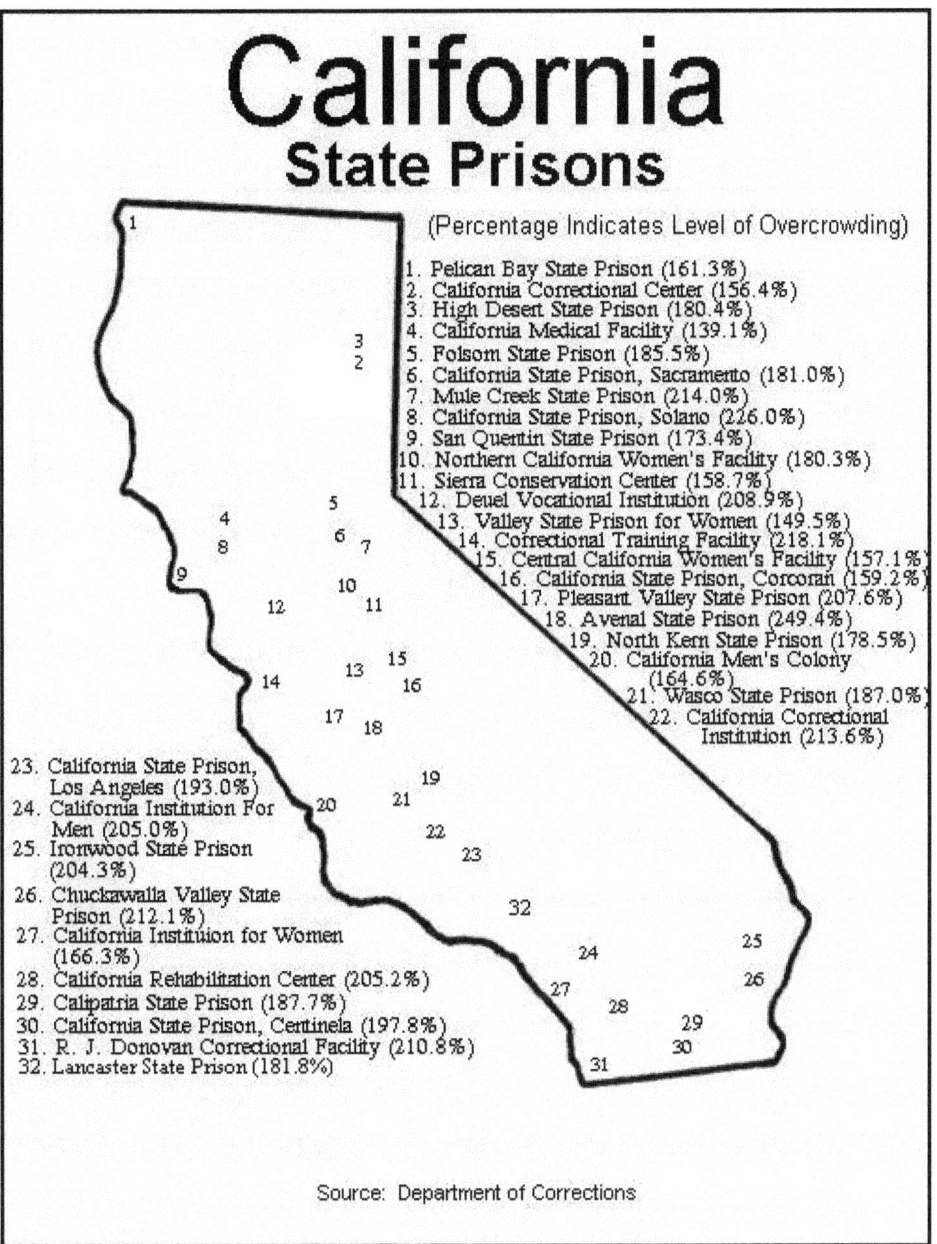
California
State Prisons
(Percentage Indicates Level of Overcrowding)
1. Pelican Bay State Prison (161.3%)
2. California Correctional Center (156.4%)
3. High Desert State Prison (180.4%)
4. California Medical Facility (139.1%)
5. Folsom State Prison (185.5%)
6. California State Prison, Sacramento (181.0%)
7. Mule Creek State Prison (214.0%)
8. California State Prison, Solano (226.0%)
9. San Quentin State Prison (173.4%)
10. Northern California Women's Facility (180.3%)
11. Sierra Conservation Center (158.7%)
12. Deuel Vocational Institution (208.9%)
13. Valley State Prison for Women (149.5%)
14. Correctional Training Facility (218.1%)
15. Central California Women's Facility (157.1%)
16. California State Prison, Corcoran (159.2%)
17. Pleasant Valley State Prison (207.6%)
18. Avenal State Prison (249.4%)
19. North Kern State Prison (178.5%)
20. California Men's Colony (164.6%)
21. Wasco State Prison (187.0%)
22. California Correctional Institution (213.6%)
23. California State Prison, Los Angeles (193.0%)
24. California Institution For Men (205.0%)
25. Ironwood State Prison (204.3%)
26. Chuckawalla Valley State Prison (212.1%)
27. California Instituion for Women (166.3%)
28. California Rehabilitation Center (205.2%)
29. Calipatria State Prison (187.7%)
30. California State Prison, Centinela (197.8%)
31. R. J. Donovan Correctional Facility (210.8%)
32. Lancaster State Prison (181.8%)
Source: Department of Corrections

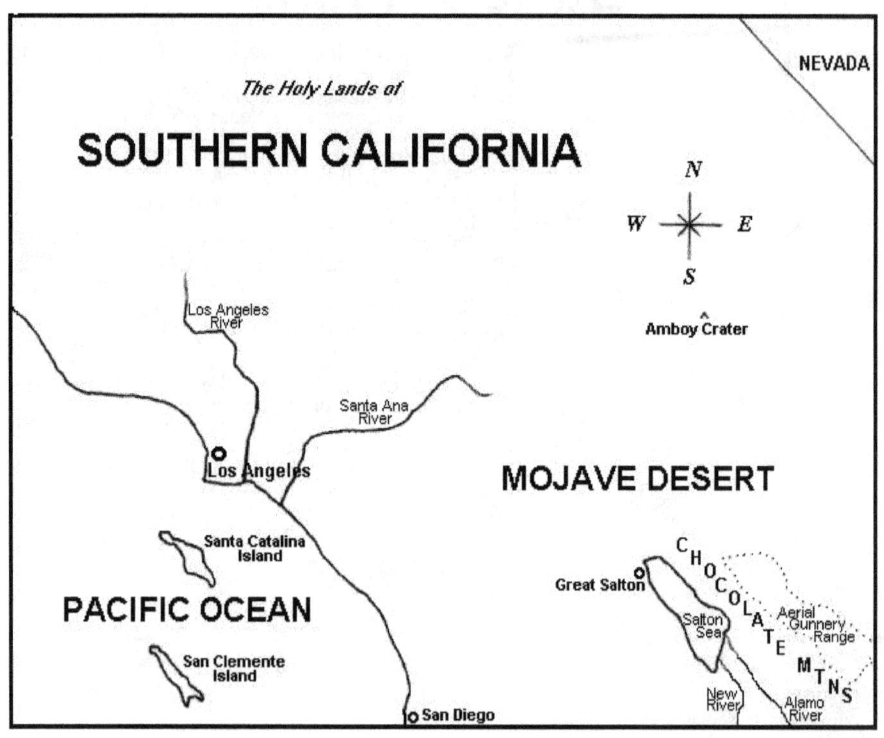

Comments? Please e-mail me at: fdungan@fdungan.com

ABOUT THE AUTHOR

I am a 100 percent service-connected disabled veteran. I can't stand or walk. My faith in Jesus Christ gives me the strength to go on; He is my Savior and my guide. This is a work of fiction, yet it is loosely based on the story of Jesus Christ as related by the four Gospels: Matthew, Mark, Luke, and John in the New Testament. I thank God for inspiring me to write it. My faith is all encompassing and limitless. With God's help, all things are possible.

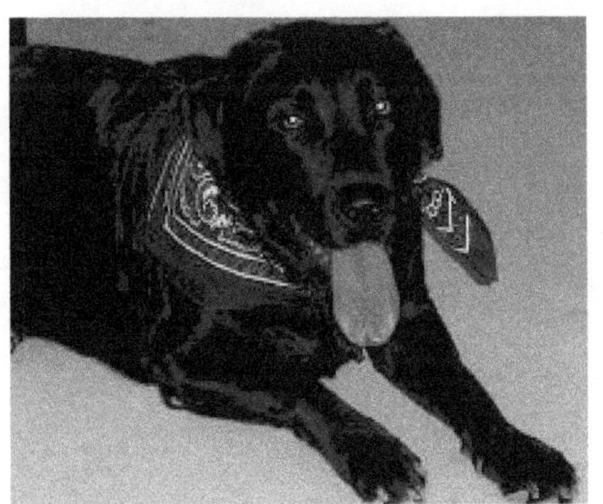

Lady, my assistance dog, is my constant companion and helpmate. She loves children and likes to play ball. Unlike Major League ballplayers her muscles are not the result of steroids.

My websites are online at fdungan.com and dunganbooks.com.

www.ingramcontent.com/pod-product-compliance
Lightning Source LLC
Chambersburg PA
CBHW031145270326
41931CB00006B/145